EAST ASIAN CINEMAS

TAURIS WORLD CINEMA SERIES

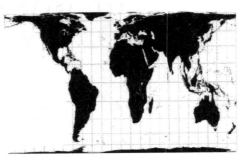

Series Editor: Lúcia Nagib, Professor of World Cinemas, University of Leeds
Advisory Board: Anthony Minghella (UK), Laura Mulvey (UK), Donald Richie (Japan), Robert Stam (USA), Ismail Xavier (Brazil)

The aim of the **Tauris World Cinema Series** is to reveal and celebrate the richness and complexity of film art across the globe. A wide variety of cinemas will be explored, both in the light of their own cultures and in the ways they interconnect with each other in a global context.

The books in the series will represent innovative scholarship, in tune with the multicultural character of contemporary audiences and designed to appeal to both the film expert and the general interest reader. It will draw upon an international authorship, comprising academics, film writers and journalists.

Prominent strands of the series will include **World Film Theory**, offering new theoretical approaches as well as re-assessments of major movements, filmmakers, genres, technologies and stars; **New Cinemas**, focusing on recent film revivals in different parts of the world; and **new translations** into English of international milestones of film theory and criticism.

Books in the series include:

Brazil on Screen: Cinema Novo, New Cinema, Utopia
By Lúcia Nagib

East Asian Cinemas: Exploring Transnational Connections on Film
Edited by Leon Hunt and Leung Wing-Fai

Lebanese Cinema: Imagining the Civil War and Beyond
By Lina Khatib

Queries, ideas and submissions to:
Series Editor, Professor Lúcia Nagib – l.nagib@leeds.ac.uk
Cinema Editor at I.B.Tauris, Philippa Brewster – p.brewster@blueyonder.co.uk

EAST ASIAN CINEMAS
Exploring Transnational
Connections on Film

Edited by

Leon Hunt and Leung Wing-Fai

I.B. TAURIS

LONDON · NEW YORK

Reprinted in 2011 by I.B.Tauris & Co Ltd
6 Salem Road, London W2 4BU
175 Fifth Avenue, New York NY 10010
www.ibtauris.com

In the United States of America and Canada distributed by
Palgrave Macmillan, a division of St. Martin's Press,
175 Fifth Avenue, New York NY 10010

Published in 2008 by I.B.Tauris & Co Ltd

ISBN: (PB) 978 1 84511 615 6
ISBN: (HB) 978 1 84511 614 9

A full CIP record for this book is available from the British Library
A full CIP record is available from the Library of Congress

Library of Congress Catalog Card Number: available

Designed and typeset by 4word Ltd, Bristol, UK.
Printed and bound in India by Replika Press Pvt. Ltd.

Contents

Part Three: Made in Translation – Transnational Identities

Part Four: How the West Was Won? Asianisation and Beyond

Notes on Contributors

Rayna Denison is a lecturer in Film and Television Studies at the University of East Anglia, Norwich. She has recently completed a PhD titled 'Cultural Traffic in Japanese Anime: The Meanings of Promotion, Reception and Exhibition Circuits in *Princess Mononoke*'. She has published articles on anime in *Scope: An Online Journal of Film Studies* and on transnational uses of stars in *Critical Survey*. She has chapters in *Japanese Cinema: Texts and Contexts* (forthcoming) and in *Film and Comic Books*. She is currently editing a collection titled *Mysterious Bodies*, with Mark Jancovich, on the body in television.

David Desser is Professor and Director of the Unit for Cinema Studies, University of Illinois at Urbana-Champaign. He is the author of *The Samurai Films of Akira Kurosawa* and *Eros Plus Massacre: An Introduction to the Japanese New Wave Cinema*, and the co-author of *American-Jewish Filmmakers*; the editor of Ozu's *Tokyo Story*; and the co-editor of *The Cinema of Hong Kong: History, Arts, Identity; Hollywood Goes Shopping: Consumer Culture and American Cinema; Cinematic Landscapes: Observations on the Visual Arts and Cinema in China and Japan; Reflections in a Male Eye: John Huston and the American Experience*; and *Reframing Japanese Cinema: Authorship, Genre, History*.

David Scott Diffrient is visiting lecturer at the University of Michigan. His essays have appeared in several journals and anthologies, including *Film Quarterly, Cinema Journal* (Fall 2005), *Horror Film: Creating and Marketing Fear* (University of Mississippi Press,

2004), *South Korean Golden Age Cinema* (Wayne State University Press, 2005), *New Korean Cinema* (NYU Press, 2005), and *Beyond Life is Beautiful: Comedy and Tragedy in the Cinema of Roberto Benigni* (Troubador Publishing, 2004).

Theresa L. Geller teaches at Rutgers University. Her publications include 'Queering Hollywood's Tough Chick: Subversions of Sex, Race, and Nation in *The Long Kiss Goodnight* and *The Matrix*', *Frontiers: A Journal of Women Studies* (Winter 2004), 'The Cinematic Relations of the Sex-Gendered Subject', *Rhizomes 11*, Special Double Issue, 'The Becoming-deleuzoguattarian of Queer Studies', edited by Michael O'Rourke (Fall 2005), '"The Film-work does not Think": Re-Figuring Fantasy for Feminist Film Theory', *Gender After Lyotard*, edited by Margret Grebowicz (2005), and 'Deconstructing Postmodern Television in *Twin Peaks*', *Spectator: The University of Southern California Journal of Film and Television Criticism* 12.2 (Spring 1992).

Chris Howard is a PhD candidate at the School of Oriental and African Studies, University of London. His research interests include contemporary Japanese and South Korean cinema, particularly in relation to their international distribution and marketing.

Leon Hunt is a Senior Lecturer in Film and TV Studies at Brunel University. He is the author of *British Low Culture: From Safari Suits to Sexploitation* (Routledge, 1998) and *Kung Fu Cult Masters: From Bruce Lee to Crouching Tiger* (Wallflower Press, 2003). His essays have appeared in *British Crime Cinema* (Routledge, 1999), *Action TV: Tough Guys, Smooth Operators and Foxy Chicks* (Routledge, 2001), *British Horror Cinema* (Routledge, 2002), *Defining Cult Movies* (Manchester University Press, 2003), *Action and Adventure Cinema* (Routledge, 2004) and *The Spectacle of the Real* (Intellect Press, 2005). He is currently writing a book about *The League of Gentlemen* for the British Film Institute's 'TV Classics' series.

Adam Knee is Assistant Professor in Ohio University's School of Film. He was awarded a Fulbright grant to lecture and research in Thailand. His writing on Thai cinema includes a recent essay on Pen-ek Ratanaruang in *Asian Cinema* and a chapter on Thai horror films in the forthcoming anthology *Horror International* (Wayne State UP, 2005), and he recently edited a special issue of the Taiwanese journal *Tamkang Review* on the topic of 'Asian Cinemas/Transnational Frameworks'.

Charles Leary is a Doctoral Candidate and Adjunct Professor in Cinema Studies at New York University's Tisch School of the Arts. He has written on the cinemas of China, Taiwan and Hong Kong for various publications, and is currently completing a dissertation on the films of John Cassavettes.

Nikki J.Y. Lee is a Lecturer in Culture & Gender Studies at Yonsei University, Seoul, South Korea. She has contributed to *Cine21*, a South Korean weekly film magazine, and is currently researching the transcultural consumption of East Asian films in the UK and on the social and cultural significance of the 1980s Korean 'Ero' (erotic) films.

Leung Wing-Fai is a writer and lecturer specialising in East Asian cinemas, and currently Research Assistant at the Creative Industries Research and Consultancy Unit, University of Hertfordshire. Her articles can be found in *Ten Thousand Li* (W.F. Leung and D. Chan (eds) 2002), *Hong Kong Express*, *Contact Sheets*, *In the Picture* magazine and *Firecracker* magazine. She is completing a doctoral thesis at the School of Oriental and African Studies, University of London.

Sheng-mei Ma is Professor of English at Michigan State University, specialising in Asian Diaspora/Asian American studies and East-West comparative studies. His book, *Immigrant Subjectivities in Asian American and Asian Diaspora Literatures* (1998), is published by the State University of New York Press. *The Deathly Embrace: Orientalism and Asian American Identity* (University of Minnesota Press, 2000) is completed under the auspices of the Rockefeller Foundation Fellowship for 1997–8. Ma's book, *East-west Montage: Reflections on Asian Bodies in Diaspora*, is forthcoming.

Gary Needham is lecturer in media and cultural studies at Nottingham Trent University, where he teaches film. He is the co-editor of *Asian Cinemas: A Reader and Guide* (Edinburgh University Press, 2006).

Brian Ruh is author of *Stray Dog of Anime: The Films of Mamoru Oshii* (Palgrave Macmillan, 2004). He has also contributed to the collections *Cinema Anime* (Palgrave Macmillan, 2006) and *The Japanification of Children's Popular Culture: From Godzilla to Spirited Away* (Scarecrow Press, forthcoming). He is currently working on his PhD in the department of Communication and Culture at Indiana University.

Gary G. Xu is Assistant Professor of Chinese, Comparative Literature and Cinema Studies at the University of Illinois, Urbana-Champaign. He has published several articles on Hou Hsiao-hsien, Zhang Yimou and global cultural politics, and has recently published *Sinascape: Contemporary Chinese Cinema*.

1

Leon Hunt and Leung Wing-Fai

Introduction

Bong Joon-ho's monster movie *The Host* was one of the most talked-about 'crossover' films of 2006. The film broke box office records in South Korea, and a warm reception at Cannes culminated in a multiple-territory purchase by American distributor Magnolia pictures,[1] a company with an eye for Asian cult potential (Thai martial arts film *Ong-Bak*, for example). Unlike *My Sassy Girl* (South Korea, 2001), a regional box office hit that is being remade in Hollywood but was denied a Western release in its original version, *The Host* seemed destined for, if not *Crouching Tiger, Hidden Dragon*-sized global success, then at least cult acclaim. English-language reviews cited *Jurassic Park*, *Jaws*, or earlier Hollywood creature features like *Creature From the Black Lagoon*, while Bong allegedly pitched the film by photoshopping the Loch Ness Monster onto the Han River.[2] But it was hard not to think of an earlier East Asian monster created by the American military, *Gojira* (Japan, 1954), who would become arguably the region's first transnational icon when he was re-named *Godzilla, King of the Monsters* (1956).[3] While the atomic lizard would sometimes acquire American co-stars in export versions, in addition to a name change, *The Host* looked to Western cinema for special effects expertise – Peter Jackson's Weta Workshop and the smaller Orphanage. Its anti-American elements notwithstanding, *The Host* was clearly designed to travel as well as conquer the local, and regional, box office. Pre-sold to Japan, already predisposed to Korean popular culture and probably spotting the connections to its own *kaiju eiga* (monster movies), here was a South Korean creature feature with effects via New Zealand and California, and enough 'local' resonances to distinguish it from its

Japanese and North American counterparts – welcome to transnational East Asian cinema.

Cinema from East Asia has arguably never had a more visible presence in the West than it does at present (although some might argue that this has been at the expense of more 'challenging', less globally ambitious, films). With the success of Chinese martial arts blockbusters, Japanese horror cycles (and their Hollywood remakes), Korean and Thai action films in the West, contemporary East Asian cinema has transcended geographical, cultural and theoretical boundaries. This success has not been evenly distributed, however. Hong Kong cinema, once one of the 'tigers' of East Asia (and a significant presence in Film Studies), is currently in crisis, in spite of isolated box office hits such as the *Infernal Affairs* series (HK, 2002–3) and *Kung Fu Hustle* (HK/China, 2004). At the same time, formerly 'peripheral' Asian cinemas have achieved an unprecedented visibility, circulated through mainstream distribution, the festival/arthouse circuit, as well as cultification on DVD, often championed by cinephiles like Quentin Tarantino. East Asian cinema has achieved an additional international presence through the 'flexible citizenship'[4] of film-makers and aesthetic traditions. Recently, Japanese directors Nakata Hideo and Shimizu Takashi are the latest Asian film-makers to pursue Hollywood careers, while 'Asianised' Hollywood films range from *Kill Bill* to the remakes of *Dark Water* and *Oldboy*. Is this evidence of the West 'yielding' to the East, or (as Gary Xu argues in this volume) an opportunistic outsourcing of talent and ideas? The talents migrated from Hong Kong to the US in the 1990s (such as Chow Yun Fat and John Woo) were largely absorbed into studio productions. Remakes used to mean copying (or plagiarising) of American movies by Asian commercial cinema. This relationship between the West (especially Hollywood) and East Asian cinemas has since evolved. In 2007, the Oscar for Best Motion Picture was awarded to *The Departed,* a bloated remake of *Infernal Affairs* – an ambivalent reflection of the cultural impact of East Asian genre cinema.

East Asian Cinemas: Exploring Transnational Connections on Film considers developments in the globalisation of East Asian cinema and the 'Asianisation' of Western cinema, with particular emphasis on crossovers, remakes, hybrids and co-productions. This collection of essays examines the changing cinematic traditions in Asia, including Japanese horror, martial arts, the emergence of 'new' cinemas from Korea and Thailand, and the global circulation of East Asian films as arthouse, independent, cult and even 'extreme' cinema.

The word 'transnational' is used more often than it is defined, and definitions remain abstract by nature. Insofar as there is a consensus, transnationality is usually taken to have something to do with: the cultural and economic flows of globalisation, the erosion of the nation-state, a 'borderless world', de-territorialisation, debates about whether we live in a 'global village' or are witness to ever more sophisticated forms of 'global pillage'. Aihwa Ong expresses a preference for the transnational over the 'global' (the two words are sometimes used interchangeably):

> *Trans* denotes both moving through space or across lines, as well as changing the nature of something ... (it) also alludes to the *trans*versal, the *trans*actional, the *trans*lational, and the *trans*gressive aspects of contemporary behaviour and imagination that are incited, enabled, and regulated by the changing logics of states and capitalism.[5]

To this one might add the *trans*vergent, recently given a provisional push as an alternative way of conceptualising the transgression of 'national cinema':

> A transvergent cinema suggests that no cinema is a complete a-priori artefact in and of itself. This cinema ... crosses lines, zigzags, derails, rerails, reroutes, jumps from one continent to another, relies on artifice to create its imaginary spaces.[6]

This use of the term 'transvergent' is derived from the digital designer Marcus Novak, whose preference for the 'trans' prefix in some ways echoes Ong's; he finds in it an 'incestuous intellectual restlessness and conceptual mobility'.[7] If 'transvergent cinema' is being offered as an alternative to the transnational – which stands accused of being either too vague or too obvious[8] – it nevertheless sounds very like the definition of the 'transnational' that we find being discussed in the essays in this collection. The possibility of 'trans'-formation for both Western and East Asian film productions means that the definitions of 'transnational' cinema remain open and contingent. These films, genres and film-makers zigzag, derail and reroute, sometimes leap across continents – so that 'East Asian cinema' might be discerned in Hollywood or French *film d'action* as well as the region itself – they frequently create 'imaginary spaces'. Suggestively, a number of accounts of the transnational stress its imaginary qualities – the 'imagined communities of modernity' created by contemporary geopolitics[9] and global media-scapes.[10] Arjun Appadurai identifies the imagination as a 'space of contestation in which individuals and groups seek to annex the global into their own practices of the modern',[11] constructing worlds that are 'chimerical, aesthetic, even fantastic'.[12] The recent anthology *Hong Kong Connections* offers a focused consideration of 'Transnational Imaginings', as cinemas ranging from India to Hollywood find a 'contact zone of transnational discussion' through the global influence of Hong Kong action cinema.[13]

There are, however, particular dimensions of transnationality that need to be stressed in this collection, given that definitions of transnational cinema can either be broad enough to include any film that has ever been exported or narrow (and ethnocentric) enough to mean any non-Hollywood film that has a significant presence in the West. On the other hand, an oft-used film studies term 'world cinema' posits precisely the power dichotomy: Hollywood versus the rest of the world, without considering the subtle and complex power relationships within and between film-producing territories. Nevertheless, we might point here to Charles Leary's notion of 'worldliness' in his chapter – transnational East Asian cinema transforms world film culture in some way, however large (Hong Kong action, Japanese horror) or comparatively small (an arthouse film or auteur, 'cult cinema'). While we might want to pause before uncritically celebrating the 'Gross National Cool' that Douglas McGray discerns in Japanese popular culture (and which might be extended more recently to the so-called 'Korean Wave'),[14] the notion of 'soft' power (economic and cultural)[15] has some currency here. Both Japan and Hong Kong have legacies of 'soft power' in world cinema, not only measured by their global impact (admittedly modest compared to Hollywood's) but their status as 'peripheral' cultural empires in regional markets, dominating, transforming and sometimes damaging less 'worldly' cinemas.[16]

If the transnational violates the 'national' in national cinema, then one might expect that the authentic is a likely casualty of these multilateral connections and influences. One might take as a case in point two Asian auteurs discussed in this volume, Kurosawa Akira and Park Chan-wook. The British critic and Asian cinema expert Tony Rayns suggests that 'Park (Chan-wook) has clearly figured out that archetypes play better in foreign markets than cultural specifics. He has also opted to aim at the overgrown "lad" audience which gets off on his hyperbolic violence'.[17] Whatever the politics of Park's 'extreme' reputation, the film or director who crosses over (or looks as though they have *tried too hard* to appeal to Western audiences) is vulnerable to accusations that they do not fully belong to a national cinema. One does not have to look far to find similar critiques of Kurosawa: Americanised, Self-Orientalising, less fully 'Japanese' than Ozu or Mizoguchi. On the other hand, this is not to say that the search for global currency is without its casualties; Gary Xu argues in his essay that the 'Asian remake' trend has led producers to make projects that can be easily sold to Hollywood for adaptation. A particular interest of this book is the mutating *currencies* of transnationality – the remake, the arthouse film, the cult film/ genre/auteur, the blockbuster. These currencies are by no means fixed within a given historical moment as movies travel – the 'blockbuster' becomes a cult or arthouse film, or an 'extreme' film-maker such as Park accumulates layers of meaning as his films circulate at film festivals or on niche DVD labels.

Having offered some tentative definitions of the transnational, what, and equally importantly *where,* is 'East Asian cinema'? The 'Idea of Asia' has attracted a considerable amount of critical attention even before one attempts to subdivide it into more specific regions (and consider the interrelationship between those regions). As Milner and Johnson put it, Asia is a 'free floating signifier – a term the exact meaning of which is not yet settled'.[18] The history of this 'idea' is subject to ongoing redefinitions of 'regional relationships and identities'.[19] Factors in this ongoing redefinition might include:

> colonialism, post-colonialism, multinational capitalism, globalisation, the complex and multifaceted interplay between the Asia Pacific and the Euro-American Pacific, and their diverse and intersecting discursive productions.[20]

East Asia is a case study in mutable regional identities. One can identify at least two 'East Asias'. Arguably the most familiar maps onto the north-east Asia that emerged out of a post-war (Western) distinction from south-east Asia, and includes China, Hong Kong, Taiwan and Japan. However, another East Asia was imagined by Malaysian Prime Minister Dr Mahathir in his notional East Asian Economic Caucus, 'a crescent of prosperous nations extending from north-east Asia to south-east Asia ... from Tokyo to Jakarta'.[21] Symptomatically, this book blurs these two East Asias. Thailand belongs to Mahathir's East Asia, but it is the only national cinema discussed here that is not part of (north)-east Asia. We offer three rationales here, as well as emphasising that the 'new' Thai cinema was always seen as a key part of the collection. Firstly, if Asia is already an 'idea in process ... just one among many types of experiment with concepts of identity and community',[22] one might assume that its regional subgroupings will be similarly mobile. Secondly, as a 'new' cinema with a comparatively recent global and regional identity, Thai cinema joins those transnational film-making territories that have traditionally been located in (north)-east Asia. Thailand has a growing global profile, based on its arthouse auteurs (Pen-ek Ratanaruang, Apichatpong Weerasethakul) and cult crossover films like *Tears of the Black Tiger* and *Ong-Bak*. Thirdly, this collection's titular emphasis on *connections* links Thailand to already established East Asian cinematic cultures. Most noticeable is the Thai-Hong Kong connection, manifested in cultural, ethnic and economic relations between the two cinemas. Hong Kong distribution companies like Fortissimo and Applause have played a key role in the transnationalisation of Thai cinema, while one might point to Hong Kong director-producer Peter Chan (ethnically Thai) and Danny and Oxide Pang, ethnic Chinese usually linked to the 'New Thai Cinema' that emerged in the late 1990s. As Brian Ruh's essay on *Last Life in the Universe* demonstrates, one can also find connections to Japanese cinema in individual Thai films. While neither the editors or the authors are naive enough to see the influx of Asian stars, film-makers and genres into Western cinema as taking place on a level playing field, this does again suggest that East Asian Cinema needs to be taken as an 'idea in process' rather than a 'geographical given'.[23]

The first section of this collection, 'Global Encounters of the First Kind', adopts a historical perspective on transnational East Asian cinema. When did East Asian films become transnational? The term poses a challenge to uni-directional cultural influences, but, as a fashionable term in film studies, implies a comparatively recent phenomenon. There is an equal danger, however, of interpreting the term so broadly and vaguely that it loses its sensitivity to key historical moments in global film culture. If transnational cinema is 'worldly', then Japan represents the first wave of 'soft' cinematic power in the 1950s. If *Godzilla* became East Asia's first global icon, then Kurosawa is arguably the first transnational Asian film-maker. David Desser's essay examines the cultural impact of *Seven Samurai,* a case study in a film's 'classic' status resting partly on constantly being 'remade, reworked, referenced and relied upon in global cinema', albeit least of all in Japan itself until the recent anime *Akira Kurosawa's Samurai 7*. Kurosawa's 'wordliness' has compromised his reputation as a 'Japanese film-maker' for many commentators, visibly influenced by Hollywood westerns; in the case of *Seven Samurai*, Desser extends the founding myths of his homosocial action film to Greek myth. The impact of *Seven Samurai* is similarly trans-cultural, ranging well beyond the Hollywood western (*The Magnificent Seven*) to Hindi action cinema (*China Gate*), and the 'new style' Chinese martial arts films of the 1960s (*The Magnificent Trio*) that would take their lead from films like Kurosawa's. To Desser's extensive list, one might add *The Seven Steptoerai* (1974), an episode of the British situation comedy *Steptoe and Son* that simultaneously responds to the international impact of Bruce Lee and Hong Kong action cinema. Kurosawa would start another trend in the 1960s, with *Yojimbo* (1960) taken as the first 'cruel *jidaigeki*' (period drama/samurai film).[24] Mifune Toshiro's stubbled, cynical *Ronin* would pave the way, of course, for Clint Eastwood's *Man with No Name*, and, with his laconic attitude towards death, Sean Connery's James Bond.

Gary Needham examines a less 'masculine' Asian cinema, in contrast with the international image of Hong Kong fostered by its kung fu and gunplay films, but one equally engaged in a dialogue with Western filmmaking models – in this case the Hollywood musical. Chinese cinema has its own culturally distinct musical traditions, such as the *huangmei* Opera, but the 'Hollywood-style' musicals of the late 1950s and early 1960s seem to embody both a localisation of and resistance to the dominant generic model. Needham offers a 'fashionable encounter' between Hong Kong and Hollywood that precedes what many take to be the former colony's first transnational moment – the *wuxia* and kung fu films of the 1960s and 1970s that progressed from regional to global success. Martial arts films were both masculinist and Sino-centric, while the Hollywood-style musical seemed to celebrate a Hong Kong of modernity, affluence and fashion, equated particularly with the female stars who dominated Hong Kong cinema before the start of the '*Wuxia* century'. The films are characterised by promiscuous musical and cinematic borrowings – both Chinese and Western – their romantic narratives tempered by culturally specific values and priorities. Charles Leary, too, considers the Hong Kong-Hollywood musical as part of his study of a film industry that has played a part in re-shaping world film culture (as the *Hong Kong Connections* collection attests). Hong Kong cinema, he argues, is characterised by the 'imagination of access to the world and to the power of film to shape our perception of the immediate space in the world'. Leary offers a 'flight' through Hong Kong cinema, with the plane and the airport as metaphors for its 'worldly' outlook. As in Needham's account, films like *Air Hostess* point to an emerging culture of cosmopolitanism and modernity. But it also points to a cinema that would soon be characterised by its ability to travel, to see the world as 'small' enough to conquer.

Part two of the collection, 'All Changes on the Eastern Front', explores the industrial implications of the globalisation of East Asian cinema that has been in a state of flux, exported, re-articulated and manipulated for local, regional and international consumption. As one of the most successful commercial cinemas, Hong Kong has long made films for global consumption. Whilst East Asian cinemas have become increasingly visible (evidenced by the international blockbusters the various countries in the region are producing and the Asianisation of Western cinema), the Hong Kong film industry has been in decline since the mid-1990s. Leung Wing-Fai's chapter argues that the crisis of Hong Kong cinema is closely related to the overwhelming changes in the way feature films are consumed, such as the rise of home entertainment, and the re-structuring of local, regional and global film markets. She examines two local blockbusters as survival strategies for the ailing film industry, the *Infernal Affairs* trilogy (Andrew Lau and Mak Siu-fai, 2002–3) and *Kung Fu Hustle* (Stephen Chow, 2004). The choice of a Hong Kong blockbuster-turned-Hollywood remake and a Hong Kong/China co-produced regional hit provides empirical evidence for the shifting paradigms in the study of contemporary commercial film practices.

Hollywood domination is supposed to universalise and homogenise cinematic experience. However, Wilson and Dissanayake suggest that this is a 'new world-space of cultural production and national representation which is simultaneously becoming more *globalized* (unified around dynamics of capitalogic moving across borders) and more localized (fragmented into contestatory enclaves of difference, coalition, and resistance)'.[25] American blockbusters are widely scrutinised in film studies, whilst relatively little has been done to explore commercially successful films from other parts of the world in depth. Rayna Denison's chapter examines the intermedia commentaries in Japan closely, as 'a home grown "blockbuster" [*Princess Mononoke*] was proving its worth against all foreign and domestic competition'. Does a blockbuster by any other name (in this case, *daihitto* or 'big hit' in Japan) remain the same Hollywood-tinted phenomenon? Denison asserts that the language of the blockbuster is not a discourse that solely comes from and relates to film-making in the US, but has its own industrial and cultural particularities as it traverses to other film markets in the world.

Korean blockbusters are the starting point for Howard's chapter on contemporary South Korean cinema. Since *Shiri* (Kang Je-gyu, 1999), a succession of domestic record-breaking films firmly established the Korean film industry as an emerging force, triumphing over Hollywood imports and infiltrating Asian markets. Rather than simply accepting the phenomenon as a model of non-American film practice, Howard examines the themes of patriotism, nationalism, screen dominance (by oligopolistic majors) and (the effects on) diversity in Korean cinema. One of the most interesting elements of the success of the Korean film industry is the overwhelming state support, which is perhaps the most significant difference to the American studio model. The lessons in Korea in the 'national conjunction' and 'creative industries' paradigms are highly relevant to film industries such as the UK, which are inevitably posited against Hollywood titles in the domestic markets.

In the next section, 'Made in Translation – Transnational Identities', the collection turns to issues raised by the transnational crossover of film texts; in particular, the implications for the representation of national identities. We have already argued against the notion of authentic national identities, but suggest that it should be examined as unfixed historical moments, in the 'imploding heteroglossic interface of the global with the local'.[26] Adam Knee's chapter on *Suriyothai* (Prince Chatrichalerm Yukol, 2001) functions as such a case study. The film's expressive attempt to assert a traditional Thai identity goes through a subsequent journey of mutation as it is exported and consumed: 'It is no small irony, however, that the version of this film eventually prepared for export (*The Legend of Suriyothai*, 2003) was subject to the editorial contributions of a foreigner – Francis Ford Coppola.'

The availability of a film in different formats, across territories, also erodes the concept of the original 'text'. Brian Ruh explores the issues of nationality, technology and authorship, asking what the various formats that circulate a film in the international market place do to viewing practices. The choice of *Last Life in the Universe* (Pen-Ek Ratanaruang, Thailand, 2003) is an exemplary case in point. It was Thailand's official submission for Best Foreign Language Film to the 76th Academy Awards, stars a Japanese cult film favourite Asano Tadanobu and was filmed by Chris Doyle, a cinematographer who has worked most famously with Wong Kar-wai, as well as other Asian and Western auteurs. To complicate the worldliness of the film in terms of nationalities, the DVD versions for the different markets emphasise the transgressive power in a film such as *Last Life*: a Thai production that demonstrates not only the flexible citizenship of the film-makers but the medium itself.

Focusing less on the actual crossing of national boundaries, David Scott Diffrient's essay on *Tokyo Godfathers* (Kon Satoshi, 2003) explores a 'network of cross-cultural references – antecedent texts that suggest a truly transnational array of audiovisual material drawn from Asian, European, and American contexts'. The original 'text' traverses from Peter B. Kyne's 1913 western novel *The Three Godfathers*, via several Hollywood films, to a Japanese animated production. Rather than literal translation of texts, *Tokyo Godfathers* creates a transnational and intertextual imaginary space that provokes the cosmopolitan, global unconscious. As eclectic a translation of cross-cultural references is Hayashi Kaizo's film, *The Most Terrible Time in My Life* (1994), examined in Theresa Geller's essay. Geller focuses on the noir as a film style and argues that *The Most Terrible Time in My Life* is a homage to the American film noir of the 1940s, as well as the French New Wave. The underlying post-war nihilism present in these earlier currents resonates with the Japanese experience of post-war reconstruction and informs the sensibility evident in Hayashi's film. The film is therefore at once the product of criss-crossing cultural histories, 'colonial antagonisms' and the constant flux of international cinematic references that become the transnational identities of many East Asian films today.

The title of the final section 'How the West Was Won?' might sound unduly triumphalist, its qualifying question mark notwithstanding. Hollywood seems in little danger of 'losing' the struggle for global domination of the world's cinemas. On the other hand, the 'soft power' of Hong Kong, Japan and (more recently) South Korea has left its transformative mark on Western popular culture, a reminder that 'Americanization cannot be the only embodiment and carrier of cultural power'.[27] In his study of the 'Asian remake' trend, Gang Gary Xu seems to support Kwai-cheung Lo's view that the 'Asian invasion' is 'simply a new face of the old hegemony, as white America dresses itself up in a new representation of its old self and of the world'.[28] The remakes of *Ringu* and *Infernal Affairs* (as *The Departed*) mobilise a 'remaking of ethnicity' that erases their Japanese and Hong Kong identity; an 'identity', Xu argues, that has already been 'Hollywoodized'. The remaking trend represents not a yielding to East Asia, but a cost-effective outsourcing, with stories tested as box office hits in their local markets and as cult films by Asianised Western cinephiles.

Nikki Lee examines a different kind of 'Asian invasion', the arthouse and cult success of director Park Chan-wook, whose international profile peaked with the revenge drama *Oldboy*. Lee provides a compelling account of transnational auteurism, contingent on international institutions and strategies of circulation. Park's acclaim took different forms at home and abroad. In the West, he was the 'auteur of vengeance' and jewel in the crown of British distributor Tartan's 'Asia Extreme' brand. In South Korea, recognition hinged increasingly on international acclaim, a success measurable in festival prizes, 'the director who won the award at Cannes'. But as Lee demonstrates, domestic and international success were interrelated, so that Park's films acquired levels of significance and value as they passed through different sites of reception.

Xu's and Lee's essays each identify 'gatekeeper' figures in the crossover of East Asian cinema to the West – Korean-American producer Roy Lee, who facilitated the remakes of various East Asian films, and Quentin Tarantino, who gave cinephile approval to Park Chanwook at Cannes (and to *Hero* in Miramax's publicity campaign). Lee and Tarantino respectively conform to the two types of gatekeeper discussed by Leon Hunt – the disinterested producer who sees a gap in the market and the Asiaphile who absorbs cinematic influences from Asian genre cinema. Tarantino is one of the two central figures in Hunt's essay. The other is Luc Besson, whose engagement with East Asian films has been in his role as producer rather than director. If this suggests a perspective as opportunistic as Roy Lee's (or producers like Joel Silver's), then the liminality of Besson's production base – both connected to and competing with Hollywood – perhaps points to a more complex relationship with Hong Kong and Thai cinema. If *Kill Bill* is simultaneously reverential and proprietorial, blurring the desire to *be* and to *have* 'Asian', then the Besson-produced *District 13* represents a different kind of Franco-Asian action cinema, arising not out of diasporic film-making talent or cinephile referentiality, but a dialogue in how to generate a 'global' action cinema.

In the final essay, Sheng-mei Ma traces the tropes of brush and blade of Asian literature and film – calligraphy and swordsmanship – from Western colonial literature to the 'global film style' displayed by *Kill Bill, Ghost Dog* and *The Last Samurai*, as well as the 'Martial Arthouse' films of Zhang Yimou. The contemporary swordplay film is linked to the persistence of Orientalism, fantasies of the 'savage Orient' now feeding into the Asiaphilia of global action cinema. Ma discerns a Hollywood that has 'gone Orientalist', projecting longing rather than loathing onto the 'Orient', while effectively working within the same colonial imaginary.

East Asian cinema challenges existing conceptions in film studies such as textuality, authorship, Hollywood domination, third cinema and national allegory. Approaches to understanding contemporary film-making need to be re-assessed, re-imagined and (literally) re-mapped. The articles in this collection examine films from the Far East and their transnational consumption as an ever-changing process, presenting new perspectives that contest existing frameworks in film studies.

References

1   Roddick, Nick, 'Red River', *Sight and Sound* 16/12 (2006) p.33.

2   Roddick: 'Red River', p.32.

3   For more on Gojira/Godzilla's transnational career, see William M. Tsutsui and Michiko Ito (eds) *In Godzilla's Footsteps: Japanese Pop Culture Icons on the Global Stage* (New York and Houndmills: Palgrave Macmillan, 2006).

4   Ong, Aihwa, *Flexible Citizenship: The Cultural Logics of Transnationality* (Durham and London: Duke University Press, 1999).

5   Ong: *Flexible Citizenship*, p.4.

6   Transvergence and Francophone Cinema Conference, SFC 2006, <http://www.ncl.ac.uk/crif/sfc/downloads/abstracts06.doc> accessed 13 March 2007.

7   Novak, Marcus, *Speciation, Transvergence, Allogenesis: Notes on the Production of the Alien*, <http://www.mat.ucsb.edu/~marcos/transvergence. pdf> accessed 13 March 2007.

8   Transvergence and Francophone Cinema Conference, SFC 2006.

9   Wilson, Rob and Dissanayake, Wimal, 'Introduction' in Wilson and Dissanayake (eds) *Global/Local: Cultural Production and the Transnational Imaginary* (Durham: Duke University Press, 1996) p.6.

10 Appadurai, Arjun, *Modernity at Large: Cultural Dimensions of Globalization* (Minneapolis: University of Minnesota Press, 1996).

11 Appadurai: *Modernity at Large*, p.4.

12 Appadurai: *Modernity at Large*, p.35.

13 Morris, Meaghan, 'Introduction: Hong Kong Connections' in Siu Leung Li Morris and Chan Ching-ku Stephen (eds) *Hong Kong Connections: Transnational Imagination in Action Cinema* (Durham and Hong Kong: Duke University Press/Hong Kong University Press, 2005) p.13.

14 McCray, Douglas, 'Japan's Gross National Cool', *Foreign Policy* (2001), <http://www.chass.utoronto.ca/~ikalmar/illustex/japfpmcgray.htm>

15 The term is political scientist Joseph Nye's, adapted by Napier, Susan, 'When Godzilla Speaks' in Tsutsui and Ito (eds) *In Godzilla's Footsteps*, p.12.

16 On Hong Kong as (former) regional empire, see Lii, Ding-tzann, 'A colonised empire: reflections on the expansion of Hong Kong film in Asian countries' in Chen Kuan-hsing (ed) *Trajectories: Inter-Asian Cultural Studies* (London and New York: Routledge, 1998). On Japan, see Ching, Leo, 'Imaginings in the Empires of the Sun: Japanese Mass Culture in Asia' in Rob Wilson and Arif Dirlik (eds) *Asia/Pacific as Space of Cultural Production* (Durham and London: Duke University Press, 1995) and Ching, 'Globalizing the Regional, Regionalizing the Global: Mass Culture

and Asianism in the Age of Late Capital' in Appadurai, Arjun (ed) *Globalization* (Durham and London: Duke University Press, 2003).

17 Rayns, Tony, 'Shock Tactics', *Sight and Sound* 15/5 (2005) p.84.

18 Milner, Anthony and Johnson, Deborah, 'The Idea of Asia', <http://dspace.anu.edu.au/bitsteam/1885/41891/1/idea.html> p.1, accessed 30 January 2007.

19 Milner and Johnson: 'The Idea of Asia', p.3.

20 Lim, Shirley Geok-lin and Dissanayake, Wimal, 'Introduction' in Lim and Dissanayake (eds) *Transnational Asia Pacific: Gender, Culture and the Public Sphere* (Urbana and Chicago: University of Illinois Press, 1999) p.3.

21 Milner and Johnson: 'The Idea of Asia', p.3.

22 Milner and Johnson: 'The Idea of Asia', p.10.

23 Lim and Dissanayake: 'Introduction', p.3.

24 Standish, Isolde, *A New History of Japanese Cinema* (New York and London: Continuum, 2005), pp.287–93.

25 Wilson and Dissanayake: 'Introduction', p.1.

26 Wilson and Dissanayake: 'Introduction', p.3.

27 Ching: 'Globalizing the Regional, Regionalizing the Global', p. 295.

28 Lo, Kwai-cheung, *Chinese Face: The Transnational Popular Culture of Hong Kong* (Urbana and Chicago: University of Illinois Press, 2005), p.171.

PART ONE

GLOBAL ENCOUNTERS OF THE FIRST KIND

2

David Desser

Remaking *Seven Samurai* in World Cinema

In June 2004, GONZO studios released *Samurai 7* to Japanese TV. Its 26 individual episodes are reportedly among the most expensive television anime yet produced in Japan, a reported $300,000 per episode.[1] With major promotion in the US by FUNimation, which licensed the rights to show the series on US satellite and cable outlets (especially the influential Independent Film Channel) and distributes the series on high-quality DVD box-sets divided, appropriately enough, into seven volumes, *Samurai 7* found an equally receptive audience outside of Japan. It has also led to the marketing of related merchandise (beginning with deluxe editions of the DVD box-sets) and the sorts of internet fan sites in which message boards discuss the series, and self-described *otaku* produce artwork inspired by the series and assume character identities.[2] The obvious derivation of *Samurai 7* (which is the Japanese title, as well) is, of course, *Seven Samurai*, Kurosawa Akira's 1954 classic. At almost 650 minutes in total running time, the anime is almost three times as long as Kurosawa's lengthy action spectacular, making it not only the latest, as we will see, in a long line of adaptations of *Seven Samurai*, but also the longest. Such is the fame of Kurosawa's original film in the US and elsewhere that the official English-language title of the series is 'Akira Kurosawa's *Samurai 7*' (Figure 1).

Seven Samurai was not immediately quite the acclaimed classic it has become in subsequent years. As often happens, the film itself becomes more popular and respected when others acclaim it – in this instance by the number of remakes and reworkings. It perhaps did not help that the film was distributed overseas in a vastly truncated 160-minute version (although I would suggest that overseas audiences at the time in any

Figure 1. *Samurai 7* – the clear link to Kurosawa

case preferred the more picturesque period films then winning awards at Venice, Cannes and the American Academy). Even at its full 200+ minutes running time in Japan, *Seven Samurai* was a film that was quite literally too much for the context in which it was released. The longest film made in the post-war era, the longest period film since Mizoguchi Kenji's far different *The Loyal Forty Seven Retainers of the Genroku Era* (Japan, 1941), which was released in two parts, and, most importantly, a film that unsparingly looked at the chaos of the Sengoku period (1478–1600) as a metaphor for the societal breakdown of the post-war period. Kurosawa refused to engage in the kind of sentimentalism becoming increasingly popular in dealing with the Pacific War. Even Mizoguchi's masterpiece, *Ugetsu* (1953), participates in the process of self-victimisation, allegorising the Second World War through the Sengoku era to claim victimhood for ordinary Japanese. Kurosawa refuses to let the Japanese off the hook, refuses to allow the heroism of the seven samurai to repress their own complicity in a social system of vast inequality. While the farmers are indeed victims of a feudalistic/militaristic culture, they are equally hardly innocent bystanders in their own destiny. Moreover, Kurosawa's film marked a vastly different treatment of the samurai genre. Try as one might, it is difficult to find many forebears to Kurosawa's film. Regardless of the historico-cultural dimensions of the film (about which we will have more to say), in terms of genre it appears to be a complete break from the pre-war samurai film and absolutely *sui generis* in the post-war period. Although *jidai geki* featuring samurai certainly had a tradition of social engagement, adult orientation and artistic integrity, with many top directors of the pre-war period working in the form, few films combined the unabashed reliance on sword play and other action set-pieces with such seriousness of purpose. So unprecedented was *Seven Samurai* that it would be seven years before any Japanese director would attempt a samurai film of such scale and with anything like a similar theme. In this instance, veteran director and fellow Toho employee Inagaki Hiroshi would pay tribute to his younger colleague's film with *Bandits on the Wind* (Japan, 1961). The talented Gosha Hideo would work a deft combination of *Seven Samurai* and *Yojimbo* (Japan, 1961) for his feature film debut, *Three Outlaw Samurai* (Japan, 1964). Yet for all that, as we will see, *Seven Samurai* has been remade, reworked, referenced and relied upon in global cinema, the Japanese themselves have been far less interested than one might expect in remaking such a transcendental masterpiece. We can compare this situation with a Hollywood film that is a veritable Rosetta Stone for understanding subsequent American cinema.

It is probably inarguable that *The Searchers*, John Ford's classic western of 1956, has had not just an incalculable influence on post-Classical American cinema, but has been overtly remade and reworked more times than any other American film. Hollywood's major film-makers of the post-studio era, including the likes of Sam Peckinpah, Steven Spielberg, George Lucas, Martin Scorsese, John Milius and Paul Schrader, have continually found Ford's film to be fair game for cinematic reinterpretation. The acclaim meted out to the film, especially since the 1970s, may partly be owed to the respect it commands from these directorial notables, but it may also be owed to the way the film itself so centrally participates in one of the founding myths of the American experience. And the propensity of film-makers to draw inspiration from Ford's film may itself have something to do with the continuing power such a foundational story continues to exert on the American imagination. Interestingly, the number of overt remakes is very small; indeed, it may be argued that it has never been remade the way, say, another genuine classic like *King Kong* has been redone twice, or *A Star is Born*, to take a completely different sort of example, which has similarly been tackled on more than one occasion. Instead, *The Searchers* is referenced, reworked, reimagined – often, given the demise of the western in post-Classical Hollywood, in other genres, from the urban thriller to sci-fi to fantasy to war. One may say that at the heart of Ford's film lies the 'captivity narrative' – a potent metaphor (one derived from historical reality, to be sure) for the White European encounter with the Native in the New World.[3] Although this theme can be found in numerous westerns both before and after *The Searchers*, Ford's film highlights the racial dynamics in a particularly piquant way and reveals much of the ambiguity, the attraction/repulsion, revolving around the White/Native interaction. The specifically racial dimension to this captivity narrative lies interestingly at the heart of many of the 'remakes' in ways that have perhaps not been sufficiently acknowledged: in *Taxi Driver* (US, 1976), in *Star Wars* (US, 1977), in *Conan the Barbarian* (US, 1982). The point is that the foundational myth of the captivity narrative still exerts a force on the American imagination, even when the narrative events are transposed from the American West into the contemporary city, the Vietnam War (e.g. *Uncommon Valor*, US, 1983) or a galaxy far, far away.

If it is true, as I have claimed, that *The Searchers* has become something of an urtext for Post-Classical Hollywood, has Ford's film similarly been the object of veneration and recapitulation in world cinema? I believe not. If the essence of Ford's film is the captivity narrative, then perhaps such a structure has little resonance in the many more homogeneous societies that have produced major cinemas. In other words, the cultural dimension of *The Searchers* has made it less an object for reworking in global cinema than a film of significant stylistic influence or cinephiliac intertextuality. What then of *Seven Samurai*, which, on the one hand, has been little remade in Japan, yet, on the other hand, has been so frequently reworked on global screens? Antecedents to Kurosawa's film may indeed be found in Classical antiquity, however, in particular Aeschylus's *Seven Against Thebes*. *Seven Samurai* may draw its number of protagonists from this work, along with the idea of fighting for one's conscience. The Homeric epics, *The Iliad* and *The Odyssey*, may also have some claim to be structural underpinnings of Kurosawa's film. Is the film, then, less 'Japanese' and therefore of relatively little interest in Japan, but of major interest outside of the country?

If *The Searchers* draws some of its power from the American foundational myth of white/native interaction and conflict in the form of the captivity narrative, from what wellspring of national mythology does *Seven Samurai* draw? Obviously, the group-protagonist structure may owe something to *Chushingura*, the archetypal Japanese group-oriented master narrative. Yet I would argue that it is precisely the setting in the period of Civil Wars and not the more static Tokugawa era that makes *Seven Samurai* less a complex story of feudal loyalty and implied feudal criticism, but in a certain way a more simple story of individual morality, of doing what is right regardless of the consequences, of the strong protecting the weak in the face of social chaos and rampant immorality.

The shift from individual or dual-hero to group hero may reflect the circumstances of the post-war world, where individual initiative seems unlikely to solve complex social problems, not to mention the recent past of massed armies wreaking unprecedented destruction, not only on military but civilian targets as well. Some of this shift is visible in the Hollywood western, for instance, Ford's *My Darling Clementine* (US, 1946), where the Earp Brothers and Doc Holiday oppose the Clanton family and gang, or Ford's cavalry trilogy (*Fort Apache*, US, 1948; *She Wore a Yellow Ribbon*, US, 1949; *Rio Grande*, US, 1950), which brings the Second World War combat film to the Wild West. Kurosawa's film may, in fact, be closer to the war film than the samurai film, after all. It is therefore time to think about what is the essence of the film, what are the fundamental structures that are being brought to bear in the numerous remakes, and what, thereby, do we mean by a remake in this instance.

A scene-by-scene analysis of *Seven Samurai*, followed by obvious comparisons and contrasts with films one might claim to be remakes, would be time consuming and tedious. The mere mechanistic notation of similarity and difference would no doubt reveal what we already suspect: that a particular group of films may be seen as remakes of *Seven Samurai*. Instead, we might divide our thinking into highlighting structural features that Kurosawa's film relies upon and analysing the major thematic components that give the original its universal significance.

Major Narrative Patterns

1) A small, isolated, powerless community is menaced by outside forces.
2) The community has failed in its attempt to deal with the menace on their own.
3) The members of the community decide to hire mercenaries to protect themselves and their property.
4) A leader is found who agrees to protect the community. He enlists or otherwise engages a small group of other fighters in the community's support.
5) The interaction between the mercenaries and the community begins immediately and continues back at the community.
6) The mercenaries begin to sympathise with the community members, as they live with and train them to aid in their own protection.
7) A series of minor skirmishes or small victories are achieved.
8) The climactic battle ends in the utter defeat of the villains, the death of some of the mercenaries, and the return to normalcy for the community.

Major Actants

1) The emissaries: the members of the village who leave to seek out the mercenaries.
2) The mercenary leader.
3) Other individual members of the hired group:
   a) the trainee
   b) the liminal figure (a mercenary with ties to both groups)
   c) an old friend of the leader
   d) a clever warrior who also exhibits leadership
   e) a jokester or playful figure
   f) the consummate warrior/fighter.

4)   A love interest from the community.
5)   The bandit leader.
6)   A community member hostile to the group.

To remind us of these character types, I will recall *Seven Samurai* in this format.

1)   The emissaries: Manzo, Rikichi and Yohei, the members of the village who leave to seek out the mercenaries

Menaced by a bandit troupe numbering some 40 outlaws, a small farming village, under the advice of the village leader, sends out three townsmen. The villagers must travel to a larger, more open town, which itself is characteristic of lawlessness and violence.

2)   The mercenary leader, Kambei

The three townsmen come upon Kambei as he rescues a kidnapped child. They enlist his help, which he reluctantly agrees to provide.

3)   Individual members of the hired group

Kambei gathers various warriors through various means, including:

a)   the trainee;
   Among the gathered group watching Kambei rescue the child is a young man, Katsushiro, who desires to be taught by Kambei.
b)   the liminal figure: a mercenary with ties to both groups;
   Kikuchiyo, an undisciplined youth, joins the group initially against the group's wishes, but through persistence, humour and some skill is made a full member. It is revealed that he shares a farmer's background, thus aligning him structurally with the townspeople.
c)   an old friend of the leader;
   Kambei meets up with Shichiroji, a former companion in the civil wars.
d)   a clever warrior who also exhibits leadership;
   Kambei enlists Gorobei to the cause due to the man's natural fighting abilities and leadership skills. Gorobei agrees to join the fight because he is intrigued by Kambei.
e)   a jokester or playful figure;
   Gorobei enlists Heihachi to the cause. Although he is a second-rate swordsman, he is a first-rate companion.
f)   the consummate warrior/fighter;
   Although only interested in perfecting his skill, Kyuzo, a master swordsman, agrees to the farmers' cause.

4)   The love interest
Shino, Manzo's daughter and one of the young women hidden by
the town, is discovered by Katsushiro. They become both sexually
and romantically involved.

5)   The bandit leader
Though he is given relatively little characterisation, he is frequently singled out for visual emphasis, and it is clear that he is a
competent leader of desperate men.

6)   The community member hostile to the group
Here it is Manzo, Shino's father, who forces her to cut her hair and
persuades the townspeople to hide the young women. Hostility or
distrust between farmers and samurai remain, though there is no
betrayal of the town to the bandits, only a continued suspicion of
the samurai.

I would suggest that most films which may qualify as remakes of *Seven
Samurai* hardly reproduce all of the actants in the exact same formations and some films may not even reproduce all of the narrative patterns. Thus we will also later need to return to the thematic concerns
that seem to inhabit Kurosawa's structural features.

I cannot go through each of the films on the (necessarily incomplete)
list of titles that I have compiled (see Appendix), in order to demonstrate how they reproduce enough of the major narrative patterns and
actants which may qualify them as remakes of *Seven Samurai*. Instead,
I will make reference to a number of films and a number of their most
significant features, in order to begin a discussion of the ways that
Kurosawa's film has been reworked both structurally and thematically.
Before undertaking that survey, however, I would like to take the best
known and most influential remake of the film and once again rehearse
the major narrative patterns and actants.

Perhaps by virtue of it being so close a remake of Kurosawa's film,
John Sturges's *The Magnificent Seven* (US, 1960) is among the best
known and most respected of the many remakes one can point to. I
would argue that given Hollywood's presence then as now in global cinema, it is arguable that many subsequent remakes of the Japanese film
are actually sifted through the American version. Let us see how closely
it adheres to the model outlined above.

1)   The emissaries
The members of the village who leave to seek out the mercenaries. Menaced by a bandit troupe numbering some 40 outlaws, a small farming village, under the advice of the village elder, sends out three of its members in a pattern exactly the same as in Kurosawa's film. At the thematic level, the fact that it is a Mexican village that sends its members north of the border to enlist gringo gunfighters adds specifically American racial and cultural dimensions. But the narrative and actantial pattern is precisely the same.

2)   The mercenary leader
The three townsmen discover Chris and Vin as they drive a hearse up to boot hill. This is the equivalent of Kambei's rescuing the child from the kidnapper in that the men act completely altruistically and their actions introduce them, so to speak, to the farmers. The three farmers approach Chris and Vin, although Vin initially declines to help. Chris becomes the de facto leader, the one who agrees to help and who will gather other fighters.

3)   Other individual members of the group
a)   the trainee;
b)   the liminal figure; a mercenary with ties to both groups.
The character of Chico functions as both the trainee – the young man who so admires the mercenary leader that he wants to be taken under his wing – and the liminal figure – the farmer-turned-fighter.
c)   an old friend of the leader;
Harry Luck is Chris's old friend. His motives for rejoining his buddy are never altruistic until the moment of his death, but in an odd way he, like Shichiroji, is rather frozen out of much of the decision making.
d)   a clever warrior who also exhibits leadership;
e)   a jokester or playful figure;
Vin functions as both an assistant to Chris (as he did in the scene when they drive the hearse), but also as the jokester, delivering many humorous lines of dialogue.
f)   the consummate warrior/fighter;
This is the character of Britt, first introduced, as in *Seven Samurai*, answering the challenge to a duel. And like Kyuzu, his interest seems more personal than altruistic.

The character of Bernardo O'Reilly is introduced in much the same manner as Heihanchi, chopping wood, but they otherwise share few characteristics. Nevertheless, it is interesting that the screenplay for the American film would use the exact same motif of a down-on-his-luck fighter discovered chopping wood for a day's pay. Similarly, Bernardo is given some of the attributes of Kikuchiyo in that he befriends some of the village children. Only Lee, the cowardly gunfighter who seeks redemption on the battle-field, is a wholly original character. Anyone familiar with *Seven Samurai* would immediately recognise the members who comprise the magnificent seven.

4)   **The love interest from the community**
Petra, a farmer's daughter, found hiding in the woods by Chico, becomes not only the love interest for the young gunfighter but, in one of the biggest variations from Kurosawa's original, manages to hold onto her lover at film's end.

5)   **The bandit leader**
The bandit leader is not only given a name, Calvera, but a rather significant role. Although this is a departure from Kurosawa's film, it is not a significant one in terms of the film's structure or on the actantial level. Interestingly, many subsequent remakes take their cue from the American remake and endow the bandit leader with more individuality and personality. This provides subsequent films with a climactic battle in which not only the bandits, but the bandit leader, is defeated, thus allowing for even greater catharsis through violence.

6)   **The community member hostile to the group**
One of the farmers, afraid of Calvera's revenge on the village, betrays the farmers' plan and the gunfighters are captured. This is a plot point completely absent from Kurosawa's film, one which is taken up in some remakes, but by no means the majority.

Variations on a Theme

Many of the films on the list of direct remakes make changes of some significance. *Battle Beyond the Stars* (US, 1980), with its script by John Sayles, nods in the direction of *Seven Samurai* by calling the planet which functions as the isolated community 'Akira' and its inhabitants the Akiras, and nods also toward *The Magnificent Seven* by casting Robert Vaughn, one of the original cast members of John Sturges's film. Like *The Magnificent Seven*, its bandit chief is far more personalized, here in the form of John Saxon. This Sci-Fi variation (the Japanese were the first to turn *Seven Samurai* into SF with *Message from Space*, 1978) utilises only one emissary, here in the form of Richard Thomas, and this emissary figure also functions as the liminal figure, the Akira who longs to fight alongside the warriors. (*Battle* is also a variation on *Star Wars*, which also owes much to Kurosawa and *Seven Samurai*.) The film uses a love interest, Darlanne Fluegel as Nanelia, but is the first of the *Seven Samurai* remakes to introduce a woman warrior. *Message from Space* utilises women far more significantly than any previous remake, more so even than the Kurosawa original. It is very much worth thinking of a line of descent from *Seven Samurai* to *Star Wars* to *Message* to *Battle*. Women warriors are taken up in B-feature remakes like *Dune Warriors* (US/Philippines, 1990) and *The Bad Pack* (US, 1998). *Dune Warriors* not only borrows the woman warrior, but also utilizes a single emissary figure and combines this function with the love interest, as the woman seeks out warriors and falls in love with one of them who, like Chico at the end of *The Magnificent Seven*, but unlike Katsushiro in *Seven Samurai*, chooses to remain in the village. This pattern also appears in *China Gate* (Rajkumar Santoshi, India, 1998): the woman as emissary and love interest who falls in love with the trainee figure, who in turn remains in the village. Although I will return to it in some detail later, it is worth mentioning *Samurai 7*, with which this essay began. It is another Sci-Fi variation on Kurosawa's original; it also uses the female emissary figure, but eschews the woman warrior of so many later variations. And although it is not the first animated version of Kurosawa's film (that distinction belongs to *A Bug's Life*, US, 1998), it is at once the most clear cut version of the film and the most extensively revised.

Another interesting variation may be found in prolific producer-director Tsui Hark's *Seven Swords* (HK, 2005). The film is based on *Seven Swordsmen from Tian Mountain*, a serialised novel begun in early 1956 by popular martial arts writer Liang Yusheng. It would be worth undertaking further research to see if Liang was influenced by *Seven Samurai*; at the very least the '*shichi*' in '*Shichinin no samurai*' (*Seven Samurai*) is the same character – '*qi*' for 'seven'. Whether or not the novel drew inspiration from the recently released Kurosawa film, there is no doubt that Tsui's version consciously alludes to *Seven Samurai*, from the simplified title to just 'seven swords', to the village menaced by larger forces, to the search for a suitable leader who helps gather various warriors, a love interest for one of the fighters, and the like. In addition, certain of Kurosawa's signature stylings are utilised – although the martial arts choreography is most definitely of the wire-work and

CGI variety Tsui himself helped pioneer. Nevertheless, in this film, as in the others just discussed, the basic patternings and character types found in Kurosawa's classic remain eminently and, I would suggest, deliberately visible, despite other generic trappings and geographical settings.

Visual Recollections and Global Film Style

Before I turn to the issue of the thematic issues with which *Seven Samurai* resonates, I would like to suggest that many films signal their relationship to Kurosawa's film through visual echoing. We not only find the same narrative patterns and character types, but many of the sequences are handled in the same way. There are, for instance, two major dramatic moments in *Seven Samurai* that seem to be particularly piquant for future film-makers. The first is the arrival of the samurai into the beleaguered community. After some days of travel, they arrive on a bluff overlooking the village (Figure 2).

Figure 2. *Seven Samurai* arrive at the village

The reality of their situation hits them: that they have indeed been hired to protect a group of farmers and that it is a less-than-glamorous locale. *The Magnificent Seven* is less interested in highlighting the poverty of the village, and the gunfighters' dismay when they acknowledge this, than it is in reproducing the other major motif of the farmers hiding from the warriors when they arrive. The dusty street of the village is mysteriously empty and this, more than the poverty, is what strikes them upon their entry (Figure 3).

In *China Gate* (which is the longest remake version until *Samurai 7*), the visual echo to Kurosawa's film is even more profound. Similarly positioned on a bluff overlooking the village, the soldiers hired to run off the dacoit Jageera and his numerous henchmen survey their new home in the company of one of the villagers sent out to meet them (Figure 4).

Another important visual echo is the use of grave markers at the films' conclusions. These markers serve not only as dramatic reminders of the cost the warriors had to pay to rescue the embattled community, but also as a kind of memorialisation within the films. Kurosawa uses the motif of digging new grave mounds as each warrior and each farmer dies over the course of the film. Most of the other films do not do that, mostly because all of the casualties come at the climactic battle scene. It is thus only at the end, when Kurosawa gives us the four grave markers of the samurai (Figure 5), that other films may find their visual echoing. Thus at the end of *The Magnificent Seven*, the three farm lads befriended by Bernardo O'Reilly come to place flowers on his grave marker, as they promised him they would (Figure 6).

Figure 3. *The Magnificent Seven* arrive at the village

Figure 4. *China Gate* – overlooking the village

Figure 5. *Seven Samurai* – four graves

Figure 6. *The Magnificent Seven* – graves

It may be that Kurosawa's unerring visual sense could not be bettered by John Sturges, and so the American film-maker liberally borrowed from the Japanese director's repertory. But there was never a question that the American film needed any bona fides to convince an audience of its high budget sheen and stylistic maturity. The same is less true of many of the remakes to follow. Here I want to suggest that film-makers outside of the US, especially those in Asia seeking a kind of global cinematic respectability, could use Japanese cinema in general and *Seven Samurai* in particular (which had, after all, been the basis for a Hollywood film – no higher standard in the global marketplace) as a kind of shorthand announcement. Intertextual references and visual echoes of this film thus function for local audiences as the arrival of their own cinemas. This is the case, for instance, with *The Magnificent Trio* (HK, 1966), an early film of the soon-to-be influential Hong Kong martial arts master Zhang Che.

The Magnificent Trio represents in some ways the culmination of a process of globalising attempts on the part of Hong Kong film-makers, led by both Loke Wan Tho, head of MP&GI Studios (later Cathay), and Run Run Shaw, production chief at the Shaw Brothers Studio. From the middle 1950s onward, Hong Kong films looked to Japan and Japanese cinema as both a model and a competitor for transnational markets and global film prestige. They engaged in a pattern of shooting films in Japan (sometimes with all Chinese casts playing Japanese characters as, for instance, *Madame Butterfly*, starring Li Lihua, and *Miss Kikuko*, starring Lin Dai, as the eponymous heroines of their respective 1956 films); co-productions with Japanese studios, especially Toho (as, for instance, Chiba Yasuki's trilogy *A Night in Hong Kong*, 1961; *Star of Hong Kong*, 1962; *Hong Kong-Tokyo-Honolulu*, starring

Yu Ming and Takarada Akira); or the importation of Japanese directors and cinematographers into Hong Kong.[4] Another strategy involved
the formation of a regional film festival, co-founded by Nagata
Masaichi, head of Japan's Daiei Studios, and Run Run Shaw. Though
it began as the Southeast Asia Film Festival in 1954, it was renamed the
Asian Film Festival in 1957.[5] The Japanese saw this festival as a chance
not only to enter Southeast Asian markets, but also as an attempt to
redeem their image tarnished by the Pacific War. For Hong Kong film-
makers, it meant not only increasing their share of overseas markets (on
which Hong Kong films have long been dependent), but a chance,
through the Mandarin language cinema, to garner a prestige for the territory's films that had previously been lacking.[6]

Eventually Shaw came to dominate the Hong Kong market and
attract overseas audiences in ever-greater numbers, through the production of Mandarin language martial arts films highly influenced by
Japanese samurai films. Both King Hu and Zhang Che fell under the
influence of Japanese swordplay styling. But for Zhang Che, the influ-
ence was both more direct and obvious: *The Magnificent Trio* is a direct
remake of *Three Outlaw Samurai*, as indicated above, itself a remake of
Kurosawa's *Seven Samurai* and *Yojimbo*. In remaking *Three Outlaw
Samurai*, *The Magnificent Trio* also alludes to *Seven Samurai* and *The
Magnificent Seven* through its English language title.[7] The Shaw
Brothers made no secret of their use of samurai films as models for the
'New Style' martial arts films, but at the same time bought up the rights
of Japanese swordplay dramas and showed them only sparingly, if at
all, in Hong Kong theatres. More particularly, their directors and writ-
ers studied the films, and many personnel were even sent to Japan to
learn production techniques. This is not to say, by the way, that *The
Magnificent Trio* or subsequent films by Zhang (or those of King Hu)
are mere imitations of Japanese samurai movies. Particular uses of
Beijing Opera and Chinese acrobatics definitely 'sinicize' these films.
The point is that *Seven Samurai*, by way of *Three Outlaw Samurai*, was
fundamentally influential in the beginning of Shaw Brothers' dominance of Hong Kong markets and Hong Kong cinema's success in
capturing more global audiences.

For the Hindi cinema (often known as Bollywood), globalization has
proven a more elusive goal. Though Hollywood films have long been
both a model of and source for Hindi films, since the 1970s, Asian
cinema has been no less an avatar of globalization. *China Gate* is not
only a fairly close rendering of *Seven Samurai* (more so than it is
The Magnificent Seven), but it also one of the few Bollywood films to
acknowledge its source material (Figure 7).

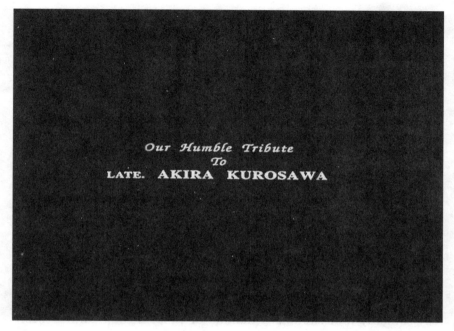

Figure 7. *China Gate* – Kurosawa acknowledgement

China Gate has received almost no critical attention in the increasingly voluminous literature on Hindi cinema. One notable exception is a thoughtful on-line essay by Andrew Grossman. He notes that '*China Gate* may be that rare Bollywood extravaganza that can be evaluated not just as a generic masala, but as a film situated within the transnational arena of artistic influence and canonical film education'.[8] Though not a major hit in India, it was acknowledged as one of the most expensive Indian films ever produced and, though it obviously borrows heavily from *Sholay* (India, 1975), perhaps the most popular Hindi film ever made, reviews were respectful. Interestingly, the review in *Planet Bollywood* (one of the most influential publications devoted to Bollywood cinema) notes the connections the film has with *Sholay*, but says nothing about its equally obvious connection to *Seven Samurai* despite the film's own overt acknowledgement.[9] The transposition from Japanese brigands to Indian dacoits is a natural one, while the displaced *ronin* equally find a suitable counterpart in the group of disgraced former Indian Army officers and enlisted men.[10] It may be argued that Hindi cinema's uses of Hollywood, Hong Kong and Japan are attempts to modernise the Indian cinema for domestic audiences, while at the

same time trying to enter a transnational marketplace increasingly dominated by a global film style and themes. Grossman's idea, then, that 'a
"transnationalized" Hindi production such as *China Gate* is probably
as user-friendly an introduction to popular Indian cinema as one could
wish for', is a clear acknowledgment of the 'transnationalized' (what I
am calling 'globalized') image of *Seven Samurai*.

It's a Man's (Globalised) World

If, as I indicated above, aspects of Japanese culture seem to have been
evacuated by *Seven Samurai*, then it has proven unsurprising that the
film has been so amenable, so available, for reworking. The narrative
structure and character patterning may then be filled up with thematic
concerns that easily find equivalents elsewhere. Almost *sui generis* as a
genre entry, the film also reproduces little of the traditions of Japanese
culture which underpin the samurai film. Chinese martial artists,
American gunfighters, space jockeys or ex-Indian Army soldiers easily
substitute for *ronin*, and the protection they afford to besieged farmers
may similarly translate to any number of isolated communities. More
to the point, the specificities of the feudal system, upon which the
bedrock of the samurai film rests, may similarly be evacuated in favour
of more generalised issues of lawlessness, corruption or simply *laissez
faire* capitalism. By the same token, the feudal class system of Japan
may find some homologies in other Asian cultures (Hong Kong films
often rely on this feature), but it may also be completely ignored inside
and outside of Asia. The same is true of one of Kurosawa's most typical motifs, which is a characteristic of Asian culture, but one particularly resonant with Kurosawa: the master/apprentice or teacher/pupil
relationship. Indeed, one could reasonably ask what martial arts movies
would be without this motif, but for Kurosawa it extends well beyond
his period films. And even the motif of the young warrior seeking guid-
ance leads more to the homo-social than the educational in many films
which reproduce this element.

   One element that is never ignored is perhaps the one element that
translates into the global most easily: the male group. Although we have
noted the introduction of a woman warrior into the basic pattern beginning in 1978, the majority of direct or partial adaptations of *Seven
Samurai* retain this feature. I have suggested elsewhere that Shaw
Brothers Studio dominated Hong Kong cinema and made their
inevitable push toward a global presence when the films of Zhang Che
began the shift away from the traditional reliance on women stars.[11]

The male-dominated films of Hollywood beginning in the late 1960s (I would suggest the increasing reliance on male stars was as much a factor in the so-called Hollywood Renaissance as the increasing focus on youth) became the first sign of a globalised cinema, and any cinema thereafter, especially those operating more in the commercial realm than in the art cinema mode, was obligated to follow this model. Even today there is an attendant 'masculinism' to many of the globalised genres of Hollywood, Hong Kong, Japan and South Korea: the action film, neo-noir, martial arts. The homosocial world that Kurosawa created transcended its origins or recollections in the Second World War combat film and John Ford's cavalry westerns. In particular, Kurosawa extended the worldview of Howard Hawks – the all-male group bonded by professionalism – into a universe where male camaraderie was perhaps the highest value. Where Ford and Hawks underpin (and grow out of) American cultural values, Kurosawa's masculinist vision proved more universal and could even be retranslated into the American cinema. Of course, such values do not exist outside of history and culture – the samurai homo-social tradition, for instance, may be seen operating within Kurosawa's universe. The point is, rather, that the male homosocial group became a sign of global cinema, a rejection of the female-dominated Classical cinema – whether Hollywood, China, Japan to some extent – and a signature of the new transnational mode. Thus to work with and within this new male cinema was to work with and within the new global cinema.

Another element that is never ignored and which translates easily, even if it is not so universally homogeneous, is the community in peril. The major point here is not simply the act of heroism that the warriors must perform or even the cost to them in fulfilling the obligation they have taken on. Any story of heroism involves a sacrifice, or at least a potential one. What Kurosawa is after is the gap between warriors and villagers, a gap that the best of the remakes must somehow reproduce. In fact, we might claim that the best remakes are those which manage to add the dimension of difference between the saviours and the saved, lending their respective films a greater cultural specificity and richer thematic terrain. It is not for nothing that the low budget 'B' feature remakes tend to be inferior. It is not simply a matter of finances, but expansiveness of vision; or, to put it another way, such minor remakes as *World Gone Wild* (US, 1988) or *Dune Warriors* (US, 1990) merely reproduce the surface characteristics of *Seven Samurai* and little of its deeper structures.

Kurosawa's film relies on feudal class divisions to highlight *difference* between the rescued and the rescuers. Lacking the overt class structures of Japan, the American *Magnificent Seven* relies on a racial divide, although I would suggest the real divide is First World/Third World, North/South.[12] It is a matter of access to power and the kind of technological resources possessed by America and lacking in Mexico/the Third World. Still, crossing the boundaries of class and race is hardly much easier in *The Magnificent Seven* than it is in *Seven Samurai*. If the liminal figure of Chico remains in the farming village at the end of the Hollywood film, where Katsushiro does not in Kurosawa's original, it may be that Chico's Mexican background (though not the actor's) more easily allows such a movement. The divide in *China Gate* is not quite a feudal class system, while neither overtly is it a First World/Third World divide. One could make the case for a kind of Mumbai-based First World-ism that the former soldiers represent, compared to the more obvious rural and 'backward' Third-World-styled village. Instead, the film plays on communal divides *within* the group (Hindu vs. Muslim), while technological and experiential divides separate the soldiers from the villagers. *China Gate*, then, becomes an interesting variation on *Seven Samurai* for its focus on the dynamics within the warrior-group.

One might, were space to permit, go through many of the remakes and reworkings I have uncovered, and see just how the group element and the issue of difference is handled in particular films. In doing so, one might indeed come upon a way of quantifying just why some remakes are more effective than others.

Originary Returns

Few anime devoted to the exploits of samurai have achieved anything like the cult status of *Samurai 7*. Indeed, when one thinks of the anime of greatest fan-boy and girl appeal, samurai seem remarkably absent. None of the visionary anime of Miyazaki Hayao or Otomo Katsuhiro deal with samurai; the groundbreaking television anime in the US, like *Pokemon* and the *Dragon Ball* series, are similarly samurai-free. Samurai, perhaps understandably, have little intrinsic appeal to young fans outside Japan. Yet I would suggest that, although samurai anime are hardly uncommon, Japanese youth are also little invested in those remnants of either feudal culture or classical cinema. In order to rework a samurai drama in anime form, it is perhaps, then, no surprise for Japanese producers to take a work that is already a globalised text and not simply a classical Japanese one. Similarly, to enter the global arena with a samurai drama, the globalized form of anime might be the best route to take.

A full analysis of *Samurai 7* would be worth undertaking at a later date, both for its fascinating similarities and revealing differences from *Seven Samurai*, as well as for its monumental achievement more generally as a hybrid of classical samurai film and various strands of anime. It is, to my mind, the most thorough re-imagining of Kurosawa's classic, at once simply a lengthy retelling (with added subplots) and a complete re-conceptualisation. In its basic outline it reproduces the fundamental plot, the essential nature of the characters, and many of the basic thematic motifs and structures so fundamental to the success of the original. A farming village is imperiled by marauding former samurai and, unable to defend themselves, they send a small group to the nearby city to recruit samurai to their cause. The samurai they recruit undertake the mission for varied motivations, from sheer heroism, to a desire to prove oneself in combat, to the camaraderie among warriors or the desire to test oneself against impossible odds. The characters retain the same names in the anime as they do in the original and they have many of the same characteristics. Kambei is the leader, first met as he rescues a child from a kidnapper. Initially reluctant to help the farmers, he is eventually won over to their cause and agrees to recruit other warriors. Katsushiro is the earnest, would-be samurai who begs Kambei to take him on as a pupil; Kikuchiyo, the bombastic fighter more loud than he is skilled; Shichiroji is Kambei's old companion from a previous campaign; Kyuzo is the master swordsman, etc.[13] The romantic attraction between a village girl and Katsushiro is also reproduced, although, typical of anime, she is something of a magical girl. The gradual formation of a relationship between protector and protected, the development of a defensive strategy for the village, even the subplot of Rikichi's wife, are all reproduced.[14]

It is not hard to see the appeal that *Samurai 7* has to anime fans. In re-imagining Kurosawa's original, the anime now belongs to the sci-fi genre so typical of the form and, even more definitively, participates in the prevalence for mecha – the mechanical/technological hybridisation of the human body. The samurai fighter Kikuchiyo is a mecha-warrior, part man, mostly cyborg, while all of the bandits, called Nobuseri, are no longer human, having traded in their human bodies for android status. Similarly, the characters possess fighting skills and abilities far in excess of even the most outrageous live action drama; indeed, the film derives a lot of its fight choreography and picturization from post-1990s Hong Kong martial arts movies. Character iconography is typical of anime, too – Kyuzo now sports blond hair while Katsushiro is highly androgynous, for instance. Yet fans of the samurai film will also profit from investing in this series. It wonderfully imagines medieval Japan in a post-industrial landscape, with typical anime iconography drawn from Fritz Lang's *Metropolis*. And in its imaging of the bandits as mecha-warriors, can we not see an apt metaphor for a samurai's loss of status, along with larger questions about what it means to be human in a chaotic, amoral world? Of course, this is precisely what Kurosawa's classic original is about. Set in the future, *Samurai 7* sees the world suffering after a massive war; set in the past, *Seven Samurai* was also about a massive war, but was also clearly referencing a war more lately fought. If wars, and the men (and women) who fight in them, seem inevitably to recur throughout history, perhaps *Seven Samurai*, one of the greatest films ever about war and how it is fought and died in, may similarly be constantly remade.

References

1   <http://www.animenewsnetwork.com/encyclopedia/anime.php?id=3127>
2   See, for instance, <http://www.theotaku.com/anime/samurai_7/>
3   See Slotkin, Richard, *Regeneration through Violence: The Mythology of the American Frontier, 1600–1860*. (Middleton, CT: Wesleyan University Press, 1973), for an in-depth discussion of the significance of the captivity narrative for the formation of a distinctly American literature and identity.
4   See Yau Shuk-ting, Kinnia, 'On Love with an Alien' in *The Shaw Screen: A Preliminary Study* (Hong Kong: Hong Kong Film Archive, 2003), for a discussion of the Shaw Brothers' importation of Japanese talent.
5   Yau Shuk-ting, Kinnia, 'Shaws' Japanese Collaboration and Competition as Seen Through the Asian Film Festival Evolution in *The Shaw Screen*.
6   Shaw Brothers also attempted a short-lived campaign to break out of the ethnic film circuit in New York, with a year-long series of films shown at the 57th St. Playhouse in 1965. Almost universally negative reviews put a halt to this effort.
7   *Seven Samurai* was, in fact, released in overseas markets in 1956 under the title *The Magnificent Seven*.
8   Grossman, Andrew, 'China Gate', *Scope: An Online Review of Film Studies* (February 2001), <http://www.nottingham.ac.uk/film/journal/filmrev/china-gate.htm>
9   Sunder, 'China Gate', *Planet Bollywood*, <http://www.planetbollywood.com/Film/chinagate.html>
10 The title refers to a campaign fought years earlier, for which the men were court-martialled due to their supposed cowardice in fleeing the battle.

11 Desser, David, 'Making Movies Male: Zhang Che and the Shaw Bros. Martial Arts Movies, 1965–1975' in Pang Laikwan and Wong Day (eds), *Masculinities and Hong Kong Cinema* (Hong Kong: Hong Kong University Press, 2005).

12 Of course there is a racial dimension to the global North/South divide.

13 Actually, Kyuzo's character here is more clearly drawn from *Three Outlaw Samurai* than *Seven Samurai*, in that Kikyo, in Gosha's film, is, like Kyuzo in *Samurai 7*, originally in the employ of the local, oppressive magistrate.

14 One of the most moving and brilliantly handled of all the sequences in Kurosawa's film is the raid on the brigand's fort and the death of Rikichi's wife; it is one of those moments that is rarely reproduced in subsequent versions.

Appendix: Remakes of Seven Samurai

Direct Remakes
The Magnificent Seven (US, 1960)
Beach of the War Gods (HK, 1973)
Message from Space (Japan, 1978)
Battle Beyond the Stars (US, 1980)
World Gone Wild (US, 1988)
Seven Warriors (HK, 1989)
Dune Warriors (US, 1990)
The Wild East (Kazakhstan, 1993)
China Gate (India, 1998)
The Bad Pack (1998)
Samurai 7 (anime, Japan, 2005)

Significant borrowings
Three Outlaw Samurai (Japan, 1964)
The Magnificent Trio (HK, 1966)
The Dirty Dozen (US, 1967)
Sholay (India, 1975)
Steel (US, 1980)
The Mission (HK, 1999)
The Anarchists (Korea, 2000)
Seven Swords (HK, 2005) (serialised novel begun in early 1956)

Parodic remake/reworking
The Wild Bunch (US, 1969)
Three Amigos (US, 1986)
A Bug's Life (animation, US, 1998)

Captivity Hybrid
Return of the Seven (US, 1966)
Star Wars (US, 1977)
The Wild Geese (US, 1978)
Uncommon Valor (US, 1983)

3

Gary Needham

Fashioning Modernity: Hollywood and the Hong Kong Musical 1957–64

In 1965, when the Hong Kong film studio Shaw Brothers announced in their magazine *Southern Screen* the launch of the forthcoming New *Wuxia* Century, it was the beginning of an enduring relationship between Hong Kong Cinema, the martial arts genre and an obsession with masculinity.[1] In the martial arts film, Hong Kong cinema found its voice, both cultural and economic, in a genre that placed emphasis on Chinese history, tradition and myth, all of which were reified through modern cinematic technologies, images of the male body and the steady development of an anti-colonial ideology. Since the early 1970s the martial arts film has almost been synonymous with Hong Kong cinema, through the wide dissemination of the kung fu film in the international film market up to the more recent cross-fertilisation of Hong Kong aesthetics in Hollywood action cinema. However, the martial arts film is only one genre in an industry previously dominated by musical genres, melodrama and a star system largely consisting of women. The more recent globalised context of film production in Asia is partly a consequence of this earlier period of cultural and cinematic contact between Asia and the West. Recent cultural exchanges have engendered a new dynamic of power relations and appreciations between Hollywood and its Asian others, but the former still maintains its aura of innovation in its encounter with Asia, for example *The Matrix* (US, 1999) and *Kill Bill* (US, 2003, 2004), while the latter is often declared imitative and derivative. In just one of many examples, the UK's most popular film magazine *Empire*, in its review of Stephen Chow's *Shaolin Soccer* (HK, 2001), writes that the film has 'all the finesse of a *Pokemon* episode', in addition to having a 'cheap look'.[2]

Popular Asian cinema is rarely taken seriously beyond the loyal fan base and cult audience, except for those auteurs whose work is formally opposed to classical film-making and not thought of as popular, that is, generic.

An implicit concern of this chapter is to understand the different engagements between Hollywood and Hong Kong, through the musical in the moment before the martial arts film takes hold both regionally and internationally. The recent focus on aspects of global and transnational film-making and the flow of talent between Hollywood and Hong Kong after 1997 can lead to an obscuring of the historical dimension of the interaction between the two as if it were an entirely recent phenomenon. Therefore, it is important to explore the relationship between Hong Kong cinema and Hollywood before the renaissance of the martial arts films in the mid-1960s.

It is equally important to specify what exactly is being exchanged between film industries and genres when Hong Kong and Hollywood interact with one another. Ana López has already suggested with reference to Mexican popular cinema that outside Hollywood any national cinema producing popular film is always having to 'face up' to Hollywood in some way, through either a process of localising Hollywood models of entertainment or resisting it altogether through art cinema strategies.[3] Dimitris Eleftheriotis's work on genre also reveals that the analysis of popular genre outside Hollywood works to destabilise the concept of film genre itself, especially when certain genres such as the western so closely associated with Hollywood are produced elsewhere.[4] For Eleftheriotis, an examination of popular genre outside Hollywood offers a series of challenges to the normative alignment between Hollywood and genre in both film studies and the popular imagination. This chapter hopefully contributes to debates about genre in Asian cinema, and through the musical hopes to challenge the hegemonies that both Hollywood and the martial arts film hold over Hong Kong cinema in Anglo-American criticism.

Genre Production from Musicals to Martial Arts

The reason I want to begin this chapter on the Hong Kong musical by contextualising the martial arts film is to create a critical dialogue between Hong Kong cinema and genre in light of a long-running history of 'facing up' to Hollywood that precedes that martial arts film. A number of concerns about Hong Kong cinema's relationship to both Hollywood and genre vis-à-vis the martial arts film, such as generic hybridity, experimentation, imitation and innovation, can be observed much earlier in Hong Kong cinema. In the Hong Kong genres of the 1950s and 1960s, and even prior to these decades, the issue of imitation and innovation and the working through of Hollywood genre conventions and an industrial base of mass culture production were in place. The post-war new *wuxia* film was only possible because the Hong Kong film studios that dominated at the time, Shaw Brothers and MP&GI (Motion Pictures and General Industries, later renamed Cathay in 1965), had already put into operation an industrial system of mass genre production. The Hong Kong film studios had implemented the industrial base of organisation for genre production modelled on classical Hollywood's system of vertical integration, in which production, distribution and exhibition is managed by the one studio. The adoption of the model of vertical integration by Shaw Brothers and MP&GI is the first step towards an adaptation of Hollywood by Hong Kong cinema at an industrial level. However, Stephanie Chung Po-yin does point out that although the studios were Fordist in their industrial organisation, they were also structured according to the family-based Asian business tradition.[5] In addition to the industrial dimension of film production what also needs to be considered is the extent to which the classical paradigm of film-making is taken as a major influence in the formal and stylistic process of film production. The majority of popular films outside Hollywood do organise time and space through the parameters set out by the classical paradigm. The rule of narrative economy, causality and the system of continuity editing perfected in the early period of the Hollywood studio era was, and perhaps still is, in Miriam Hansen's term, 'the first global vernacular'.[6] What is essentially being adopted by popular film production outside Hollywood during this period is both the industrial and aesthetic models of film-making established in the studio era as the relationship between a mode of production and formal and stylistic convention.[7]

Before the ascendancy of the martial arts film in the mid-1960s, Hong Kong cinema was dominated by the melodrama and the musical as the two key genre trends of the Mandarin studios. The musical genre in Hong Kong cinema also accounts for a number of variations and subgenres that include melodramas which feature songs (*It's Always Spring* (Evan Yang, HK, 1962), *Love Without End* (Doe Chin, HK, 1961)); traditional Mandarin *huangmei diao* or yellow plum operas (*Love Eterne* (Li Han-hsiang, HK, 1963), *Kingdom and the Beauty* (Li Han-hsiang, HK, 1959), *Maid From Heaven* (Ho Meng-hua, HK, 1963)); the southern Cantonese opera films (*The Gold Braided Fan* (Jiang Weiguang, HK, 1959), *The Swallow's Message* (Zhu Ji, HK, 1959)); and the focus of this chapter, the contemporary 'Hollywood style' musicals (*Mambo Girl* (Wen Yi, HK, 1957), *The Wild Wild Rose* (Wang Tianlin, HK, 1960), *Because of Her* (Wang Tianlin, HK, 1963), *Love Parade* (Doe Chin, HK, 1963), *Hong Kong Nocturne* (Umetsugu Inoue, HK, 1966)). The genre also incorporates a range of musical influences and traditions including Western and Chinese opera, jazz, classical and mambo, as well as the important legacy of the musical and nightclub cultures of 1930s Shanghai. Wang Tianlin's *The Wild Wild Rose* incorporates nearly all of these musical influences, and is inspired in equal amounts by Bizet's opera *Carmen* and *The Blue Angel* (Germany, 1930), with Marlene Dietrich. The Shanghai influence also, with its own set of connections with Hollywood, should be considered a cultural influence of the contemporary formation of the Hong Kong musical, and although it is not discussed here is a logical link in the history of musical film production and Mandarin popular song between Shanghai, Hong Kong and Hollywood.

The majority of contemporary musicals, and the best examples of the Hollywood influenced genre, were produced between 1957 and 1964 by the MP&GI studio. The Shaw Brothers did produce a significant number of contemporary musicals in order to compete with their rival studio, but their musicals exhibited less commitment towards the genre's exploration of Hong Kong's modernity and the space of the city than it was an exercise to simply compete with MP&GI's innovation with the genre. Shaw Brothers' real focus during the musical phase was on the period *huangmei diao* opera musical films, with their cultural roots and commitment firmly located in a cinematic fantasy of pre-communist mythical China. The *huangmei diao* films are in themselves a cinematic hybrid of film form and traditional folk culture adapted from the songs sung by the tea picking girls in the Anhui province of China. Despite their appearance of essentialist cultural authenticity, Edwin Chen, in his preliminary study of the genre, considers the *huangmei diao* as a 'highly cinematic genre ... comparable to the American classical musical theatre established on Broadway in the early 1940s'.[8] More recent studies of the *huangmei diao* film have begun to look at the complex dynamic of cross-gendered performances as the site of potential queer moments.[9] During this period, MP&GI of Malaysian origin was committed to exploring contemporary Hong Kong and East Asia in the context of modernity with an eye towards an international future evident in films such as *Air Hostess* (Wen Yi, HK, 1959). Shaw Brothers, on the other hand, with its strong company links not only with Malaysia but importantly with the pre-war Shanghai film industry from whence it came, was entrenched in fantasies of the past demonstrated by the over production of period films that include the *huangmei diao* and the later *wuxia* films. Shaw Brothers was selling the 'China Dream' to its diasporic Chinese audience,[10] looking backwards to Chinese literary and cultural tradition and history, folklore and myth, that it so expertly mediated through colourful widescreen spectacle. Shaw Brothers caught on much later to MP&GI's international ambitions and would eventually become Asia's international player in film production during the 1970s, with American (*Cleopatra Jones and the Casino of Gold*, 1975), British (*Legend of the Seven Golden Vampires* and *Shatter*, both 1974), Japanese (*Zatoichi Meets the One-Armed Swordsman*, 1971) and Italian (*The Stranger and the Gunfighter* and *Crash che botte!*, both 1974) co-productions, but it would appear that Shaw's key concerns were in reifying Chinese history and mythical fantasy through genre as the ideological embodiment of a China lost to politics and revolution. The contemporary MP&GI musicals appear to be implicitly positioned in opposition to the sino-centrism of Shaw Brothers through their engagement with the appropriation and adaptation of an American rather than a Chinese tradition. The MP&GI films are all set in Hong Kong as opposed to China, are contemporary rather than historical, and are important in establishing Hong Kong as the location for the narrative and the characters, as well as conveying themes of internationalisation and travel. Along with the smaller Cantonese film industry operating at the same time and in the shadow of the Mandarin language studio giants, MP&GI was given over to making Hong Kong the subject of Hong Kong cinema.

The Musical Between Hollywood and Hong Kong

The Hong Kong musical is the genre most closely associated with Hollywood and perhaps one of the most conducive to an analysis of what might be called the Hong Kong-Hollywood discourse. Also, a significant number of musicals are liberally remade from classical Hollywood films. The most common strategy in the musicals as a form of remaking and appropriation is to borrow and adapt important plot devices and narrative tropes from well-known Hollywood musicals, comedies and melodramas, rather than directly transpose an entire film's plot into a Hong Kong context. Many of the Hong Kong musicals combine elements from different films to produce a bricolage of familiar narrative conventions and sequences from a wide and varied Hollywood canon. For example, the much debated key scene at the end of King Vidor's classical melodrama *Stella Dallas* (US, 1937) is

reproduced with less melodramatic intensity in Wen Yi's *Mambo Girl*.
The audience for the Hong Kong film also share the point-of-view shot
of the estranged lower class mother, who in *Mambo Girl* watches in
exclusion her daughter and her adoptive family in a happy reunion. In
addition to its melodramatic influences, *Mambo Girl* also takes two
songs from the Hollywood film *Rock and Roll Revue* (US, 1955) and
remakes them as Mandarin pop, and the general milieu of the teenage
world takes its inspiration from the wholesome end of 1950s Hollywood
teen movies.

One of the key differences between Hong Kong and Hollywood versions of the musical genre is the role occupied by gender and sexuality
in relation to the structuring of narrative and number. This significant
difference in the number and sexual politics is how the Hollywood
genre becomes localised and managed within its Asian context. The
genre can look like a classical text, as they often do, but it is ideologi-
cally separate from what can be easily understood in classical
Hollywood cinema as the drive to collapse generic pleasure into couple
formation. Hollywood cinema privileges the formation of couples
through narrative closure as evidence of its heteronormative logic.
According to Yingchi Chu, who makes reference to *Mambo Girl*, Hong
Kong cinema of this period had 'a focus on Confucian values' and foregrounded 'the theme of *lunli*'.[11] *Lunli* or Confucian ethics govern
relationships especially within the family and between genders,
expressed through the concept of patriarchal filial piety. *Lunli* in the
Hong Kong musical strongly informs the trajectory of relations
between characters and their development in the plot, and how any res-
olutions within the family and between genders will resolve the narrative. From a structural point of view, the restrictions (both romantic
and sexual) and deferrals in the formation of couples or the ability to
have an independent agency that runs counter to the ethics of *lunli* is
perhaps what allows many of the films from *Mambo Girl* to *Cinderella
and Her Little Angels* to be overwhelmingly melodramatic. The
coincidences, the temporalities of delay, denial and deferment and the
structural gaps between the knowledge and power of character and
spectator are central to definitions of classical Hollywood melodrama
and the woman's film.[12] Through the organisation of a character's
gendered and familial relations, one can understand how the processes
of hybridity between the Hollywood musical as a film-making model
(vertical integration, genre production, the classical paradigm) and
the ideological and cultural specificity of its adaptation and localisation
as a Hong Kong genre unfold. The Chinese influence on the genre is
ideological rather than generic and would explain one of the key

structural differences between the Hong Kong and Hollywood musicals, namely the dual-focus narrative structure detailed by Rick Altman in his influential study of the Hollywood genre.[13] A principle concern of the Hollywood musical is towards couple formation and the narrative closure is resolved through the utopia of heterosexual union that escalates in the progression of the musical numbers. As a key element of the Hollywood musical, the genre is structured around a set of opposing parallel gender relations in character, style and form that the musical works to resolve by the final number. As Altman explains:

> Pairing-off is the natural impulse of the musical, whether it be in the presentation of the plot, the splitting of the screen, the choreography of the dance, or even the repetition of melody. Image follows image according to the nearly iron-clad law requiring each sequence to uphold interest in male–female coupling by including parallel scenes and shared activities.[14]

The dual-focus narrative and its dependency on closure through couple formation and the playful oppositions between gender is an aspect that needs to be overcome in the ethics and ideology that informs the Hong Kong musical and its emphasis on moral virtue and filial piety. This difference between genders and the resolution of these differences in the Hong Kong musical is often resolved through processes of displacement. The dual-focus narrative and the formation of the couple is often displaced onto more platonic relations between family members and friends, and the initial germination of a possible but very off screen union between a couple is overshadowed by an alternative source of the film's generic plenitude. The final number in the Hong Kong musical does not conform to the type of closure essential to the generic and ideological pleasure of the Hollywood model in always producing a couple. In *Mambo Girl*, the potential of heterosexual romance between Kailing (Grace Chang) and Danian (Peter Chen Hou) is explicitly displaced when the adopted Kailing runs away from the family home to try and find her birth mother. The film's narrative closure ends with a dance and song motivated by the reunion of Kailing's adoptive family and friends, rather than her male college friend and reluctant dance partner. *Mambo Girl* is one of the earliest examples from 1957, but the later musicals such as Doe Chin's *Love Parade* (HK, 1963) make a move towards exhibiting more confidence in the role of heterosexual coupling. *Love Parade*, whose English title refers to the Ernst Lubitsch musical from 1929 of the same name, is clearly modelled on the

Hollywood comedy of the sexes, and the adoption of both *Pillow Talk* (US, 1959) and *Designing Women* (US, 1957) is evident in the conflict and repartee of rival fashion designers, played by Lin Dai and Peter Chen Hou. Although a number of Hong Kong musicals eventually work towards gendered pairings in terms of romance and structuring oppositions, the final musical numbers rarely, if ever, are used in service of couple formation as narrative closure. Furthermore, the most spectacular number in the Hong Kong musical is not always the last number, as would often be the case in the Hollywood genre. Directed by Cathay veteran Huang Tang in 1959, *Cinderella and Her Little Angels* is a typical example of both the structure of gendered oppositions in the musical genre and the specificity of the Hong Kong displacement or resistance of romantic heterosexual closure being directed away from the couple as the film moves towards resolution. *Cinderella and Her Little Angels* has a fairly simple premise organised around the two characters of Danning (Peter Chen Hou) and Xiaolin (Lin Dai). The film borrows from the 'orphan plot' familiar in the Shirley Temple milieu of films like *Curly Top* (US, 1963), and the numerous versions of the 'orphan with secret rich benefactor' plot of *Daddy Long Legs* (US, 1931, 1955).

Xiaolin is from a girls' orphanage, where she both lives and teaches younger orphans. The orphanage makes clothes for a local clothing shop, where the male shop assistant Danning works. He regularly makes the trips between the clothes shop and the orphanage and is secretly in love with Xiaolin, which is expressed through his attraction to the store's mannequin that also resembles her. It should be noted that the closest he ever physically gets to Xiaolin in the film is through a displacement of her actual body in the inanimate dummy that he talks to, dresses and kisses. Through the course of two charity fashion events for which Xiaolin is the star model, the couple eventually come together through the suggestion of romantic possibility, but are faced with the obstacle of the strict and unsympathetic orphan madam who opposes every move that Xiaolin makes to be involved with the clothing store and Danning. One night a thunderstorm damages the orphanage almost beyond repair and the madam has to admit that she was overly strict, and she accepts some of the charity money from the fashion show to repair the orphanage. The repairing of the orphanage is used to resolve the structured oppositions between genders that were organising the narrative and style of the film according to how Altman defines the Hollywood musical's dual-narrative focus. The main oppositions in *Cinderella and Her Little Angels* are the following:

Male	Female
Danning (Chen Hou)	Xiaolin (Grace Chang)
The clothing boutique	The orphanage
Shop assistant	Teacher/Model
Shop Manager	Orphanage Madam

The film works through these oppositions at a structural and stylistic level through mise-en-scène and alternating musical numbers sung by Xiaolin and Danning, although they never once sing to each other in a duet. This structural opposition is typical of the Hollywood model, but where the American genre would conclude with a show stopping number that resolves those differences and oppositions through song, dance and couple formation, *Cinderella and Her Little Angels* does not carry the dual-focus narrative through to its logical conclusion. Instead of unifying the couple through the concrete representations of heterosexuality in classical cinema, the kiss, an embrace and/or marriage, *Cinderella and Her Little Angels* ends with the joyous repair of the storm damaged orphanage as the locus of generic plenitude. The pleasure of narrative closure is diverted away from couple formation and instead onto the building of bridges between the community of female orphans and the fashion and clothing world. The orphanage takes precedence over the couple, as does the female mannequin take the place of actual bodily contact in dance or romance between the male and female lead. However, in the final moments of *Cinderella and Her Little Angels*, in a shot-reverse-shot structure between Xiaolin and Danning, and the shop manager and orphan madam, the film makes a formal gesture towards closing the gap between two potential couples, although it is something that must be inferred in the story's future rather than in the film's plot.

Cinderella and Her Little Angels resists the actual representation of couple formation. The possibility of reading any kind of union based on gendered oppositions is through the formal function of shot-reverse-shot as a formal displacement for the union that cannot be represented within a single shot. In the 'Brides of June' musical number, a charity fashion show in which numerous types of national wedding costume and ceremony are displayed, Xiaolin and Danning are unified but only within the confined limits of role-playing in the number's fantasy of marriage which, unlike the American musical, does not later translate to anything beyond what the number can only represent as wishful thinking. The number is rarely used to cement a coupling; therefore, the Hong Kong musical avoids the collapsing of the ideology of heterosexuality into the generic pleasures of song and dance. Individuals do sing about each other, but rarely do they get to dance together or duet in a way that works through the oppositions and differences between genders intrinsic to the Hollywood musical. Furthermore, in the Hong Kong musical there is no equivalent to the Ginger Rogers and Fred Astaire pairing. The absence of a consistent pairing thus confirms that the heterosexual couple are not a dominant structural convention of the musical's Hong Kong variation.

Fashioning Modernity and the Musical Number

I have established that the number in the Hong Kong musical is not necessarily tied to the dual-focus narrative structure pointing towards a significant difference between the Hollywood and Hong Kong versions of the genre. In addition to the question of couple formation, there is another set of significant differences in the function of the musical number. One of the first and most notable differences between the Hollywood and Hong Kong musical is the absence of complex dance choreography, and in many instances such as in Huang Tang's *Cinderella and Her Little Angels* there is no dancing at all. The absence of dance and choreography in the musical is a revelation since Hong Kong cinema has gained its international reputation through the sophisticated and complex staging of fight choreography in the martial arts film. It is also worth noting that the ability of female martial arts performers to succeed in the genre is often understood as a consequence of their background in dance. Furthermore, the action scenes in *wuxia* films with graceful choreography, from *Come Drink With Me* (King Hu, HK, 1966) to *Crouching Tiger, Hidden Dragon* (Ang Lee, HK/China/ US/Taiwan, 2000), are often described as balletic. Aside from the romantic Austen-esque plotting of *Crouching Tiger, Hidden Dragon*, one of the many reasons given for its apparent appeal for female audiences often alienated by the martial arts genre obsession with masculinity was that the scenes of action and combat were experienced as embodying the representation and sensation of dance on screen.

Balletic, the term frequently used to describe the action scenes in *Crouching Tiger, Hidden Dragon*, also recalls earlier Anglo-American descriptions of John Woo's Hong Kong films and the hero genre as 'bullet ballets'. One has to assume that the absence of complex choreography and dance in the Hong Kong musical is not simply because there was no creative talent to direct and construct dance-based numbers. The new *wuxia* films of the 1960s, like *Come Drink with Me*, *Temple of the Red Lotus* (Chui Chang-wang, HK, 1965) and *The Knight of Knights* (Sit Kwan, HK, 1966), are from their inception beautifully choreographed works of action cinema, and the tension between the action scenes and the narrative similarly works along the same lines as the tension between narrative and spectacle in the musical.

The musical numbers in the contemporary Hong Kong films place emphasis on music, lyric and costume rather than dance and movement, and I would argue that the number is instead tied to expressing and conceptualizing discourses of modernity. To return to *Cinderella and Her Little Angels*, this is readily apparent in the two musical numbers that convey modernity through the spectacle of a fashion show. The most spectacular number in *Cinderella and Her Little Angels* appears midway through the film and is a seven-minute fashion show spectacular encapsulated in the song lyric 'to look modern is to look sexy'. Lin Dai's character Xiaolin takes the diegetic audience and the spectator through a series of fashions both traditional and modern, marked by different cultures, stereotypes and locations. The song conveys the purpose of some of the fashions as well as indicates their appropriate context, alluding to the role that consumption and an international sensibility plays in the desire for modernity. The number does not involve dance, but it does involve movement and the spectacle is organised around the clothes and the mise-en-scène, which changes with each outfit to contextualise the fashion with different cities (Paris), cultural contexts (skiing, shopping, parties), cultures (Chinese, Japanese) and Hollywood (the Western). The globe-trotting fantasy of tourism and fashion in the number corresponds to notions of internationalisation and the status of Hong Kong itself in constructing discourses of otherness. In the musical number the spaces of foreign cultures, especially of the West, are offered up as spectacles to be visually and commercially consumed by local audiences. Similarly, Wen Yi's globe-trotting MP&GI film *Air Hostess* places as much emphasis on style, appearance and getting the right 'look' as it does on air travel and the ability to speak several languages. During the interviews for the hostess job, itself a parade of contemporary 1950s fashions, Grace Chang, when asked by a fellow interviewee if she made her snappy dress, is quick to interject that her dress is in fact prêt-à-porter.

Fashion is one of the most important elements of the Hong Kong musical, not just in the costuming of the many female stars but the musical number where it occupies the main source of spectacle. The Chinese title of *Cinderella and Her Little Angels – Yunchang Yanhou –* is more fashion friendly and translates as *Cloud Dress Beauty Queen*. The fashion show is a regular feature in the Hong Kong musical not only in *Cinderella and Her Little Angels*, but also in other fashion and design set musicals like Shaw Brothers' *Love Parade* which opens with a spectacular ten-minute fashion show in radiant Shawscope. One has to assume that many of these Hong Kong films follow in the wake of the fashion musicals *Vogues of 1938* (US, 1937), *Hollywood Party* (US, 1937) and *Fashions of 1934* (US, 1934), conspicuous in 1930s Hollywood and featuring 'fashion numbers'.

Fashion might appear as trivial, camp and frivolous, but its importance should not be overlooked, as an attention to fashion in the context of the Hong Kong musical actually reveals its role in the particular processes of modernity. Fashion is connected to notions of change and the development of consumption and material culture brought about through the transformation in social, economic and cultural spheres, the result of industrial capitalism. Identification with modernity as a process of social and cultural change can be explicitly tied to fashion as a signifier of the modern and the affluent in terms of an upward mobility of cultural identity and aspiration. An intensity of fashion discourses emerge when there is a need to demarcate social mobility or the appearance of social mobility most famously demonstrated in Europe by Christian Dior's New Look of 1948. The nipped in waist of the Dior Silhouette that followed the formless clothing representative of the austerity of wartime styles was how fashion embodied Europe's post-war transformation in the 1950s. Fashion can be reduced here to being about change, as the affluence to buy in to the fashion world is marked through annual trends and seasonal changes, brands and silhouettes, being up-to-date and moving forward with the times is how fashion can turn modernity into style and help make visible contemporary cultural identities through consumption and the body.

The relationship between fashion, consumption and Hong Kong film genre was also conspicuous in the cinema magazine culture throughout the 1960s and 1970s. The studios like MP&GI and Shaw Brothers produced monthly film magazines like *International Screen, The Milky Way Pictorial* and *Southern Screen* (Figure 1), with star profiles, news and reviews of upcoming studio films and international hits and, importantly, fashion shoots and beauty tips. Alongside information about film releases the studio magazines often included photo shoots of the latest Grace Chang star fashions, how to apply eye make-up like Betty Loh Ti, and included a wealth of advertisements for boutiques, hair products, perfumes and cosmetics. The photo magazine *One Plus One* was completely devoted to film star fashions and style related gossip, and news about the Hong Kong film industry was very much in the background.

在上期本刊裏，列出了一帮「明星秋日試新裝」的圖片，包括有：凌波、泰萍、井莉、于倩、沈依、林嘉、金霏等的新裝。這些新裝又包括有日常服、旅行裝和晚禮服等。款式設計新潁，顏色配色調和，很受影友們喜愛。

由於篇幅所限，尚有多位影星的新裝未及在上期本刊登出，故此本期繼續介紹幾位影星的新裝，計有：李菁、何莉莉、邢慧、潘迎紫、舒佩佩、陳依齡等。她們所穿的新裝除了有些是日常服裝之外，也有些是在她們主演的新片裏的戲裝，例如李菁、邢慧、陳依齡所穿的新裝中，有幾襲是她們演的新片「愛」中的服裝。將來這部新片公映時，影友將有機會更仔細地看清楚。這些服裝雖然是在戲裏穿着，但實際上中可在日常穿着。因為它們在設計上是很適合一般少女穿用的緣故。

至於本期所列出的明星新裝，仍由名作家亦舒小姐逐一介紹其款式和色調，讓愛好時裝的影友欣賞。

2

Figure 1. Fashion, modernity and cinema in *Southern Screen* magazine (1963)

Conclusion

Hong Kong cinema's interaction in transposing the Hollywood musical comes at a time when the region was undergoing rapid change. In her argument about classical Hollywood as vernacular modernism, Miriam Hansen suggests that the popular success of Hollywood cinema throughout the world was due to it being able to provide 'modes of identification for being modern'.[15] It would seem then that the appropriation of Hollywood mode of production and its aesthetic model evident in the Hong Kong musical was one potential way of facilitating the encounter with modernity and identification with the modern. Through stylised tropes of modernity, the musical's context of transformation makes visible the space of the Hong Kong, its culture and new forms of identity engaging spectators in ways that Hansen perceives to be intrinsic to Hollywood's global hegemony and appeal. In numerous films and not just musicals and Hong Kong cinema, modernity is signified through discourses of mobility as tourism and travel and consumption through fashion and style as both physical and social movement that address the desires and aspiration of spectators. This is evident in MP&GI's non-musical films also such as Wen Yi's *Our Dream Car* (HK, 1959), where the narrative's focus is organised in a couple's desire to own a motor car. In *Our Dream Car*, the husband also works on an industrial construction site, a setting that further emphasises the themes of change and prosperity in Hong Kong. The objects of desire in modernity, for example the car in *Our Dream Car*, the giant refrigerator in Wang Tianlin's MP&GI comedy *The Greatest Civil War on Earth* (HK, 1961) and fashion in the films discussed above, suggest the ways in which mobility is explicitly tied to consumption trends, material production and style consciousness as symbolic entry points of social and cultural modernity.

However, and what makes the musical an important genre in Hong Kong cinema, is that modernity also comes to be related to femininity and female stardom. Mary Wong also argues that femininity and female stardom are explicitly tied to travel, tourism and border crossing in MP&GI's films that my analysis also correlates in terms of the fantasies of travel expressed in *Cinderella*'s musical numbers.[16] The modern musical is in many ways exploring new forms of identity as the consequence of modernity, and it does this to some degree through the engagement and adaptation of classical Hollywood, the musical genre and its address to the spectator. The musical in some sense accounts for the emergence of the martial arts film, which is a reaction to the apparent 'cult of femininity' and female stardom in post-war Hong Kong cinema of the 1950s and 1960s. In his memoirs, Zhang Che (Chang Cheh) is openly hostile towards the musical.[17] Zhang's line of thought is that there were no good roles for men in cinema during this period and the actors in the musical films were all deemed to fall short of the ideological ideals of Chinese masculinity, typified by the muscular heroes of the *yanggang* martial arts films that he later pioneered. Stephen Teo also refers to the men in Hong Kong musicals as 'weak and sissified' and that 'the musical was responsible for showing up the weak and effeminate nature of man'.[18] Both Teo and Zhang can barely conceal their anxieties around men who quite simply do not measure up to the highly regulated notions of masculinity in the martial arts film.

What comes to be established is an antagonism between the musical and the martial arts film as an opposition between on the one hand femininity, female stardom and fashion, and on the other hand masculinity, male stardom and the male body. The martial arts look back to history and tradition and the films often construct masculinity as natural and timeless, hence the representation of the hero with little or simple clothing and an emphasis on the beauty of the male torso. The contemporary musicals are instead focused on the future and towards a cultural modernity that places great emphasis on commodities, material culture and the contemporaneous styles of fashion and glamour.

It seems that after this period of the Hong Kong musical, femininity and the female agency it engenders get clawed back once women have played their part in the region's social and economic progress. The contemporary musical becomes an almost forgotten part of Hong Kong cinema because femininity, stardom, fashion and music, which were the cinematic sites of its historical and cultural progress, become suppressed and transformed through the macho self-representation of the national imaginary in the martial arts film. The Hong Kong musical needs to be understood on the one hand in the context of regional modernity and on the other through strategies of appropriation and adaptation of classical Hollywood, when the gap between Hong Kong and Hollywood was a very close but fashionable encounter.

References

1 Law, Kar, 'The origin and development of Shaw's colour *wuxia* century' in Wong Ain-Ling (ed), *The Shaw Screen: A Preliminary Study* (Hong Kong: Hong Kong Film Archive, 2003).

2 Empire Online, <http://www.empireonline.com/reviews/reviewcomplete. asp?DVDID=10475> accessed 6 December 2006.

3   López, Ana M., 'Facing up to Hollywood' in Christine Gledhill and Linda Williams (eds), *Reinventing Film Studies* (London: Arnold, 2000).

4   Eleftheriotis, Dimitris, 'Genre criticism and the spaghetti western' in *Popular Cinemas of Europe* (New York: Continuum, 2001) and 'Genre criticism and popular Indian cinema' in Eleftheriotis and Gary Needham (eds), *Asian Cinemas: A Reader and Guide* (Edinburgh: Edinburgh University Press, 2006).

5   Chung, Stephanie Po-yin, 'A Southeast Asian tycoon and his movie dream: Loke Wan Tho and MP&GI' in Wong Ain-Ling (ed), *The Cathay Story* (Hong Kong: Hong Kong Film Archive, 2002).

6   Hansen, Miriam Bratu, 'The mass production of the senses: classical cinema as vernacular modernism' in Christine Gledhill and Linda Williams (eds), *Reinventing Film Studies* (London: Arnold, 2000), p.340.

7   Bordwell, David, Janet Staiger and Kristin Thompson (eds), *The Classical Hollywood Cinema: Film Style and Mode of Production to 1960* (New York: Columbia University Press, 1985).

8   Chen, Edwin W., 'Musical China, classical impression: a preliminary study of Shaws' *huangmei diao* film' in Wong Ain-Ling (ed), *The Shaw Screen*, p.51.

9   Aw, Annette and Tan See Kam, '*Love Eterne*: almost a (heterosexual) love story' in Chris Berry (ed), *Chinese Films in Focus: 25 New Takes* (London: British Film Institute, 2004).

10 Sek, Kei, 'Shaw movietown's "China dream" and "Hong Kong sentiments"' in Wong Ain-Ling (ed): *The Shaw Screen*.

11 Chu, Yingchi, *Hong Kong Cinema: Coloniser, Motherland and Self* (London and New York: Routledge, 2003), p.34.

12 Doane, Mary Ann, *The Desire to Desire: The Woman's Film of the 1940s* (Bloomington: Indiana University Press, 1987).

13 Altman, Rick, *The American Film Musical* (London: The British Film Institute, 1989).

14 Altman: *The American Film Musical*, p.32.

15 Hansen: 'The Mass Production', p.344.

16 Wong, Mary, 'Women who cross borders: MP&GI's modernity programme' in Wong Ain-Ling (ed): *The Cathay Story*.

17 Chang, Cheh, *Chang Cheh: A Memoir* (Hong Kong: Hong Kong Film Archive, 2004).

18 Teo, Stephen, 'Oh, karaoke! Mandarin pop and musicals' in Law Kar (ed), *Mandarin Films and Popular Song 40s–60s* (Hong Kong: Hong Kong Film Archive, 1993), p.36.

4

Charles Leary

Electric Shadow of an Airplane: Hong Kong Cinema, World Cinema

What is cinema – doing in this world?

Nicole Brenez, 'For It Is the Critical Faculty That Invents Fresh Forms'[1]

What is Hong Kong cinema doing in this world? Hong Kong cinema is, for one, a multinational enterprise, and you can find it produced in many places: Singapore, Shanghai, Taipei, Tokyo, Guangzhou, San Francisco and Hong Kong. The first Hong Kong film is generally considered to be the 1913 comedy short *Zhuangzi Tests His Wife*, never actually released in Hong Kong but shown in Los Angeles.[2] Filmmaking in Hong Kong did not resume until 1924 and, two years later, the French art critic Elie Faure wrote, prophetically, of a vision of the future for the cinema:

> There will someday be an end to the cinema considered as an offshoot of the theatre ... Otherwise, we must look to America and Asia, the new peoples as those renewed by death, to bring in – with the fresh air of the oceans and the prairies – brutality, health, youth, danger, and the freedom of action.[3]

Situated on either side of the Pacific Ocean, one now indeed finds two of the biggest film industries in the world, both renowned for their 'freedom of action', in Hollywood and Hong Kong. With such a bi-continental, coastal outlook in mind, I want to query the resurgence, within film criticism, of the term 'world cinema' and how it can be related to the cinema of Hong Kong, often discussed in a worldly fashion. How can one reconcile the early 'world cinema' texts in the discipline of film studies, the rubric of globalisation surrounding Hong Kong and Hong Kong cinema, the resurgence of 'world cinema' encyclopedias, and the discourse of transnationalism? Is there something particularly 'worldly' about Hong Kong cinema?

One can catalogue a number of recent film study publications that use the term 'world cinema,' while one can also find a number of books on Hong Kong cinema that use, as a descriptor, words like 'world', 'planet', or 'global'.[4] Hong Kong is a popular subject for transnationalism because of its history existing between two nations, the British Empire and China. Hong Kong was, and still is, the access point for the West to the East, and as such has drawn the reputation for being one of the world's most cosmopolitan locales. What does globalisation mean, and what does it do for us? Is it not a redundant term, to say, for example, that the world has now become globalised? Is not the globe by definition globalised? The distinction to make between a theory of world cinema and a world theory of the cinema lies in the definition of globalisation as an economic term – so it is places in the world that have been globalised, and made part of a global market where political borders (trade sanctions, nationalism, etc.) have reached their limits, or are no longer a force.[5] I am bracketing the numerous studies that associate Hong Kong cinema and transnationalism to consider the connotation more of a sense of singularity – or universality – in 'world cinema' rather than cross-cultural exchange. Terms specific to the global reach of Hong Kong cinema and its surrounding markets in Asia include 'Chinese Cinemas', 'Transnational Chinese Cinema' and 'Chinese language cinema'. Hong Kong shares a film history with many surrounding areas, particularly mainland China and Taiwan. Hong Kong and Taiwan both of course exist at 'the edge' (geographically and politically) of mainland China, and critical terminology such as 'national cinema' and 'post-colonialism' serve an ongoing integral function for understanding cultural production in both regions.

More generally speaking, comparative literature has terms like 'planetarity', 'oneworldedness', 'transnationalism', 'post-colonialism' and, of course, 'comparative literature'. Film studies have terms such as 'transnationalism', 'post-colonialism', 'third cinema' and 'world cinema'. To encourage the usage of a term like 'world cinema' is, seemingly, a step backwards, glossing over the cultural, social and political differences that distinguish national film industries and film cultures, without taking into account the bulk of literature on post-colonial theory and cultural studies, on multiculturalism and theories of globalization, much of which has been especially brought to bear upon the case of Hong Kong in interrogating its status as a 'national cinema'. World cinema does not necessarily mean an encyclopedia of national cinemas, but it may also be used to suggest the cosmopolitan nature of the cinema – its worldliness – and film's figuring of the world. The title of my essay is primarily derived from a book published in 1972 that follows such a meditation, by the American film critic Parker Tyler, entitled *The Shadow of an Airplane Climbs the Empire State Building: A World Theory of Film*.[6] Tyler approaches a theory of film realism, though not quite in the same way as, for example, Andre Bazin or Siegfried Kracauer. Rather, the attention to worldliness is more a turn to figuring the world, in attention to not so much film realism as such but rather the materiality of film and the film experience. Despite the implication of an international overview in the title of Tyler's book, his text does not work towards a definition of national cinemas, and only refers to the cinemas of the US, the Soviet Union, Hungary, Brazil, Japan, Germany, England, France, India, Italy and Sweden. Rather, with frequent dismissals of Kracauer's theory of the 'redemptive' nature of film realism – he is rather interested in how cinema films the world, film's place in 'the world'. In considering Tyler, a remnant of cinephilia's encounter with both film-making and film studies in America, I ask: how has Hong Kong cinema transformed the world, our cinematic perception of the world, and world film culture?

In a key text outlining both the industrial determinations and aesthetic of the post-classical 'high-concept' film, Justin Wyatt notes that advertising has become a fundamental 'medium of expression'.[7] Notwithstanding its intensive marketing campaign, one of Hong Kong's biggest blockbusters exemplifies this alignment of cinema and advertising – the star-studded *Infernal Affairs* series, bathed in a soothing bluish-tint and otherwise minimalist colour scheme (and set in a metallic industrial decor).[8] But of course these days, Hong Kong itself is a brand name: 'Asia's World City'. This brand name, the image of Hong Kong's 'location positioning'[9] in the parlance of the hired public relations firm, does not only position itself on the MTR or on Hong Kong television commercials: it travels with its cinema as well. For example, a recent touring programme of Shaw Brothers martial arts films in the US was sponsored by the tourism board, complete with the dragon logo present on all publicity material and complimentary postcards of the city for attendees.

David Bordwell's taxonomy of film style is notably configured on a planetary access, in his book *Planet Hong Kong*. In so titling his book, presumably in a play on the international restaurant chain named Planet

Hollywood, an alignment is made between Hong Kong and Hollywood cinemas as 'popular entertainment' and the 'classical' qualities of storytelling and action that Bordwell breaks down in lucid language. The universalism ascribed to Hong Kong cinema by Bordwell coincides with a point of contention in the criticism of Hong Kong's reception by both academics and popular audiences in the West. The action-oriented work of most Hong Kong film-makers in Hollywood leaves Ackbar Abbas, for example, to write that: 'The United States – along with Britain, Europe, and Australia – is captivated by the siren song of the Hong Kong cinema but not necessarily by listening to it. What the global media does not want to hear *it makes successful*, which is to say intelligible on its own terms.'[10] In the poor English of a self-described modern day Buster Keaton, Jackie Chan or Sammo Hung, 'sound' and 'voice' are then not so much suppressed as neutralized. Describing a process of 'deterritorialization' in Hong Kong film's subtitling, Tessa Dwyer makes a similar argument, while also ascribing a certain mobility and 'other worldliness' to Hong Kong cinema's translation for Western audiences: 'Translation constitutes a process of meaning construction that is active, on the move ... With translation, signification remains mobile and multidirectional. In this sense it extends beyond the realm of the actual.'[11] It should be noted, however, that Hollywood cinema also undergoes a certain deterritorialisation – and silencing – in its international distribution. As Franco Moretti has pointed out, in examining the box office success of particular genres in a sample decade of 1986–95, American comedies, relying upon jokes told in English, fared less well in areas outside of the US.[12]

Bordwell argues further that 'Hong Kong cinema, in its drive for clarity and impact, has revitalised silent film techniques'.[13] Hong Kong cinema's fascination with slow motion, special effects and action, and consequent reference to the silent film, is also symptomatic in part of the die-hard cinephile's search for 'pure cinema', a film in which dialogue in a local vernacular is marginal and that can thus be called, indisputably, cinematic. And this cinephiliac reference of Hong Kong contemporary cinema to the silent film returns us to Tyler, as Tyler was among a number of film critics in the 1960s who wrote general survey books of silent cinema – and world cinema – often with titles prefaced as 'a world history of ... ', 'a pictorial history of ... ', or, as in Tyler's case, *Classics of the Foreign Film*.[14] These early film texts were chiefly devoted to the history of the silent film, and can be seen as the impetus for later archiving efforts and more methodologically sophisticated historiographies in film studies. In addition, such books are not completely unlike the books many Westerners used to rely upon for information about Hong Kong cinema; for example, *Sex and Zen and Bullet in the Head, Hong Kong Action Cinema, Kung Fu: Cinema of Vengeance*, books described in the-aptly-titled collection, *Between Home and World: A Reader in Hong Kong Cinema*, as having the primary aim to 'entertain and inform ... questioning the ability of film academics and cultural critics to describe the "excitement, vitality, and electricity" of [Hong Kong] cinema'.[15] Written at the cusp of cinema's entrance into an academic discipline, these previous world cinema books I am discussing are largely forgotten, because, in a sense, they are not really needed anymore. Often written by collectors such as William K. Everson, these books appealed to a growing audience of film societies, people desperate even to see an image from a forgotten or inaccessible film. Most of these books were composed of personal film still collections, but now one might just try the video store. Bordwell, of course, insists on the use of frame enlargements (not film stills) for his books. These works rediscovered a period in which Hollywood's control was not quite as complete as it would become, while also reinforcing the concept of the universalism of silent film language with the success of the 'pictorial history' texts. A number of these books were written by cinephiles who adhered to a rigid nostalgia for the silent cinema, fervently celebrating figures like Griffith and thus, as Robert Sklar notes in his own more recent historical survey of world cinema, *An International History of the Medium*, 'Universalism implied there was only one right way to make and watch films'.[16] While no one should expect to get away with just looking at the pictures in an academic publication, I am trying to make something of a point here. The editors of *Between Home and World* position their collection in distinction from a litany of books on Hong Kong cinema mainly written by and for Western cult fans that display a 'spirit of anti-intellectualism'.[17] In the case of *Sex and Zen and Bullet in the Head*, I would also suggest there is a degree of an orientalist spirit with the running gag of cataloguing poorly translated English subtitles in Hong Kong films (this dimension is itself a bit out of date now as well, as I think it is fair to say that English subtitles have become much better in Hong Kong cinema). Such books, with their heavy use of film stills and frame enlargements, also however might be considered in a longer tradition of 'picture books' of film history, largely lying within the middle-brow market but also marking an encounter between the cinephilia of film societies and film collecting, calls for film preservation, and the discipline of film studies. A case in point is the exceptional and exhaustively researched pictorial history book *Silver Light: A Pictorial History of Hong Kong Cinema* by Paul Fonoroff, available in both English and Chinese, which, in addition to being an authoritative survey of the history of Hong Kong film, includes rare images that otherwise may have been lost forever.[18] More recent examples of pictures telling words can be found in a recent issue of the film journal *Rouge*, made up of brief reflections on particular images.[19]

The Airplane

> My plane is flying now over the land between Baghdad, Beirut, Haifa, and Tripoli, into Turkey and Romania. I am making a clandestine entry into 'Europe'. Yet the land looks the same – hilly sand. I know the cartographic marks because of the TV in the arm of my seat. Planetarity cannot deny globalization. But, in search of a springboard for planetarity, I am looking not at Marti's invocation of the rural but at the figure of land that seems to undergird it. The view of the Earth from the window brings this home to me.
>
> Gayatri Chakravorty Spivak[20]

I would like to quote here the very first sentence of Bordwell's book, in the preface that confirms the Hong Kong cinephilia that shapes in part the rest of the book. Bordwell begins: 'Some of the best books on Hong Kong start with the author flying into the old Kai Tak airport, the jumbo jet nearly scraping the rooftops of Kowloon City before wheeling around sharply to land.'[21] This perhaps is a reference to the introduction to *Hong Kong Babylon*, which describes an interview with Jackie Chan at his office near the airport, with planes rushing by overhead. Of course, Hong Kong has often been remarked to be a city of transit, or a city of transients, and the Hong Kong airport has been a defining construction project for the city.[22] In the 1950s and 1960s, air-travel provided a modernising, border-crossing subplot to a number of Hong Kong films, or, in the case of a film such as the 1959 Motion Picture and General Investment (MP&GI) production *Air Hostess*, the primary setting. The stewardess character is not entirely uncommon in Hong Kong cinema, as Wong Kar-wai's *Chungking Express* (HK, 2004) or Sylvia Chang's *20-30-40* (a Taiwan-Hong Kong co-production, 2004) can attest as more recent examples. *Air Hostess* is an excellent example of the post-war modernising project of MP&GI (later renamed Cathay Studios), a story of growing up in a cosmopolitan city, enjoying leisure activities and most importantly travel. The vertical integration this film constructs has been pointed out by both Mary

Wong and Poshek Fu with Loke Wan Tho, the chairman of MP&GI, serving on the board of Malay Airlines, while the film at times resembles an industrial film: the stewardess training scenes resembling, in fact, those safety instruction films that we are now asked to watch on television in the plane (but at that time were performed).[23] The air hostess not only crosses borders between nations, as Mary Wong describes, but crosses over the border for traditional female domestic roles, opting for a career instead of marriage.[24]

But then again, has not air-travel been a crucial element of Hong Kong cinema throughout its history. In the ability of martial artists to fly through the air, as Zhang Zhen has pointed out in Shanghai and Hong Kong films, 'what makes possible the instant bodily transportation from one location to another hinges upon the capability of losing one's gravity in space and overcoming the restraint of time'.[25] And Zhang cites an early example of a Shanghai film, *The Great Knight-Errant of Aviation* (China, 1928), depicting a martial arts hero based on the real life story of China's first long-distance pilot. The woman flying though space to traverse the world is played in *Air Hostess* by dancer and singer Grace Chang, especially famous for her role as the *Mambo Girl* (HK, 1957). In turning now to another dancer turned film star in Hong Kong, I want to note the affinity between the musical and the martial arts film, both predominant genres at this time. Both fall under the heading of 'body genres', as labelled by Linda Williams – genres that engage the senses and rely upon visceral reactions from the spectator.[26] Cathay remains well known for its modern musicals, while its competitor, Shaw Brothers, is most famous for its martial arts films. The Mandarin language films of these studios targeted audiences all across East Asia, especially reaching the Taiwan market in appealing to the Guomingdang. Of course, both tried to outdo the other at their respective specialty, and here I want to turn to that star of martial arts trained as a dancer, Cheng Pei-pei, and discuss the modern musical she made for Shaw Brothers, *Hong Kong Nocturne* (HK, 1966), in the role of Chuen Chuen, the second-oldest of three sisters who dance and sing in nightclubs as part of their father's magical act. This dense film, directed by a Japanese, features not only a modern Hong Kong, but also other settings like Japan and Thailand. But there is one curious moment, when the film seems to stop being a musical for a moment, and the world happens off screen, that is to say, a realistic event comes crashing down on the narrative, the death of Chuen Chuen's husband in a plane crash. Before she has been told of the accident, an ominous thunderstorm ensues and her husband's ghost flashes for a second in the shadows, in an image evocative of a horror film. The horror component of the film reemerges later with another apparition, of her sister appearing before a maniacal ballet teacher, reminiscent of the macabre underbelly of Michael Powell's ballet film, *The Red Shoes* (GB, 1948). To bring back her husband from the dead, or rather, to let his spirit live on, the sisters must go on television. In order to ensure the success of her husband's variety show, Chuen Chuen first must ask permission from her in-laws to leave her domestic life and return to the world of show business, with the argument that dance must be brought to the public. The film was released just as Hong Kong began in earnest to broadcast television programming, and Tyler was also writing in the wake of both the age of television and the space race, two phenomena which for him became inextricably entangled, while also figuring man's conquest of outer space with a 'super jet plane' and conquest of space in general with the cinema and television. He writes:

> Like other communication instruments, the wireless is a sign of man's pride in scientific achievement, in what is commonly referred to as 'unifying' the planet. Television at once comes to mind as the greatest human achievement of this type, insofar as a complete image of reality be concerned ... its purpose is to encyclopedize the world, the act of living everywhere at once.[27]

Thus, like airplanes, television makes the world smaller.

What I find most 'worldly' about Hong Kong cinema, I think, is not so much its status as a major film industry in the world, but rather its cinema imagination of access to the world and to the power of film to shape our perception of the immediate space in the world. To better appreciate this, one may refer to another study of the 'worldliness' of Shanghai in the Republican period, as discussed by Zhang in *An Amorous History of the Silver Screen: Shanghai Cinema, 1896–1937*. She notes the penchant for 'world fever' (*shijiere*) with numerous amusement halls, which would also serve as locales for film consumption, using the word 'world' in their naming.[28] A film like *Air Hostess* underscores this issue of access well, as the Hong Kong citizen is part of a travel network which expands beyond the region, with images of the globe in the background as constant reminders. As to the spatial perception of the world, this is perhaps represented best in Hong Kong's gift of the martial arts film to Hollywood, beginning with *The Matrix*, where gravity no longer remains a physical constraint, and, in the images of a fluid space, a character is invited to 're-shape the world as he saw fit'. As Tyler writes:

The world of the imagination, where film participates like any other art, is weightless in that it may assume either weightlessness or any weight at any time. Any single frame (that is, any instant plucked from the flow of action in a film) automatically assumes a certain 'plastic' weight, a thing of related rest and movement, depth of shadow and brightness of highlight, balanced stability and instability; this quality of the frame is both something in itself and relates to the frame preceding and the frame succeeding it. This is why violent impact, like a blow struck, a falling object or an automobile collision, is not the same in film as in life ... for on film such a violent impact is variously manipulated, and in any case we know, if in the movie house, that we are seeing, not material objects, but only their mirror images. We react to the idea of a collision, not to a collision.[29]

Such is the 'freedom of action' of which Faure wrote, not limited, by the way, to the 'weightlessness' in martial arts film, in considering two prominent auteurs of Hong Kong action cinema: John Woo and Johnnie To. In Woo's films, such as *The Killer* (HK, 1987) or *A Better Tomorrow* (HK, 1986), slow-motion governs movement. To uses slow-motion and freeze-frames less, but the world will slow down for his characters, as in *The Mission* (HK, 1999), wherein, the major action sequence of the film taking place in a shopping mall, the characters plant themselves strategically at different positions and wait. They wait, undeterred and motionless, as an enemy may slowly emerge to view from an escalator.

If the airplane can be a metaphor for the global outlook of Hong Kong cinema, we recall that the earlier mode of mass transportation, the railroad, has also been used in service of emblematizing early cinema in particular. The cinema rarely predicts a future for itself (how often has the activity of 'virtual reality' replaced film going in science fiction films?). A recent Hong Kong film offers a vision of the future as time that can be transversed as space. The train in Wong Kar-wai's *2046* (HK, 2004) takes us to a future city in the clouds where people can find their memories of the past. Tyler makes only a passing reference to the source of his book's title: 'The shadow of an airplane climbs the Empire State Building ... I saw that from my window the other day while I took a turn about my room in a moment of recess from the typewriter ... I saw then ... *that it can happen in the world too* ... this wonderful shadow existence of the film.'[30] Tony Leung's character, Chow Mo-wan, in *2046* writes what might come to be, before our eyes, in 2046, and the final image of the film is of this city of the future represented by skyscrapers bathed in coloured neon light, as the focus repeatedly shifts, one may wonder if this end of the film shows an actual physical space, or electric shadows flashing by in the imagination of this future. As Hong Kong film travels across the world, we can be reminded that in doing so it renews and transforms our very perception of the world as well.

References

1   Brenez, Nicole, 'For It Is the Critical Faculty That Invents Fresh Forms' in M. Temple and M. Witt (eds), *The French Cinema Book* (London: British Film Institute, 2004), p.230.
2   Wong, Mary (ed), *Hong Kong Filmography*, vol. 1, 1913–41 (Hong Kong: Hong Kong Film Archive and Urban Council, 1997), pp.3–4.
3   Faure, Elie, 'The Art of Cineplastics' in R. Abel (ed), *French Film Theory and Criticism: A History/Anthology*, vol. I, 1907–29 (Princeton: Princeton University Press, 1988), p.259.
4   On the one hand, such recent film studies' publications include Dennison, Stephanie and Lim, Song Hwee (eds), *Remapping World Cinema: Identity, Culture and Politics in Film* (New York: Wallflower Press, 2006); Chapman, James, *Cinemas of the World: Film and Society from 1895 to the Present* (London: Reaktion Books, 2003); Hill, John and Church Gibson, Pamela (eds), *World Cinema: Critical Approaches* (Oxford: Oxford University Press, 2000); Badley, Linda, Barton Palmer, R. and Schneider, Steven Jay (eds), *Traditions in World Cinema* (Edinburgh: Edinburgh Press, 2006); Grant, Catherine and Kuhn, Annette (eds), *Screening World Cinema: A Screen Reader* (London and New York: Routledge, 2006), and Nowell-Smith, Geoffrey (ed), *The Oxford History of World Cinema* (Oxford: Oxford University Press, 1996). As for books on Hong Kong and Hong Kong cinema, on the other hand, recently published works include McDonogh, Gary and Wong, Cindy, *Global Hong Kong* (New York: Routledge, 2005); Bordwell, David, *Planet Hong Kong: Popular Cinema and the Art of Entertainment* (Cambridge: Harvard University Press, 2000); Cheung, Esther M.K. and Chu Yiu-wai (eds), *Between Home and World: A Reader in Hong Kong Cinema* (Hong Kong: Oxford University Press, 2004).
5   Balibar, Etienne, *We the People of Europe: Reflections on Transnational Citizenship*, trans. James Swenson (Princeton: Princeton University Press, 2004), p.102.
6   Tyler, Parker, *The Shadow of an Airplane Climbs the Empire State Building* (New York: Doubleday, 1972).
7   Wyatt, Justin, *High Concept: Movies and Marketing in Hollywood* (Austin: University of Texas Press, 1994), p.23.

8   I discuss the 'high-concept' aspect of *Infernal Affairs* at greater length in my essay 'Infernal Affairs: High Concept in Hong Kong,' *Senses of Cinema* 26 (2003).

9   *Report of Commission on Strategic Development, Hong Kong's Long-Term Development Needs and Goals*, Hong Kong, 2004.

10 Abbas, Ackbar, 'Dialectic of Deception', *Public Culture* 11/2 (1999), p.361.

11 Dwyer, Tessa, 'Straining to Hear (Deleuze)' in I. Buchanan (ed), *A Deleuzian Century?* (Durham: Duke University Press, 1999), p.176.

12 Moretti, Franco, 'Planet Hollywood', *New Left Review* 9 (2001), pp.90–101.

13 Bordwell: *Planet Hong Kong*, p.7.

14 Some examples are Rotha, Paul and Manvell, Roger, *Movie Parade, 1888–1949: A Pictorial Survey of World Cinema* (London: Studio Publications, 1950); Tyler, Parker, *Classics of the Foreign Film: A Pictorial Treasury* (New York: Citadel Press, 1962); Tyler, Parker, *A Pictorial History of Sex in Films* (Secaucus: Citadel, 1974); Everson, William K., *The Bad Guys: A Pictorial History of the Movie Villain* (New York: Citadel Press, 1964); Everson, William K., *A Pictorial History of the Western Film* (Secaucus: Citadel Press, 1969).

15 Cheung, Esther M.K. and Chu Yiu-wai, 'Introduction: Between Home and World' in *Between Home and World*, p. xii; Hammond, Stefan and Wilkins, Mike, *Sex and Zen and Bullet in the Head* (New York: Simon and Schuster, 1996); Logan, Bey, *Hong Kong Action Cinema* (Woodstock: Overlook Press, 1995); Glaessner, Verina, *Kung Fu: Cinema of Vengeance* (London: Lorimer, 1974).

16 Sklar, Robert, *Film: An International History of the Medium* (New York: H.N. Abrams, 1993).

17 Cheung and Chu: *Between Home and World*, p.xii.

18 Fonoroff, Paul, *Silver Light: A Pictorial History of Hong Kong Cinema, 1920–1970* (Hong Kong: Joint Publishing, 1997).

19 'The Image Issue', *Rouge* 5 (2004) at <http://www.rouge.com.au>

20 Spivak, Gayatri Chakravorty, *Death of a Discipline* (New York: Columbia University Press, 2003), p.93.

21 Bordwell: *Planet Hong Kong*, p.ix.

22 Abbas, Ackbar, *Hong Kong: Culture and the Politics of Disappearance* (Minneapolis: University of Minnesota Press, 1997), p.4.

23 Wong, Mary, 'Women Who Cross Borders: MP&GI's Modernity Programme' in Ai-ling Wong (ed), *The Cathay Story* (Hong Kong: Hong Kong Film Archive, 2002); Fu, Poshek, 'Hong Kong and Singapore: A History of Cathay Cinema' in *The Cathay Story*.

24 Wong, Mary: 'Women Who Cross Borders', pp.162–75.

25 Zhang, Zhen, 'Bodies in the Air: The Magic of Science and the Fate of the Early "Martial Arts' Film" in China', *Postscript* 20/2&3 (2001), p.54.

26 Williams, Linda, 'Film Bodies: Gender, Genre, and Excess', *Film Quarterly* 44/4 (1991), pp.2–13.
27 Tyler: *The Shadow of an Airplane*, p.93.
28 Zhang, Zhen, *An Amorous History of the Silver Screen, Shanghai Cinema, 1896–1937* (Chicago: University of Chicago Press, 2005), pp.58–64.
29 Tyler: *The Shadow of an Airplane*, pp.276–7.
30 Tyler: *The Shadow of an Airplane*, p.284.

PART TWO

ALL CHANGING ON THE
EASTERN FRONT

5

Leung Wing-Fai

Infernal Affairs and *Kung Fu Hustle*: Panacea, Placebo and Hong Kong Cinema

The decline of Hong Kong cinema since the mid-1990s is closely linked to the overwhelming change in the way feature films are consumed and the re-structuring of local, regional and global film markets. As a result, film-makers look for new ways to cater for the mainland Chinese and international audiences, tactics that are seen as vital for future survival. This chapter examines two local blockbusters as survival strategies for the ailing film industry, the *Infernal Affairs* trilogy (Andrew Lau and Mak Siu-fai, 2002–3) and *Kung Fu Hustle* (Stephen Chow, 2004), and empirically considers Hong Kong cinema within shifting paradigms in the study of contemporary commercial film practices.

Hong Kong Cinema 1980–95

The 1980s were the commercial peak of Hong Kong Cinema. From 1988 to 1996, an average of 153 films were made each year.[1] Through the 1980s to the mid-1990s, Hong Kong films dominated the local box office. In 1992, for instance, all top ten films were Hong Kong productions. On the other hand, only three local productions were in the list of top ten titles at the box office in 1998.[2]

During the 1980s and early 1990s, Hong Kong films also dominated the export markets in Asia to the extent that Lii argues that Hong Kong cinema was a 'marginal empire'.[3] Productions were exported to Taiwan, South East Asia, and Chinese-speaking audiences beyond Asia. For instance, since Taiwan had stringent import rules against foreign films from which Chinese language productions from Hong Kong were exempt, Taiwan represented 30 per cent of Hong Kong films' export market.[4] The prominent position of Hong Kong cinema in the regional markets meant that little regard was given to specifically catering for the culturally diverse audiences. The most popular genres for exportation were action and comedy: therefore, it was relatively easy to sell homogeneous products to a variety of markets. The end result was a cinema that was largely apolitical and imminently suitable for exporting to diverse cultures without making an effort to be market-specific.

In Hollywood, the flow of product is maintained by what is called vertical integration, major companies controlling production, distribution and exhibition. Shohat and Stam argue that there has been a long tradition of film industries, including Hong Kong, imitating Hollywood.[5] In the 1980s, three major film companies existed in Hong Kong: Golden Harvest under Raymond Chow started production in the early 1970s; Golden Princess, a chain of theatres, was behind Cinema City studio to ensure the supply of titles; Dickson Poon launched D & B Films in 1984 that took over the screens owned by the Shaw studio. Golden Harvest had a 'satellite model of production' that Cinema City imitated. The latter also bankrolled the director Tsui Hark's Film Workshop. Each chain had two or three local productions each week until the decline of the industry in the mid-1990s.

The major distribution chains required around 120 films a year and therefore had enough scope to test the audiences through a variety of productions. In 1983, 51 out of 88 cinemas were controlled by the three major chains, with the other cinemas showing a mixture of foreign and local films.[6] This separation between the distribution of local and foreign films continued through the 1980s and benefited domestic productions. In 1988, 107 out of 133 theatres showed domestic films. However, from the early 1980s onwards, mini-cinema complexes began to open. Gradually, with the lack of Hong Kong films to fill the mini-theatres, many chains were forced to bring in American films. In 1989, Golden Harvest brought United International Pictures to Hong Kong, which enabled its distribution of productions by Universal, Paramount, MGM and United Artists.

The so-called break-even films were made for as little as HKD 3 million, which would be certain to recoup the cost through theatrical release and video sales.[7] On the other hand, a blockbuster in the mid-1990s cost HKD 50 million (of which the stars consumed at least a third).[8] Investment came from individuals, distribution, exhibition and overseas sales. As the industry was relatively small and insular, directors came up with ideas, sometimes worked with scriptwriters and went directly to investors to get the financing. That resulted in the practice of often filming without a complete and developed shooting script. Post-production often took only two weeks. Films 'sold' themselves, so there was no need for substantial release publicity. Generic conventions counted more than screenwriting skills, and scripts were often written with an industrial formula. Furthermore, when films became box office hits in Hong Kong, copycats of the types and genres dominated, creating fads and cycles and resulting in the highly self-referential nature of many local productions. Directors and actors worked constantly in the 1980s and early 1990s, honing their skills, a practice quite unique to Hong Kong due to the 'mass production' nature of the industry.

Rayns sums up the operation of the Hong Kong film industry at this time:

> By the late 1980s most Hong Kong films were in profit before a frame was shot: it was routine to pre-sell films (on the strength of a title, a genre and two or more star names) throughout East Asia, and a pre-sale to Taiwan alone was generally lucrative enough to cover two-thirds of the cost of making the film. These circumstances bred complacency. Many films were sloppily improvised, without shooting scripts; many actors devalued their own currency by accepting too many roles in too many lousy movies; ideas and sometimes whole scenes were freely plagiarised from other movies, local and foreign.[9]

Hong Kong Cinema as Culture Industry

At first glance, critiques of film industries by the Frankfurt School apply appropriately to Hong Kong cinema, especially the productions of the 1980s and early 1990s. Briefly, Adorno and Horkheimer assert that Hollywood studios produce formulaic mass products that serve the capitalist ideology:

> Movies and radio need no longer pretend to be art. The truth that they are just business is made into an ideology in order to justify the rubbish they deliberately produce.[10]

> Cultural entities typical of the culture industry are no longer also commodities, they are commodities through and through.[11]

According to Adorno and Horkheimer, audiences cannot distinguish between real life and movies because 'the sound film, far surpassing the theatre of illusion, leaves no room for imagination or reflection on the part of the audience, who is unable to respond within the structure of the film, yet deviate from its precise detail without losing the thread of the story'.[12] In other words, they serve to stunt the imagination of the consumers. Since the masses are moulded to understand these standardised products, characterised by 'eternal sameness' and 'inter-changeable sameness',[13] they know what they expect and they do not resist them, no matter how low the quality of popular entertainment is. The consumers of such products are reproduced in the ideology of capitalism, rendered juvenile by the lack of artistic quality. When Adorno elaborated the original thesis further in *Culture Industry Reconsidered* in 1963, Hollywood film production was about to become disintegrated with the emergence of New Hollywood and more inde-pendent productions.[14]

Film production in Hong Kong exaggerates the systematic exploita-tion of cultural products, especially at the height of its commercial success. Films are made as a manufacturing process. The Frankfurt School's culture industry thesis has been used in relation to the repro-duction of capitalist ideology: in Chun's analysis of identity and public culture in Hong Kong, for instance, he states that due to the development of a distinctive Hong Kong culture from 1967 to 1984, there is 'the flourishing of media-oriented popular culture that was financed by large capitalist interests, not unlike Horkheimer and Adorno's culture industry, which neatly reproduced the utilitarian values of a free-market society', 'where everything can be priced, even culture'.[15] Nevertheless, Adorno conceives that his observations are not the result of empirical evidence, which is precisely the importance of an enquiry such as this.[16]

The Decline of Hong Kong Cinema: 1995–2005

Since the mid-1990s, the Hong Kong film industry has been in rapid decline. The channels of disseminating feature films in Hong Kong have proliferated through the advent of the video/VCD market and satellite stations.[17] At the same time, the number of film productions in Hong Kong reduced to 63 in 2004, and 55 in 2005.[18]

In 2002, for instance, around 92 films were made, one-third of which were shot on DV (digital video) and bound for the video market. In addition, out of 62 (non-digital) films of that year, 29 earned less than HKD 1 million at the box office.[19] Given the increase in population and the rise in ticket prices over time, the figures show that the audiences have deserted local cinema. This decline since the mid-1990s has been for a variety of reasons, not least competition from Hollywood films, the shrinking local market and cheap reproductions in the form of VCDs.

Hong Kong film production has lost much of its regional markets in Korea, Taiwan and South East Asia. Since the relaxation of import regulation in 1986, Taiwanese audiences gradually abandoned Chinese films for Hollywood productions. In addition, many of these countries were badly affected by the Asian economic crisis in 1997 and never recovered. On the other hand, film industries in Korea and Thailand have taken off in the last decade and become keen competitors. In Hong Kong and the Chinese markets, piracy is a major problem.

Further proof of the Hong Kong audiences' declined interest in domestic productions can be found in quantitative data. The market share of local films has shrunk (see Tables 1 and 2).

There are two noticeable trends at the box office since 1980, illustrated by the tables. First of all, local productions have been losing the domestic market in favour of foreign, mainly Hollywood, films. In the focus groups studied by TELA,[20] participants reported that for them, cinema viewing was about special visual and sound effect. If spectacular scenes are considered important, then the local productions are less likely to compete with Hollywood blockbusters.

As seen in Table 2, the box office share of domestic products has been dropping. Exception to recent trend was the result of the commercial hit *Shaolin Soccer* (Stephen Chow, 2001) that went head to head with *Harry Potter: the Philosopher's Stone* (Chris Columbus) in 2001 and

Table 1. Box Office Record for Top Local and Foreign Films[21]

	Box Office for No. 1 Local Film	Box Office for No. 1 Foreign Film
1980	HKD 9,429,871	HKD 5,742,063
1985	HKD 30,748,643	HKD 24,649,206
1989	HKD 36,294,029	HKD 24,275,380
1996	HKD 57,518,795	HKD 49,380,096
1998	HKD 41,532,235	HKD 28,852,845
2000	HKD 35,214,661	HKD 36,138,973
2001	HKD 60,739,847	HKD 43,409,950
2002	HKD 42,430,940	HKD 31,124,971
2003	HKD 30,200,000	HKD 37,600,000
2004	HKD 25,200,000	HKD 41,600,000

Table 2. Local VS Foreign Films Box Office Ratio[22]

	Percentage of Box Office (Local Films)	Percentage of Box Office (Foreign Films)
1988	78.58	21.42
1989	72.15	27.85
1991	77.2	22.8
1995	58	42
1996	52.05	47.95
2002	40	60
2005	35.1 (estimated)	64.9

between *Infernal Affairs* and *Harry Potter and the Chamber of Secrets* (Chris Columbus) in 2002. *Infernal Affairs* represented 16 per cent of the total box office of that year. Despite that, the percentage of total box office for local films in 2002 was only 40 per cent.[23]

Mass production of the 1980s and early 1990s had the advantages of 'time-saving, flexibility, freedom of employment, ad hoc decision making, and a minimum of bureaucracy', but that became problematic and 'led the downturn of the film business since the early 1990s'.[24] Increasing cost and decreasing profit meant less investment in film, a trend that continued right through the 1990s.

Infernal Affairs: Model of a Blockbuster

In response to the crisis of the industry, the investors, usually private business interests, want safe projects, which by definition is characterised by a star cast, easily discernible genres, confidence in the film-makers and export potential. Woody Tsung Wan-chi, chief executive of the Hong Kong, Kowloon and New Territories Motion Picture Industry Association, said: 'These days, if it isn't a big production you can't pull the audience in ... Other genres, such as sitcom and drama, which were popular in the past and can be produced at a lower cost, are less likely to attract investment.'[25] There is therefore less variety in the productions. The types of production have polarised: big budget films/ blockbusters or very low budget productions that are aimed at the more locally focused, VCD market. John Chong, executive director of Media Asia, also points out that the company will focus on big budget films or star casts because they will have international appeal and therefore are not affected by the weak local market. Local film-makers have replaced creativity with cautious calculation.[26] The trend towards blockbuster production is not unlike New Hollywood of the 1970s, where:

> mainstream hits are where stars, genres, and cinematic innovations invariably are established, where the 'grammar' of cinema is most likely to be refined, and where the essential qualities of the medium – its popular and commercial character – are most evident.[27]

Infernal Affairs was the inaugural production for the Media Asia conglomerate, which previously only distributed films and videos. The film offers a twist in the gangster-undercover cop formula. It is a mixture of two subgenres. The two main characters are played by major Asian stars, Tony Leung and Andy Lau. Yan (Tony Leung) is an undercover policeman masquerading as a drug dealer and Ming (Andy Lau) is a gangster infiltrating the police force. The two men have been in their deep cover existence for ten years and both are sick of the state of affairs. Yan resorts to seeing a female psychiatrist. Ming leads a seemingly middle-class life, occupying a senior position in the police force, indicated by a minimalist apartment. When both sides find out they have a mole amongst them, Yan and Ming are ordered to root out the identity of one another.

Infernal Affairs fully uses Hong Kong's high tech, urban backdrop, producing blue and grey tones that permeate the film. The skyscrapers' glass and metal are juxtaposed with clear blue or glittering night sky. There are previous undercover cop films from Hong Kong, a subgenre that has been around since the early 1980s. The gangster and action genre as a whole is exemplified by John Woo's pre-1992 films, such as his last Hong Kong film *Hardboiled* (1992).

Infernal Affairs was perceived as the life saver of the Hong Kong film industry. Rayns notes that the promotion for the film suggested that audiences should see the film if they loved Hong Kong![28] The film was released before Christmas 2002, with competition in the theatres by way of Hollywood blockbusters including *Gangs of New York* (Martin Scorsese, 2002) and *Chicago* (Rob Marshall, 2002). It grossed over $7 million at the box office in a city of 7 million people.[29] The long holiday theatrical release was followed by timely DVD and VCD issues for the Chinese New Year holidays in 2003. Following the success, Media Asia immediately planned a prequel and a sequel that appeared in 2003, and both achieved a high level of box office success. The remaking rights were sold to Warner Brothers for $1.75 million through Brad Pitt's production company and remade as *The Departed* (Martin Scorsese, 2006).

The two leads are major stars in Asia: Tony Leung had recently acted in Wong Kar-wai's arthouse hit *In the Mood for Love* (2000), as well as Zhang Yimou's *Hero* (2002). Andy Lau was, in 2002, less well known abroad, but had been a famous actor in Asia for two decades. There is also support from the two bosses played by Anthony Wong and Eric Tsang, both established character actors. Andrew Lau Wai-Keung is the more famous of the co-directors. He directed the popular *Young and Dangerous* series in the 1990s about young triad members. Lau is also known for the two film adaptations he made from martial arts comics, *The Storm Riders* (1998) and *A Man Called Hero* (1999), both utilising CGI effects extensively.[30] Alan Mak Siu-fai is a novice compared to Lau, but he co-scripted all three films. The detailed scripts contributed to the success of the series. The commercial calculation of the film includes balanced screentime for the actors and the injection of women in the story, which evidences a lack of auteur sensibility. Andrew Lau states:

> The scriptwriters really like *The Godfather*. So they had carefully studied the structure of *The Godfather's* script. There was influence on our film. We imitated some style. We don't mind [people say that].[31]

In the past, promotion of local films was usually done with less than 5 per cent of budget, mainly through trailers, posters and newspapers only. The heavy promotion of the series was unprecedented. One of the main infotainment magazines in the city notes the marketing of *Infernal Affairs 3*: 'making of' videos all over Causeway Bay and Mongkok, as well as on the 'roadshow' channel (broadcast in a large number of buses), poster campaign in MTR stations, features in all the major newspapers and magazines.[32] Movie tie-ins were also previously rare in Hong Kong, but the *Infernal Affairs* series boasted special edition DVDs, merchandise, novels and scripts, even a first day cover.

Surprisingly, not all three films reached the official Chinese market. Andrew Lau explains:[33]

> If you are brave, you can leave the mainland market. Without the mainland market, it'd still be okay. The first one [*Infernal Affairs*] didn't make the cinemas in China. The ending did not consider the mainland. They had already said no. Lots of countries[34] have these rules, you have to go along with them, to change these things. In terms of commercial consideration, I feel there's no problem. Of course, there are people who are insistent, then you have to make other calculations. Making commercial products, you have to consider your markets.

Infernal Affairs 3 is such a compromise, produced firmly with the Chinese market in mind. The plot includes a mainland businessman, played by Chen Daoming (an actor famous for television roles and as the emperor in *Hero*), and a clear anti-crime message.

Infernal Affairs is the closest to a major, high-concept, blockbuster that emerged out of Hong Kong recently (as suggested by Schatz's typology). Leary asserts that there is a shift in Hong Kong from the assembly line mode of production towards high budget, high concept film-making.[35] It also signals the emergence of Media Asia, a conglomerate set up by the businessman Peter Lam. Media Asia has adopted a Hollywood-style management tactic, requiring completed scripts and detailed budget plans before shooting, and early and cross-media promotions. After noting the production values, Leary also suggests that the middle-class milieu, high tech, cool colours and office environment speak to the projected audience.[36] It moves away from the depiction of working class that is the norm in the action films of the 1980s.

Paradoxically, the attempts to create blockbusters further divide the industry. Audiences continue to wait for the occasional high budget releases at the movie theatres. Despite successes such as the *Infernal Affairs* series, the number of productions and the market share of domestic products continue to fall. Hollywood studios have large, varied slates, where losses are compensated by blockbusters and occasional breakout hits. However, the production companies in Hong Kong, financed by private capital, do not have the same capacity for diversifying products.

Kung Fu Hustle: The International China-Hong Kong Co-production

The recent trend in the Asian film industries, especially since the success of *Crouching Tiger, Hidden Dragon* (Ang Lee, 2000), is the attempt to replicate cross-over, co-produced blockbusters. Hong Kong film-makers also look for new ways to cater for the mainland Chinese and international audiences, tactics that are seen as vital for future survival. *Crouching Tiger, Hidden Dragon* was financed by Sony's Asian initiative Columbia Pictures Film Production Asia (based in Hong Kong), pre-sold to major territories in Europe and had producers in China and Hong Kong. With CEPA (Closer Economic Partnership Agreement),[37] all the major film producers in Hong Kong set their eyes on the Chinese market.[38] In 2004, nine out of 61 films were

China-Hong Kong co-productions, although only *Kung Fu Hustle* and *New Police Story* (Benny Chan, 2004) had significant box office performance.[39]

Co-productions, with other Asian countries or American studios, have a chequered history. Several recent English language productions (for instance, a Columbia Tristar production, *So Close* and *Naked Weapon*, both 2002) have failed at the box office. These films are presented in English and have little local flavour. *Silver Hawk* (Jingle Ma, 2004, starring Michelle Yeoh), produced by Media Asia for the Chinese New Year market in 2004, only took HKD 2.4 million at the box office after a week, a big loss against the HKD 20 million production cost.[40]

Nevertheless, co-productions ease the problem of cost (for high-quality crew and stars), as well as the sharing of production cost, potential markets and choice of locations. Law suggests that Hong Kong cinema, facing a shrinking market, should become 'a cinema exhibiting "special Chinese characteristics" but "without borders"' to compete internationally and to recapture Chinese audiences.[41]

Stephen Chow is one of the most bankable stars in Hong Kong and has been for about 20 years. He came from local television, most unglamorously as a children's programme host. In the early 1990s, he began making films most well known for its *mou lei tou* humour.[42] A typical character in Chow's early film is a penniless country bumpkin (from the mainland) who arrives in the big city and accidentally becomes the successful hero. Chow 'specialises in improvised wisecracks and absurdist non-sequiturs and respects nothing', humour which is limited to Cantonese speakers understanding.[43] Chow's breakthrough film, *All for the Winner* (Jeff Lau, 1990), took HKD 41 million at the box office and broke the previous records.[44] The commercial success was repeated through the early 1990s. Most notably, he made 'low-budget genre parodies (eight of them in 1990 alone, six more in 1991)'.[45]

All through the 1990s, Chow consistently achieved high-level box office records. *Shaolin Soccer* (2001), his film prior to *Kung Fu Hustle*, made HKD 60 million.[46] Merchandise followed, including manga and a computer game. Unlike *Kung Fu Hustle* though, this previous international hit could not be released theatrically in China.[47] Miramax released *Shaolin Soccer* in 2004, in an English dubbed version, under a storm of criticism. The original score was discarded in favour of a hip hop version (including the Carl Douglas song 'Kung Fu Fighting'). Twenty-six minutes of footage was cut and release in the UK was delayed by three years. Chow reportedly said: 'I like the long version, but Miramax know the audience. I can accept them making it shorter.'[48]

The local box office record of *Shaolin Soccer* was matched by *Kung Fu Hustle*. Nevertheless, Chow chose to work with Sony Colombia instead on *Kung Fu Hustle*. Chow wrote, directed and acted in the film. The crew included renowned international martial arts choreographers Sammo Hung and Yuen Wo Ping. Entering the international market was a well-stated aim for the production team. Chow commented that the CGI effects should create a sense of freshness and shock factor for the film's success.[49]

Kung Fu Hustle is a film in which Stephen Chow tones down his *mou lei tou* humour and local sensibilities to please the American investors. His locally coloured comedy is tamed in favour of more universal, cartoon-like physical gags. The Bruce Lee references play on Lee's local/global fame. Nevertheless, Chow also retains elements that aim to resonate with the domestic audiences. For instance, Srinivas suggests that *Kung Fu Hustle* uses 'highly localized cinematic language ... which addresses the spectator as if she is a member of an in-group'.[50] This is further enhanced through the use of martial arts stars from the 1970s (some of them had 'retired' from acting for many years). Chow has said that the film is a tribute to the local kung fu movie tradition: 'Inspiration for this film comes from all Hong Kong kung fu movies, from the 60s to the 90s, that I've watched in all these years. I made this film as a tribute to local kung fu movie production.'[51] Though never becoming a kung fu star, Chow practises martial arts daily and has named Bruce Lee as an important influence. *The South China Morning Post* notes that the filming and post-production took months longer than the usual Hong Kong movie and extols it as an example of good film-making.[52]

Concluding Remarks

The decline of the formulaic productions is evidence against the thesis of Adorno and Horkeimer, although the preference is shifted in favour of another culture industry: Hollywood studios. Despite isolated successes such as *Infernal Affairs* and *Kung Fu Hustle*, the once healthy film industry in Hong Kong has not revived. Law & Bren sum up the situation in 2004:

> What is clear is that Hong Kong film could still [*sic*] not compete with Hollywood on an equal footing, although it had been accepted in the international market as a legitimate provider of mass-appeal action products and high-end art films. Closer to home, the coveted Chinese

market remained largely out of reach and its government nowhere near implementing fundamental reform. Hong Kong film was thus looking at a period of hardship ahead as it sought transformation from an autonomous regional cinema to being a part of the Greater Chinese cinema.[53]

The changes in the Hong Kong film industry open up discourses on the failure of mass production. The industry can no longer support emerging film-makers or actors. Stars such as Andy Lau and Tony Leung are repeatedly employed as box office guarantees. The practice leads to high budget and audiences' boredom.[54] Hong Kong cinema, apart from the few blockbusters, has become part of home entertainment (through the flamboyant VCD/DVD markets and problems of piracy) rather than a theatrical experience. The mass cinema going habit of the 1980s and early 1990s have not returned with the infrequent box office hits that the industry is producing. The strategies to replicate box office performance, such as *Infernal Affairs* and *Kung Fu Hustle*, have paradoxically threatened the very production structure and consumption of the Hong Kong film. Many other high- and low-budget productions fail at the theatres. Investors' caution mean that fewer and fewer films are funded: the industry is in a vicious circle.

Choi further argues that the cross-over of Hong Kong film-makers, such as Jackie Chan, Yuen Wo-Ping and Chow Yun Fat, to Hollywood is evidence for the change from Fordist to post-Fordist production in Hollywood, the 'original' cultural industry.[55] The cultural industry thesis by Adorno and Horkheimer refers specifically to the 1940s Hollywood production of mass products, which 'content of the ideology is exhausted in the idolization of the existing order'.[56]

The lesson of the industrial change in Hong Kong cinema is that capitalist cultural production no longer satisfies the desire and sensibilities of individuals that it once created and tried to satiate. It challenges Adorno's assertion of the consumers of the cultural industry:

> They force their eyes shut and voice approval, in a kind of self-loathing, for what is meted out to them, knowing fully the purpose for which it is manufactured.[57]

Framed in the debates of postmodernity, production in late capitalism represents 'more flexible labour processes and markets, of geographical mobility and rapid shifts in consumption practices'.[58] The Hong Kong film industry has developed unevenly. The 1980s mode of production was a version of mass production and there were vertical integrated chains, though the film companies did not have the power of Hollywood studios of the 1940s. Hollywood has been successful in capturing diverse audiences in its exporting of films, an example of its success in maintaining the market leader position since the break up of the studio system in the 1940s and 1950s. The foreign markets have become increasingly important for the American film industry: *Harry Potter and the Sorcerer's Stone* (Chris Columbus, 2001) grossed $651 million in foreign markets and only $317 million domestically.

In Hong Kong, the break up of the larger studios indicates the problems of mass production, but the smaller companies have not ensured innovative practices as they have to rely on large private corporations for investment, distribution and exhibition. The decline of the Hong Kong film industry is not evidence of more flexible production, but a failure of the 'culture industry' to adjust to changes and maintain markets. As the industry shrinks, the contents of films have become more, not less, formulaic due to nervous caution. The range of products is not enough for the increasingly flexible markets. Jameson suggests that late capitalism is no longer about 'the primacy of industrial production',[59] and so the readjustment in the form of consumers' control of their own personal space determines the development of a once successful mass production industry.

The post-1997 economic crisis changed 'Hong Kong as the bastion of free-marketing practices',[60] as the Special Administrative Region government intervened in the market, including government support for the survival of the film industry. The rupture coincided with the handover of Hong Kong back to China in 1997, the economic crisis in Asia around the same time and Hong Kong's failure to remain a primary commercial centre in the region. The process of adjustment within the Hong Kong film industry indicates a step towards it becoming a regional cinema within Greater China, as isolated successes such as *Kung Fu Hustle* demonstrate. The attempt to create blockbusters, often co-produced, is a placebo masquerading as panacea for the ills of the Hong Kong film industry.

Acknowledgement

I was supported by the University of London Central Research Fund and BFWG Charitable Foundation Grant for this research.

References

1   Zhang, Yingjin, *Chinese National Cinema* (London: Routledge, 2004), p.156, Table 5.2.

2   City Entertainment, 'Hong Kong Cinema: Will it Revive in the Next Half Year?', *City Entertainment* (15–28 August 2002, Issue 609), pp.18–22 (in Chinese).

3   Lii, Ding-Tzann, 'A Colonized Empire: Reflections on the Expansion of Hong Kong Films in Asian Countries' in Kuan-Hsing Chen (ed), *Trajectories: Inter-Asia Cultural Studies* (London & New York: Routledge, 1998), pp.122–41.

4   Law, Kar and Bren, Frank, *Hong Kong Cinema: A Cross-Cultural View* (Oxford: Maryland, Scarecrow Press, 2004), pp.291, 295, note 1.

5   Shohat, Ella and Stam, Robert, *Unthinking Eurocentrism* (London: Routledge, 2004), p.29.

6   See Chu, Yingchi, *Hong Kong Cinema: Coloniser, Motherland and Self* (London & New York: Routledge Curzon, 2003), pp.54–6, for details.

7   HKD = Hong Kong Dollars. In November 2006, HKD 10 million = $1.3 million or £674,000.

8   See Bordwell, David, *Planet Hong Kong: Popular Cinema and the Art of Entertainment* (Cambridge, MA: Harvard University Press, 2000), pp.117–19.

9   Rayns, Tony, 'Deep Cover', *Sight and Sound* (January 2004), p.28.

10 Adorno, Theodor and Horkheimer, Max, 'The Culture Industry: Enlightenment as Mass Deception' (1969) in Simon During (ed), *The Cultural Studies Reader* (London: Routledge, 1993), p.31.

11 Adorno and Horkheimer: 'The Cultural Industry', p.32.

12 Adorno and Horkheimer: 'The Cultural Industry', p.34.

13 Adorno, Theodor, 'Culture Industry Reconsidered' (1963) in Paul Marris and Sue Thornham (eds), *Media Studies Reader* (Edinburgh, Edinburgh University Press, 1996), pp.32, 35.

14 As opposed to the studio controlled, vertically integrated system that dominated film production of the 1940s and much of 1950s.

15 Chun, Allen, 'Discourses of Identity in the Changing Spaces of Public Culture in Taiwan, Hong Kong and Singapore', *Theory, Culture & Society* 13 (1) (1996), pp.58, 63.

16 Adorno: 'Cultural Industry Reconsidered', pp.35–6.

17 VCDs are films on MPeg formats.

18 See Zhang: *Chinese National Cinema*, p.156; City Entertainment, 'Meaning of Copyright' *City Entertainment* (Issue 671, 30 Dec–12 Jan 2005), p.30 (in Chinese); Chow, Vivienne, 'Fadeout on the Set as

Filmmakers Play Safe', *South China Morning Post* (10 Jan 2005), C1; Cahiers du Cinema *Atlas 2006* (Hors-Série Special) (2006).

19   City Entertainment, 'Five Features of Hong Kong Films in 2002', *City Entertainment* (Issue 619, 2–15 January 2003), p.35 (in Chinese).

20   TELA (Television and Entertainment Licensing Authority), *The Survey on Movie-Going Habits in Hong Kong*, <http://www.tela.gov.hk/english/doc/forms/whatsnew/fullreport.pdf> 2001, accessed 10 March 2005.

21   From *City Entertainment* Issues 308 (17–30 Jan 1991), 609 (15–28 August 2002), 671 (30 Dec 2004–12 Jan 2005), 620 (16–29 Jan 2003).

22   From *City Entertainment* (25 January 1990), p.19; Chu: 'Hong Kong Cinema', p.55; *City Entertainment* (Issue 609, 15–28 August 2002), p.19; *City Entertainment* (Issue 620, 16–29 January 2003), p.15; Cahiers du Cinema: *Atlas 2006*.

23   Law, Ryan, 'Decline and Fall Hong Kong Box Office in 2002' in *Far East Film 5* (Udine, CEC, 2003), pp.12–13.

24   Chu: *Chinese National Cinema*, p.126.

25   Chow: 'Fade out on the Set'.

26   Chow: 'Fade out on the Set'.

27   Thomas Schatz, quoted in Buckland, Warren, 'A Close Encounter with Raiders of the Lost Ark' in Steve Neale and Murray Smith (eds), *Contemporary Hollywood Cinema* (London: Routledge, 1998), p.166.

28   Rayns: 'Deep Cover'.

29   Rayns: 'Deep Cover'; Youngs, Tim, 'An Affair to Remember Hong Kong Cinema' in 2002 *Far East Film 5* (Udine: CEC, 2003), pp.6–11.

30   Computer generated imagery.

31   Talk given at the Chinese University of Hong Kong on 22 March 2005.

32   *Next* (11 December 2003), p. 194. MTR is the underground train system in Hong Kong.

33   See note 31.

34   He referred to Asian countries such as Malaysia and Indonesia. The ending of *Infernal Affairs* shows the gangster seemingly getting away with it. See also note 37.

35   Leary, Charles, 'Infernal Affairs: High Concept in Hong Kong', *Senses of Cinema*, <http://www.sensesofcinema.com/contents/03/26/internal_affairs.html> 2003, accessed 10 March 2004.

36   Leary: 'Infernal Affairs'.

37   For more information about CEPA, see The Hong Kong Trade and Industry Department website <www.tid.gov.hk>. Prohibited themes by the Chinese authority include superstition, sexual taboos, explicit sex scenes, political comments, gambling, violence, 'threats' to law and order.

38   In October 2003, for example, the major investors and representatives from China Star, Emperor, Media Asia, Golden Harvest and Universe

made a three-day visit to Beijing. See *Next* (30 October 2003), pp.40–2.

39 *City Entertainment* (Issue 671, 30 Dec–12 Jan 2005), p.36 (in Chinese). *Kung Fu Hustle* took HKD 60 million and *New Police Story* HKD 21 million.

40 *Next* (29 January 2004), p.42.

41 Law, Kar, 'Crisis and Opportunity: Crossing Borders in Hong Kong Cinema, Its Development from the 40s to the 70s' in Hong Kong International Film Festival, *Border Crossings in Hong Kong Cinema* (Hong Kong: HKIFF, 2000), p.122.

42 Literally being headless: meaning a nonsensical kind of humour.

43 Rayns, Tony, 'Hard Boiled', *Sight and Sound* (August 1992), p.22.

44 *Next* (29 January 2004), p.129.

45 Rayns: 'Hard Boiled'.

46 *Next* (29 January 2004), p.129.

47 'On [*Shaolin Soccer*]'s first release in Hong Kong, its distributor neglected to take it to the Chinese censorship board; in retaliation it was banned from mainland China – one of the largest markets in the world'. Review posted by Nosemonkey, <http://unseenmovies.blogspot.com/2004/11/shaolin-soccer.html> accessed 11 January 2007.

48 Quoted in Queen, Neil, 'Dragon Loses Its Fire', *The Times: The Eye* (13 November 2004), p.8.

49 See <hk.omovies.yahoo.com/news/ent/005080206001f6cy.html> accessed 5 August 2005 (in Chinese).

50 Srinivas, S.V. 'Kung Fu Hustle: A Note on the Local', *Inter-Asia Cultural Studies* (Vol. 6, No. 2, 2005), p.290.

51 Quoted in Franklin, Erika, 'from Street Hustle to Box Office Muscle: Stephen Chow Interviewed', *Firecracker,* <http://www.firecracker-media.com/cgi-bin/moxiebin/bm_tools.cgi?print=:s=1;site=1> 2005, accessed 6 June 2005.

52 South China Morning Post, 'Without Fresh Ideas It's Curtains for Film Industry', *South China Morning Post,* 22 January 2005.

53 Law and Bren: *Hong Kong Cinema*, p.294.

54 The salary of the major stars will require guaranteed commercial success at the box office: in 2005, Andy Lau, Tony Leung Chiu-Wai and Maggie Cheung were paid HKD 8–9 million, Stephen Chow's fee was HKD 15 million in 2002. As a result of the lack of Hong Kong film stars who have 'box office clout', local film productions turn to foreign (mainly Asian) actors. These Asian stars increase the international appeal of the oft-co-productions and are reportedly cheaper than the most popular Hong Kong counterparts. See Chow, Vivienne, 'Star Shortage Forces Director to Look Elsewhere', *South China Morning Post* (8 July 2005), C3.

55　Fordist production is about mass production, mass consumption, balance of labour unions (or the lack of them), large corporate capital and minimum state intervention in industries. Choi, Wai Kit, 'Post-Fordist Production and the Re-appropriation of Hong Kong Masculinity in Hollywood' in Laikwan Pang and Day Wong (eds), *Masculinities and Hong Kong Cinema* (Hong Kong: Hong Kong University Press, 2005), pp.199–220.

56　Choi: 'Post-Fordist Production', p.212.

57　Adorno: 'Culture Industry Reconsidered', p.35.

58　Harvey, David, *The Condition of Postmodernity* (Oxford, Cambridge, Mass: Blackwell, 1999), p.124.

59　Jameson, Frederick, *Postmodernism, or, the Cultural Logic of Late Capitalism* (London, New York: Verso, 1991), p.3.

60　Abbas, Ackbar, '(H)edge City: a Response to Becoming (Postcolonial) Hong Kong' in *Cultural Studies* (Vol. 15, Numbers 3/4, July 2001), p.622.

6

Chris Howard

Contemporary South Korean Cinema: 'National Conjunction' and 'Diversity'

In the now familiar post-*Shiri* (Kang Je-Gyu, South Korea, 1999) narrative of the triumph of local films over Hollywood imports, a succession of domestic blockbusters have broken Korean box office records. By 2006, four films had also surpassed the historic benchmark of 10 million entries, an astonishing figure representing more than one-fifth of the country's entire population. But in light of these achievements a consensus has also emerged that this 'record-breaker' phenomenon is related to certain problems in South Korea's wider film culture. This reached a head in August 2006 with the public protests by European festival favourite Kim Ki-Duk that culminated in a 100-minute television debate. On this occasion, Kim aggressively asserted that the success of the latest record-breaker, Bong Joon-Ho's *The Host* (2006), was down to patriotism/nationalism, questionable audience taste and, above all, the problem of 'screen dominance'.[1] Whilst Kim's hyperbole drew vitriolic responses from some quarters, the outburst crystallised concerns about the oligopolistic practices of the so-called big three 'local majors', powerful distributors also tied to the main multiplex chains. On an immediate level these debates highlighted the increasing difficulties of non-mainstream or smaller budget films, including Kim's *Shi Gan* (2006), released at the same time as *The Host*, to gain any substantial screen space. It is against this backdrop that an almost universal accord has been reached that 'diversity' should now become a key component of contemporary Korean cinema.

The aim of this chapter, however, is to look at both the parallels and differences between the emergence of the record-breaker films and the apparent solution of diversity. In relation to the former, I introduce the idea of a 'national conjunction' to describe the intimate relation between industry, text and cinema-going practices that have led to the domestic success of the record-breaker films. Whilst I consider the role of 'patriotic consumption' in the popularity of the films, like Kim, I also stress the overarching role of the Korean majors in motoring such phenomena. But the apparent turn to diversity in, for example, a range of KOFIC (Korean Film Council) initiatives is far from a simple response. Rather than merely correcting the *social* problems of the record-breaker film, diversity in many cases also functions to complement or expand particular *commercial* activities of the film industry. If blockbusters and record-breakers have made the Korean industry dominant in the domestic market, many 'diversity policies' have a notable emphasis on increasing the regional and global reach of Korean cinema. Furthermore, even though initiatives such as the Art Plus Cinema Network Korean are helping audiences to access a wider range of films, there is still something of a national element to the 'management' of diversity. This, however, is primarily through government agencies in collaboration with SMEs (small to medium-sized enterprises) rather than through the activities of Korean majors. Instead of being something unique to Korea, however, I suggest that this particular national intervention is merely part of a more global turn towards the discourse of 'the creative industries', albeit with the South Korean case demonstrating its own distinctive elements.

The 'National Conjunction' of South Korean Cinema

In English-language materials there remains little critical reflection about researchers' own positions in relation to the seemingly 'new' object of study of Korean cinema, an object that has, of course, a far longer history. Much of the impetus for the interest in Korean cinema in this essay initially came from trying to understand why South Korean cinema had been so much more successful in attracting local audiences than, for instance, in Japan, the UK or France. Whilst commentators such as Shin have begun to plot the links between the success of the film industry and wider economic and political changes,[2] here I attempt to locate these particular record-breaker films in relation to a more concrete series of industrial and film-going practices. I put forward the idea that the record-breaker phenomenon is a national conjunction: an assemblage of film text, industry strategy and mode of consumption principally organised along 'national' lines. I use this over-determined label of the national to more specifically emphasise the continued importance of the domestic market for Korean films, principally because of the oligopolistic activities of the Korean majors. The strong position of local companies in the Korean film industry, for instance, makes an interesting comparison with the presence of Canal+ in France. The French media/film conglomerate was from its inception much more dependent on global distribution channels, particularly through the ownership of various European television channels. As Miller *et al*. demonstrate, the relationship between Canal+, government policy and co-production/inward investment by Hollywood companies is also a complex issue.[3]

Promoting Korean cinema exports has long been a focus of KOFIC. But even though there is an increasing awareness of Korean films in Europe and America, particularly through DVD, this has yet to translate into substantial box office returns. Furthermore, although Asia, and particularly Japan, has been the dominant export market for South Korean films, it is still evident that unlike the global reach of most Hollywood products, for Korean films the domestic market has a far more substantial bearing. According to KOFIC's statistics, between 2001 and 2004 the domestic theatrical market generated 74–77 per cent of Korean films' total revenue, with a mere 3.4–9.6 per cent earned from export to foreign markets (the remainder from domestic ancillary sales).[4]

It is in this geo-economic context that the record-breakers have played an increasingly important role. Since *Silmido* (Wook-Suk Kang, 2003) passed the historic benchmark of 10 million entries, the overall box office record has been broken a further three times. Most recently, *The Host* eventually ended its run after 'mobilising' 13.19 million viewers and breaking *The King and the Clown*'s (Jun-Ik Lee, 2005) six-month record of 12.3 million viewers. The last of the record-breaker titles, *The Host* was released on 620 screens out of a total number of 1,649 screens, thus taking up nearly 38 per cent of the nation's entire screen capacity.[5] As already mentioned, it is this screen dominance that has been positioned as the biggest problem with Korean cinema.

Although accounts such as Shin's mention that 'nationalism' has at least had some role in the development of contemporary Korean cinema, I wish to analyse this in relation to more concrete phenomena such as the marketing and cinema-going practices around the record-breakers. My overall claim, however, is that any manifestation of nationalism is less a 'motor' for the record-breaker phenomenon and more a 'tool' that helps the Korean majors generate these films' enormous box office rewards. The complex genealogy of Korean nationalism is dealt with in more detail by Shin Gi-Wook,[6] but it is clear that the received idea of a 'one-blood' ethnic nationhood (complete with foundation myth) has remained manifest across different time periods and in different forms. In the context of the twentieth century, such sentiment has been part of responses to the Japanese Occupation, the Korean War and also life under subsequent military dictatorships. Nationalism was also one of the main driving forces behind South Korea's economic miracle (1972–9). These historical moments are obviously emotionally charged and still, of course, within the memory of older generations of Koreans. This often makes discussions of such sentiments a delicate issue.

More recently, South Korea's first civil government of 1993, led by President Kim Young-Sam, promoted open market policies and the discourse of *Saegaewha* (i.e. the 'national movement' towards globalisation).[7] Here, however, there is also a shift away from production to also emphasise the importance of consumption. It is against this development that I want to position the sudden emergence of the 'Red Devils' phenomenon during the 2002 World Cup, a phenomenon that has, in turn, been observed as having a bearing on the record-breaker phenomenon. According to commentators such as Jeon Gyu-Chan and Yoon Tae-Jin,[8] the Red Devils phenomenon is inflected with two strands of nationalism. The first is simply an extension of older forms of state-driven nationalism based on the *minjok* (one-blood ethnic nationhood) ideology. The second is a more spontaneous form of popular nationalism. Whilst this second strand may have its positive aspects, Jeon and Yoon argue that, at least to some extent, this more festive form was channelled by the state and corporations for the purposes of 'patriotic consumption'.[9]

Returning to the record-breaker phenomenon, the astonishing popularity of the Korean record-breaker titles has, unsurprisingly, raised questions as to what degree their box office success is attributable to the purely spontaneous and popular responses of local audiences. Here the idea of patriotic consumption again begins to surface in remarks made by Kim Ki-Duk. Taking issue with the release and promotion strategy of Bong Joon-Ho's *The Host*, Kim claimed:

> When you go to the multiplexes these days, you're immediately grasped by six posters of *The Host*. Rather than propagating this kind of repressive effect, why don't you just build a cinema with 10,000 seats so everyone can see the film and chant 'Dae-Han-Min-Gook' (Viva Great Korea).[10]

One of the interesting things about this quote is that it explicitly links this patriotic consumption with the commercial aspects of the industry (multiplexes, big budget marketing), all of which I unravel as part of the national conjunction. It is worth stressing, however, that whereas Korean nationalism has usually been criticised by local dissidents according to its role in the political and ideological agendas of the state, here it is identified as part of a wider series of issues all ultimately attributable to the commercial interests of big business.

To some degree, Korean blockbusters are subject to the pressure to compete with the production values of other (principally Hollywood) blockbusters, thus leading to their dependence on stars and spectacle. In achieving such values, there is often a sense of patriotic pride in the South Korean industry for being able to compete on such terms with Hollywood. There are, however, textual features that more specifically unite the record-breaker films in their relation to the national. One unifying factor is the use of a 'multiple-address' strategy. To help attract an enormous audience, the record-breaker films benefit from being able to address *different* audiences *within the nation*. This is a feature of the films themselves, aided, rather than 'created', by subsequent distribution and marketing strategies. An awareness that, at a pre-production level, producers must identify and cater for target audiences has become a central feature of the Korean film industry since the 'planned film' production mode emerged in the 1990s. But with record-breaker films, an enormous cross-section of the domestic market is targeted by the same film. *The King and the Clown* is instructive for understanding the pre-production rationale of the film and how it ultimately succeeded in reaching a wide range of audiences. Jeong Jin-Wan, head of production company Eagle Pictures, suggests the success of the film was down to its capacity to be read in multiple ways, just like a 'Rorschach test'. Thus 'for the teens and early-mid twenties the film is mainly considered as a melodrama revolving around the figure of Gong Gil (Lee Jun-Gi), for the late twenties to thirties and forties it becomes a film about Jang Sang's (Kam Woo-Seong) challenge to the King's power, and for the over fifties it is an archetypal dynastic period drama'.[11]

The record-breakers, however, still unite these different strands within an overarching narrative that has a particular focus on articulating Korean identity. This does not, however, mean that all the films take the same approach. Here the politics of *The Host* and *The King and the Clown* take a different tack from that of *Silmido* and *Taegukgi* (Kang Je-Gyu, 2004). *The Host*, for instance, re-inscribes the politics of the 1980s student movement into what otherwise appears as a cross between traditional family melodrama and *Jurassic Park*-style monster movie. But this aspect of *The Host* also helps explain why Kim Ki-Duk's protests provoked such wide public controversy, as it highlights the way in which even a progressive, leftist film-maker like Bong is ultimately enveloped in an industrial structure in which oligopolistic practices have increasingly precluded access to smaller films without such financial backing. As those critical of Kim's comments pointed out, his protests (as an 'auteur' director and well-known participant at European festivals) have a self-serving element. But Kim's posturing also allows him to exploit his symbolic status as a representative of the great number of Korean film-makers who are not benefiting from the rewards of domestic box office success.

Kim, however, is simply one of many Koreans (whether film-goers or industry workers) critical of the structure and practices of the Korean film industry. Indeed, it is the industrial aspects of Korean cinema that makes the most fascinating comparison with Euro-American cinemas. The exceptionally concentrated nature of the Korean film industry, with so much power held by a few local distributor-exhibitors, actually allows oligopolistic activities that far exceed those available to the Hollywood studios in other territories. In Korea the control of the 'big three' local majors at the levels of distribution-exhibition has recently become so extreme that they have the ability to wide release record-breaker films on such an astonishing proportion of cinema screens as to mark them as a 'national event'.

In terms of film production, between 2001 and 2004, the average film budget rose from $2.8 million up to $4.5 million.[12] The number of films produced also increased from 65 in 2001 to 82 in 2004. This attention to production data, however, overlooks other profound changes in the industry. In 2000, annual audience attendance was 64.6 million, with an attendance of 22.7 million attendances for Korean films. By 2004 this had grown more than twofold to 135.6 million, with audiences for domestic films increasing at an exponentially faster rate to 80.1 million. But this striking growth of cinema attendance also coincides with the growth of multiplex cinemas. In 1999 (the breakthrough year of *Shiri*), cinema sites fell from 507 to 373, but the number of screens increased from 507 to 588. This is due to the initial wave of multiplex constructions. These trends have subsequently continued apace. In 2001, 818 screens were situated across 344 sites, rising by 2004 to 1,451 screens at only 302 sites.[13] Like other countries in Asia, including Japan, South Korea has experienced multiplex-isation rather later than Europe, and local companies appear to have capitalised on the situation in a much more proactive manner.

The belated but spectacular growth of multiplex cinemas in South Korea has emerged hand-in-hand with horizontally and vertically-integrated 'entertainment companies'. While venture capital investment and government sponsored film funds have played a significant role in film production after the withdrawal of Chaebol capital, the film industry has seen a more general restructuring around local majors such as CJ Entertainment/Cinema Service, Showbox and Lotte Entertainment. Although principally emerging as distributors, these companies now have stakes in the production sector through pre-sales investment and in the exhibition sector by merging with major multiplex chains. I suggest that many of the peculiarities of 'the era of 10 million audiences' are intrinsically connected to the market structure dominated by the so-called 'Big Three' investor/distributor/exhibitor 'majors' (now recognisable as CJ-CGV, Showbox-Megabox and Lotte Entertainment-Cinema). In terms of local distributors, the three majors together took 59.6 per cent of the total market share in the year 2005 (estimated by audience numbers).[14] In terms of exhibition, CGV, Megabox and Lotte Cinema also held 48 per cent of South Korea's total cinema screens (789 out of 1,648) at this time. It is not difficult to appreciate the formidable power arising from this market structure.

It is this level of control, I suggest, that has enabled such an astonishing wide release strategy for the record-breaker films. But the role of distributors is also important for their effect on another part of the national conjunction, marketing. The most conspicuous marketing strategy common to all four record-breaker titles is the encouragement of audience participation by way of a suspenseful, stage-by-stage 'countdown' in newspapers to see if the current record-breaker is still on track to beat previous national records. This was established as a paradigm for *Silmido*, with later films also becoming part of a race or competition to break the previous record, and with the audience positioned as both viewer and record-breaking participant. It would also be interesting to see how these films were constructed as national media events that in effect pressured non-viewers to go and see the film or be 'excluded' from everyday discussions with friends, workmates and family.

Additionally, there were some other 'peculiar' marketing incentives worth noting. Two months after *Taegukgi*'s release, when the 10 million audience mark had been broken, the distributor Showbox launched a special '50 per cent ticket discount' promotion across 150 screens nationwide. This lasted for three weeks, enabling everyone who had not seen the film so far a 'last chance' to see it. Furthermore, during this three week promotional event, Showbox contracted a special 'distributor-exhibitor' box office share deal, whereby the exhibitor was given 90 per cent of the ticket sales instead of the usual 10 per cent as an incentive to maintain the screens for *Taegukgi*.[15] Such practices begin to resemble a veritable 'dumping strategy'.

The description of the national conjunction is deliberately provocative. Whilst not wanting to be entirely economistic, I do wish to emphasise the motoring role of the Korean majors in the record-breaker phenomenon, and how commercial interests had a role in shaping the production, distribution and marketing of these films. There is obviously scope to debate what (or if) such a national conjunction model could help us to understand the practices surrounding blockbuster films below record-breaker status. I also suggest other questions still need to be asked of the national conjunction paradigm. Whilst many accounts are aware of the issues raised by the Korean majors, there are technical questions that (perhaps because of insufficient knowledge of finance/economics) remain unanswered. This includes details of how local majors were able to emerge so quickly, which may also involve a more detailed analysis of the effects on these companies of government taxation/investment policies. It is also important to consider the exact ways in which local Hollywood subsidiaries have been squeezed by domestic companies and how these subsidiaries responded. This has become more pressing given the ways in which the Korean conglomerates appear to be acting in more collaborative ways with the Hollywood studios.[16] Looking beyond an exclusively national model, we also need to consider the relationship between CJ Entertainment and DreamWorks and the way in which overseas companies such as Golden Harvest and Village Roadshow helped to develop South Korea's multiplex circuits.

It is clear, with such national saturation, that exporting Korean films is a future imperative. However, record-breakers are a potential stumbling block, with their patriotic or nationalist narratives. Some record-breaker films have, for instance, performed well in Japan but others have failed, and it is clear that the reliance on Japan is precarious, particularly with increasing resistance to *Hallyu* (the 'Korean Wave').[17] What is now clear is that the Korean majors are trying to expand their distribution reach outside Korea. CJ Entertainment has made ties both with China's SINA Corporation and Japan's Softbank.[18] It has also even made attempts to directly distribute films on DVD in Britain. The effects of the entry of SK Telecom and Korea Telecom into the content provision market will also no doubt institute some interesting changes in both the local and regional reach of South Korean films.

Korean Cinema and Diversity

In light of the screen dominance issue, diversity has become part of a number of KOFIC policies. The Art Plus Cinema Network is one of the centrepieces of plans to introduce diversity into film practices. Currently a network of 18 cinemas, this will be expanded in 2007 to 28 cinemas, with proposals to eventually reach 50 cinemas.[19] Although now an essential part of KOFIC's activities, the Art Plus idea initially emerged in 2001 after audiences became frustrated by the lack of screening time for small-budget local films such as *Nabi* (Moon Sueng-Wook, 2001) and *Take Care of My Cat* (Jeong Jae-Eun, 2001). It gradually gained substance between 2003 and 2006, with KOFIC giving a financial subsidy to a small number of cinemas that also agreed to adhere to certain criteria for screening non-mainstream films.

Amongst its aims the network states that it wants to deliver a 'more diverse range of titles for the audience to choose from'.[20] Thus, although 'art' may be one of the values proffered, it is diversity that is the more important keyword. This is evident in the slogan of the network, 'I see different films', as well as the term 'plus' in the moniker 'Art Plus'. As well as programming feature-length fiction films, Art Plus also emphasises the importance of screening animation, documentary films, short films and experimental films. The network nevertheless also screens so-called 'crossover' films, i.e. those films that also have a relation to more mainstream film-making. Some of these crossover films also screen in multiplex cinemas outside the Art Plus network. KOFIC has a committee that decides which films qualify as 'specialised films' and Art Cinema Plus Network cinemas are expected to screen such specialised categories of films for at least 219 days; and 70 days of these 219 days must be of Korean films.

The timeline of the emergence of Art Plus is also interesting in regards to how diversity is being conceptualised by other discourses. Here I suggest there are revealing connections (and disjunctions) between KOFIC and the discourses of Unesco and the creative industries. Until 2000 the dominant position of Unesco vis-à-vis culture was in protecting 'cultural heritage'. This was particularly evident in the rhetoric of France and Canada, where the idea of the cultural exception to neo-liberal free trade was instituted in the Uruguay round of GATT in 1993. After the Unesco meeting in 2000, there appears to have been a shift in direction away from protecting cultural heritage to preserving and promoting 'cultural diversity'. Although this is partly linked to the supposed role of respecting cultural diversity in conflict prevention, the more overarching framework, I suggest, is the productive relation between diversity and the increasing flows of people and products under globalisation.

But what is also interesting is that diversity becomes a keyword of Unesco at the same time that it becomes prominent in the paradigm of the creative industries. Indeed, the reason that diversity now has such a global provenance, I suggest, is that if the commercial imperatives of the creative industries can be aligned with the social imperatives of Unesco then this provides a powerful (and convenient) agenda for business and government. What also connects these discourses is the important role that they attribute to the nation state. In the case of Unesco, the nation state is still given sovereign power to manage cultural diversity within its national territory. In the case of the creative industries government, policy is important to make nations globally competitive both for driving exports and attracting inward investment.

The definition of what constitutes the creative industries is not, however, straightforward. Debates rage about whether it should include things beyond audio-visual content, like ICTs and other forms of Intellectual Property. The latter implicates an enormous number of industries if we take IP to involve patents and trademarks, as well as copyright. It also raises complex political questions as to which government departments and agencies should be managing the creative industries. I still suggest that the ideal of the creative industries is strongly linked to government interests, but mediated through a diffuse range of departments and agencies, each with their own internal complexities and occasionally overlapping remits.

One important aspect of the creative industries is the aim to produce new and innovative ideas. Such ideas are achieved through 'managing' the creative diversity of a team of people rather than relying on the now out-of-favour concept of the individual creative genius.[21] Such interest in innovation, however, has emerged in tandem with commercial interest in the value of the 'intangible assets', and particularly copyrights, patents and trademarks. Much of the rush to celebrate the creative industries has been down to the idea that audio-visual 'content' is an important new form of capital. With an ever-increasing number of distribution platforms (VOD, mobile phone, satellite, etc.) and with platforms having an increasing global penetration, it is assumed that audio-visual content has immense potential value. Furthermore, the new form of content-creation, whether blockbusters or art/specialist films, is increasingly considered to be a major source of national wealth as content, of course, is still copyrighted in particular territories. In many cases, such as in the UK, the strategic emphasis has been on driving the export of contents from a very early stage.

There are, however, other aspects to the creative industries model as it is manifest in cinema. The idea also demonstrates an awareness of the importance of post-production as a global service sector. Although more mobile than film production, post-production is still dependent on both technology and skills. Here the development of skills becomes a form of 'human capital', another type of 'intangible asset'. It is evident that many governments are now taking a very active interest in promoting policies for developing and managing content production for domestic consumption and export-driven sales, as well as policies that emphasise the importance of skills-creation for attracting mobile projects.

Many of these trends are evident in organisations such as KOCCA, the Korean Culture and Content Agency – another agency, like KOFIC, working under the Ministry of Culture and Tourism. KOCCA, established in 2001, deals primarily with animation, music and character industries, and explicitly links these to being a source of the nation's wealth. It aims to help young and start-up companies to produce content with export specifically highlighted. Here KOCCA also puts an emphasis on both training and developing technology.[22] The agency's remit over animation has occasionally come into conflict with KOFIC over film and because of the difficulty of defining the creative industries (as aforementioned) there are often tensions with other interested agencies, including (amongst a number of others) the Korean Agency for Digital Promotion and Opportunity (KADO) and the Korea Game Development & Promotion Institute (KGDPI). Although the national remains the overriding framework, the geographical location of creative industry companies is also attractive to city governments who often try to provide incentives for companies to work in their cities.[23] The Seoul Business Agency is thus now having an effect on the creative industries by trying to provide the infrastructure to turn part of Seoul into a 'digital media city' for SMEs working in high tech and content-production areas.[24]

In many ways the Art Plus Cinema Network is indeed providing a valuable forum for smaller budget films. But although it does give cinema-owners a degree of freedom in their programming, there is still something of a centralised imperative. The Art Plus cinemas are connected through having a collective programming and release schedule. With the production of selected projects also benefiting from finance from new film funds and KOFIC contributions to P&A budgets, some local specialised films effectively seem to be part of a vertically-integrated structure that combines production (here finance), distribution/marketing and exhibition. Interestingly, some of the

Korean films incorporated also have rather patriotic themes. The documentary *Our School* (Kim Myung-Jun, 2006), for instance, looks at the way Korean language learning is still maintained in a Korean school in Japan. The film is even given an inflection of patriotic consumption, with claims by KOFIC that in order to specifically make the film the first digital production simultaneously available in ten cinemas, they will be installing theatres with digital screening facilities.[25] There are also other aspects of the Art Plus Cinema Network that aid domestic interests. While 'animation' has been an important recent part of Art Plus programming, this has been almost exclusively in regards to Korean animation, with American and Japanese animations actually barred from distribution.

One of the most interesting questions is whether the Art Plus Cinema Network is being positioned as a test bed for larger digital screening/distribution projects across Asia. Here KOFIC's projects include contributing to a north-east Asia council on digital cinema.[26] Working with the Digital Cinema Association in Japan (DCAJ) and the China Research Institute for Fiscal Science (CRIFS), there is an emphasis on bringing together 'the content, technology, and markets of Korea, Japan, and China'. There is clearly also a hope that this will provide a more general boost to Korean IT companies working on aspects of a digital distribution/exhibition infrastructure. Thus the current emphasis on 'diverse films' still has much of the feel of a different kind of national conjunction. But here there is firstly an emphasis on state agencies working in tandem with SMEs rather than conglomerates, and secondly there appears to be a more specific long-term aim of enhancing Korea's role within a regional Asian framework. This is also a line taken by KOCCA, who state that they aim to facilitate international partnerships and joint ventures.[27] Here recent events include joint activities to promote Korean and Japanese animations in New York.[28]

It is difficult to approach these developments in a predominantly sceptical manner, as firstly there actually *is* an increased access for audiences to a wider range of films, and secondly, although Korean government agencies have high budgets and are very active in their operations, most of their projects can be mapped as being consistent with other territories following the creative industries path, such as the UK. Here the UK Film Council has had an enormous input in developing a digital cinema infrastructure.

In both cases, there are interesting questions about the long-term ownership of digital distribution channels and whether these will ultimately be run by big business. But there are also some interesting differences in the way the creative industries paradigm is developing. The British approach, for instance, more explicitly links the creative industries to the diversity of its citizenry. Initially posed as a useful tool for *enfranchising* minority groups in content creation, it has a second, rather more insidious side, in which minority groups may be *economically useful* to the nation state in global competition. Not only can minorities produce 'innovative ideas', but they may also be helpful in making global links to companies from other territories. Although it might appear controversial to say that ethnic minorities in Britain (many linked to the country's colonial past) are now an asset in global business, this is explicitly evident in some policy discussions. Although there are also 'multi-ethnic' dimensions to South Korea, many such links, and particularly any relationships with Japan, remain highly sensitive areas.

I have posed these two aspects of the national conjunction and the creative industries paradigm to highlight the interesting ways in which business and government have been extremely active, both during the boom in Korean cinema and in the current turn to diversity. In the case of the record-breakers, the situation has been very different, for example, from that of commercial film-making in the UK or France. The success of such films has been motored by the development of multiplexes and the industrial activities of the Korean majors. Elements of patriotism or nationalism (in their manifold forms) have also contributed to the national conjunction and there is evidence to suggest that such sentiment has been channelled for the commercial interests of the Korean majors. If the national conjunction has meant that Korean cinema is now dominant in its own domestic market, there are, however, changes now taking place. Whether this can be conceptualised as a 'break' or simply an expansion into additional markets is yet to be seen, particularly as the majors' oligopoly in the multiplex sector remains unchanged. There are strong commercial incentives to expand into overseas markets, particularly through the promise of digital distribution. In this regard the Korean majors are also making links with other Asian countries. But the creative industries idea is also important as another form of conjunction between government and smaller companies. This also has a 'global' agenda through the development of content and skills (though again developing a domestic market for animation and documentary appears to still be a priority). Of course, given that these industrial trends are still very much in process, how they will ultimately fit together is an open question.

Given that 'content' needs distribution, it will be interesting to see how exactly the creative industries' celebration of content production functions in relation to domestic, regional and global distribution chan-nels. It seems unlikely that KOFIC's development of a digital cinema infrastructure will remain permanently under its control. I wish, how-ever, to point to two other avenues for subsequent discussion. Firstly, it will be interesting to look at how all the issues raised by domestic suc-cess, Unesco policies and the creative industries paradigm have impacted upon debates about the Korean film quota, for a long time one of the centrepieces of Korean film policy. Secondly, I am interested in what kind of theoretical framework we should use to conceptualise the changes in the industry. Can we analyse current trends as part of a continuous process unfolding from the *saegaehwa* Korean official version of 'globalisation', or do we instead need to talk about multiple globalisations with overlapping histories? It is in this regard that I suggest we need to think even more about the various approaches to diversity, and how they have been used both in South Korean dis-courses and in discourses from other global sources.

References

1   MBC TV 100 minutes special Panel Debate at 12 pm, 17 August 2006. The event led to a frenzy of media and public debate, with much public anger vented at Kim's remarks. An official 'apology' duly followed, beg-ging for forgiveness both from *The Host*'s producer and director and the audience. For a brief English language account of this incident, see: <http://www.koreacontent.org/weben/inmarket/Ns_knews_view.jsp?news _ seq=29473>

2   Shin Jee-Young, 'Globalisation and New Korean Cinema' in Julian Stringer and Chi-Yun Shin (eds), *New Korean Cinema* (Edinburgh: Edinburgh University Press, 2005).

3   Miller, Toby, Govil, Nitin, McMurria, John, Maxwell, Richard and Wang, Ting, *Global Hollywood 2* (London: BFI, 2005).

4   Park, Young Eun, '2004 년 한국영화 수익성 분석과 영화산업 향상방안' 요약본 ('An analysis of Korean film's profit rate and an improvement scheme of the film industry in 2004', abridged edition), July 2005, KOFIC. Also note that although 2005 saw an increase of 30 per cent (from 2004 $58,284,600 to $75,994,580) in total exports, the yet to be confirmed figures of 2006 are expected to have fallen drastically. This over-dependence on the domestic theatrical market is further exacerbated by the very weak ancillary market (interestingly the DVD medium never really took off in Korea).

5   한국영화는 지각변동 중! 조이뉴스 (Korean film is fluctuating dramati-cally!), Joy News, 2 November 2006.

6   Shin Ji-Wook, *Ethnic Nationalism in Korea: genealogy, politics and legacy* (Stanford: Stanford University Press, 2006).

7   For more details, see Shin: *New Korean Cinema* (2005).

8   Jeon Gyu-Chan and Yoon Tae-Jin, 'Cultural Politics of the Red Devils: the desiring multitude versus the state, capital and media', *Inter-Asia Cultural Studies*, 5/1 (2004).

9   Indeed, as the authors point out, the main slogan 'Dae-Han-Min-Gook' was initially introduced by the conglomerate SK inc p.85.

10 MBC 100 minutes debate.

11 왕의 남자 성공 요인 [1] (The primary factor in the success of *The King and The Clown* [1]), Cine21, 25 January 2006.

12 KOFIC Annual Report 2005 (Seoul, 2005), available to download from the publications section of the KOFIC website <http://www.koreanfilm. or.kr/>. At the time of this chapter's writing, the 2006 annual report is yet to be posted online.

13 KOFIC Annual Report 2005.

14 Doh DongJoon and Rhu Heung Jin, 2005 년 극장 및 스크린 현황 분석 (An analysis of the present condition of cinemas and screens in 2005), Kofic, 2006.

15 Lee Young Jin, 인사이드 충무로, 태극기 '덤핑'에 휘날리며' (Inside Chung-Moo Roo, 'Dumping strategy of Taeguki'), Cine21, 12 April 2004.

16 CJ entertainment is now distributing films by Paramount: <http://www. variety.com/article/VR1117954672.html?categoryid=13&cs=1&nid=2564>

17 <http://www.hollywoodreporter.com/hr/content_display/international/ news/e3i293cfb6cfe266acb4f24cdc15dfd98cd>

18 <http://www.koreacontent.org/co/c/cjinternet/comp_info.html>

19 For more details on the emergence of the Art Plus idea and its aims, see *Korean Film Observatory*, Vol. 4, 2005.

20 See the Art Plus website <www.artpluscn.or.kr>

21 Bilton, Chris, *Management and Creativity: from creative industries to creative management* (Malden, Oxford and Carlton: Blackwell, 2007).

22 See <http://www.koreacontent.org/weben/etc/aboutus_sub0301.jsp>

23 For an explanation of this city-led dimension of the 'creative economy', see Richard Florida, *Cities and the Creative Class* (New York and Abingdon: Routledge, 2005).

24 <http://sba.seoul.kr/eng/activity/marketing01.jsp>

25 Kofic News Focus, March 2007, <www.kofic.or.kr>

26 See the section on support programmes for exhibition on KOFIC website <http://www.koreanfilm.or.kr/>

27 <http://www.koreacontent.org/weben/etc/aboutus_sub0301.jsp>

28 'Korean and Japanese Animation Today' at the Egyptian Theatre, Hollywood, 31 March 2007.

7

Rayna Denison

The Language of the Blockbuster: Promotion, *Princess Mononoke* and the *Daihitto* in Japanese Film Culture

Given that the Japanese film market has been acclaimed as the second most important in the world, little work has attempted to understand it as such. Although American blockbusters thrive there and even though the Japanese film industry regularly produces films that garner global success, the industrial and cultural reasons that allow for those phenomena remain unexamined. This chapter seeks to redress this imbalance, investigating Japan's film marketplace at a particular moment in time when a home grown 'blockbuster' was proving its worth against all foreign and domestic competition. Using a variety of marketing and promotional sources, this chapter will argue for a reconsideration of the industrial complexity of Japan's film culture, centred on the concept of the *daihitto* or 'big hit' film.

The term blockbuster is not used in Japan. It does not appear in any of the discussions of film circulating around the release of the record-breaking film *Princess Mononoke* (Miyazaki Hayao, Japan, 1997) in the summer and autumn of 1997. This film was the first in a series of animated (or anime) films produced by Japan's Studio Ghibli to break all box office records in Japan, before going on to garner high critical praise and some limited commercial success in the global market. While the term blockbuster may not have been directly applied to *Princess Mononoke*, a semblance of blockbuster culture resonates deeply within Japanese film culture. It will be argued here that the *daihitto* and even the *cho daihitto* (super big hit) function in a similar fashion to blockbuster culture in Japan. *Princess Mononoke* continues to be regarded as a *daihitto*, but it was in the film's advertising campaign and in discussions of its performance by journalists that the film was first identified as a 'big hit', and within these various usages it becomes possible to discern patterns of meaning ascribed to the term that link it with, and differentiate it from, its American blockbuster counterparts.

For these reasons the differences between the blockbuster and the *daihitto* are particularly germane to any discussion of Miyazaki's film. *Princess Mononoke*'s association with the *daihitto* helped to define it and support its cultural recognition as a phenomenon. Points of divergence between *daihitto* culture and blockbuster cultures are intended here to counter conceptions of the blockbuster film as a monolithically American phenomenon. Instead, Julian Stringer's conception of blockbuster film as a genre, or James Naremore's conception of film noir as an idea, form more useful approaches to what is a variegated facet of film-making.[1] This provides the beginning of a definition of the blockbuster predicated not on finite lists of qualities, but on production and consumption trends within contemporary film-making. Positing that *Princess Mononoke* was a Japanese blockbuster, or *daihitto*, this investigation will strive to discuss what kind of blockbuster film it was and whether or not it is representative of some kind of blockbuster culture. Doing so will shed light not only on how large-scale, big budget, highly consumed films operate in Japan, but also on how they are perceived and positioned in relation to one another more widely.

Daihitto Film Culture

Implicit within discussions of the blockbuster are issues of big-ness in budgetary terms and the blockbuster's worldwide reach. Size thereby becomes the most oft-cited obstacle to the recognition of blockbusters from outside America, as scale and global success act as markers of blockbuster status. As Martin Barker and Kate Brooks observe, a central feature of blockbuster films is that they are 'expensive, and publicise and celebrate their costs'.[2] This translates frequently in discussions of the blockbuster into notions of spectacle or scale; blockbusters as the biggest, the best or even on occasion as the worst.[3] Stringer posits that:

> Size is the central notion through which the blockbuster's generic identity comes to be identified. However, the exact contexts cannot be assumed or taken for granted. What may be termed a blockbuster's 'size factor' operates to distinguish something unique in the case of each individual movie.[4]

This ties into Justin Wyatt and Katherine Vlesmas's discussion of the discourses surrounding *Titanic*'s budget in the American media:

> The cost proved to be a resilient hook for journalists writing about the film, allowing for a large number of related concerns to be expressed. ... However, after the film's release, the budgetary issues became secondary to another commercial parameter: box office gross. Suddenly, the press became obsessed not with *Titanic*'s cost but with its record-breaking potential.[5]

As becomes obvious from the arguments above, money has become a key factor in the classification of Hollywood film. While the US may not boast the world's most prolific film industry, it remains the most moneyed, and debates centring on the blockbuster tend to reinforce the primacy of the American market through their very discussions of its financial clout. Wyatt and Vlesmas's investigation of *Titanic* and Stringer's recognition of size as integral to the blockbuster project support this Hollywood-centric conceptualisation of the blockbuster film.

However, as will be discussed in more detail hereafter, the Japanese media are quick to discuss their own prestige film productions in the same record-breaking terms that American journalists did with *Titanic*. Similarly, when the issue of relative or proportional size is inserted into blockbuster discourses, it becomes possible to view any number of previously excluded films as blockbuster hits. Alisa Perren's work on what she terms the 'indie blockbuster' recognises that it is not merely non-American films that have been understood as lacking the necessary size. Those 'independents' that 'on a smaller scale, replicate the exploitation marketing and box-office performance of the major studio high concept event pictures' have also been somewhat neglected.[6] Perren's assertion that 'relative' success be used as a measure of a film's blockbuster status opens the floodgates to the recognition of regionally or proportionally successful films as blockbusters.

Certainly, Japanese films would benefit from being viewed in this light, particularly given the national specificity of film products so reliant on Japanese culture and language. Also, their adoption of American and European advertising techniques has created the same furore around domestic blockbuster films as seen in relation to American blockbusters. This and the high price of tickets and recent expansions in the exhibition market have led to recognition of Japan as one of the world's largest markets for film exhibition. For example, Wyatt and Vlesmas explain that for *Titanic*, 'a premiere outside the domestic market in Tokyo seemed appropriate since Japan was potentially the most lucrative foreign market'.[7] That Japan as a 'lucrative' market should be able to produce films of a kind not dissimilar to, if somewhat smaller in scale than, its American blockbuster counterparts should not therefore come as a surprise. Considered in relative terms, a *Princess Mononoke* is not so different from a *Harry Potter* or a *Titanic*.

However, it is not enough to simply make the case for *Princess Mononoke* as a blockbuster in isolation. In place of such a narrow purview this investigation will attempt to broaden its scope, to contextualise the release of *Princess Mononoke* by considering its relationship with contemporary film releases in Japan. This should enable a more thoroughly historical materialist approach to the film, albeit in a synchronic moment.[8] It is hoped that, by comparing *Princess Mononoke*'s promotion to that of the many films it shared market space with on its release, it may be possible to better ascertain its status within the domestic marketplace. To this end, the film advertisements that appeared alongside the print campaign for *Princess Mononoke* will be examined. Further to these promotional advertisements, publicity for the film in the form of reviews will be used to explicate *Princess Mononoke*'s status.

Advertising: Selling *Princess Mononoke*

The process of creating *Princess Mononoke* as a *daihitto* began long before the film's promotional phase of production. In comparative terms, *Princess Mononoke* had a massive budget, one of the largest in anime history at ¥ 2.4 billion.[9] This, following Wyatt and Vlesmas's argument, helped to mark the film's blockbuster proportions. However, unlike most American blockbuster films, the term *daihitto* was only applied to *Princess Mononoke* fairly late in its production cycle. The first instance of the *daihitto* in *Princess Mononoke*'s advertising campaign appears at the end of its first week in exhibition. This indicates that its studio waited for *Princess Mononoke* to prove itself at the box office before appending the *daihitto* label to it, in contrast with Hollywood blockbusters, which are usually promoted as such before release. What this further implies is that the calculated element of *Princess Mononoke*'s blockbuster success was not in fact taken as a surety.

However, *Princess Mononoke* is not the only film for which this is the case. Following the same pattern as its release in the United States, Disney's *Hercules* (US, 1997), although clearly marked as a blockbuster through its large scale, yet multivalent style of advertising, was rarely, if ever, labelled as such in its home market. On 22 August 1997 an advertisement in the *Asahi Shimbun* newspaper,[10] one of Japan's most popular broadsheets, proclaimed that *Hercules* would make 'This Summer, the Best in Memory ...'.[11] This tagline follows Disney's practice of denying the blockbuster nature of their animated features, although the 'Best in Memory ...' tagline implies the status of the film as a hit. The animated nature of both *Princess Mononoke* and *Hercules* may point to a reason for their slow recognition as blockbuster-style films. The animated blockbuster has, as Steve Neale observes, gone 'largely unnoticed', even though it 'has, in its own specific and particular way, helped revive not just biblical epics ... but ... the traditions of the Broadway-oriented musical as well'.[12]

One of the central reasons for this critical omission may stem from the typical orientation of Disney's and many other animated films towards children, resulting in attempts to avoid the commercial discourses that routinely circulate around live action blockbusters. In the case of *Princess Mononoke*, however, it seems more likely that the lack of a *daihitto* declaration or label had more to do with Studio Ghibli's lack of confidence in their project. This said, however, their expansive advertising campaign reveals that they desired and aimed for the film to become a blockbuster-style hit.

It was only six days after *Princess Mononoke*'s release on 12 July 1997 that advertisements began to appear proclaiming the film a *daihitto*. However, the films that *Princess Mononoke* was advertised alongside at this early stage of its mature promotion phase (around either side of its release date) proclaim it as a rather different kind of film from the American blockbuster. The first time *Princess Mononoke*'s advertisements appeared alongside other blockbusters was on 11 July 1997, when it appeared in conjunction with *The Lost World: Jurassic Park* (US, 1997). Previously, *Princess Mononoke* was balanced between 'art house' and anime film advertising. On 4 July 1997, for instance, a quarter page advertisement was taken out in the *Mainichi Shimbun*. The remaining quarter page of advertising (on what the newspaper calls its 'PR Page') was made up of advertisements for the 'sleeper hit' *Sleepers* (US, 1996) and the British 'indie' hit *Trainspotting* (1996). Of the three, *Sleepers* was the one declared as a *daihitto*, described with the phrase 'Overwhelming Big Hit!'. This begins to show how widely the term *daihitto* is applied in Japanese film advertising, as *Sleepers* made only roughly twice its budget at the worldwide box office. However, that indie favourite *Trainspotting* does not declare itself in the same manner also indicates the limits of the *daihitto*'s elasticity. Instead, the advertisement declares the film grossed over ¥ 229 million, with audience figures and awards also listed making appeals to it as a popular hit, if not as a *daihitto* 'big hit'.[13]

In another advertisement placed in the *Asahi Shimbun* on the same day (4 July 1997), *Princess Mononoke* also appears alongside numerous Japanese animated films. A variety of small advertisements, including a double bill of popular TV anime movie adaptations *Sureiyaazu Gureeto* (*Slayers Great*, 1997) and *Tenchi Muyo! Manatsu no Ebu* (literal translation: *Useless Angel!: Midsummer Eve*, 1997) and anime *Erumaa no Bouken* (*My Father's Dragon*, 1997), are juxtaposed with *Princess Mononoke*. They signify the appeals to the anime 'niche' market in Japan, an audience much larger and more varied in Japan than it is in many other markets. The variety of exhibition styles displayed in these advertisements is remarkable: with old-fashioned double bills and anime fairs, as well as *Princess Mononoke*'s large-scale, and by comparison, wide release. This illustrates the diversity in the animated film market in Japan, ranging in this example from Miyazaki's brooding historical fantasy to action adventure TV serials such as the film adaptation of *Rettsu ando Gou!* (*Let's and Go!*, 1997). Indeed, this juxtaposition is almost certainly purposeful. Putting the large and high concept advertisement for *Princess Mononoke* next to the relatively rag-tag presentations of other anime on this page acts to heighten perceptions of *Princess Mononoke*'s quality in relation to the other anime in the marketplace. That *Princess Mononoke*'s advertisement is almost twice the size of the other advertisements is similarly a deliberate attempt to outclass the anime with which it had to compete on its release.

Daihitto Queen: *Princess Mononoke* becomes a 'Big Hit'

While *Princess Mononoke* was not presented as a *daihitto* initially, it is significant that neither were the anime films it was juxtaposed with. This changed dramatically after the film's release, however, with *Princess Mononoke*'s advertising being placed in increasingly close quarters with Hollywood's calculated blockbusters, and with the term regularly recurring. The transition took place over the course of a month, roughly from 25 July to 22 August 1997. In the meantime, the film consistently brushed shoulders with big Japanese films, including anime such as a re-release of Osamu Tezuka's *Jungle Emperor* (1989) and, increasingly, blockbuster American films like the *Star Wars* trilogy re-release and the new *Batman and Robin* (US, 1997). Even after *Princess Mononoke* was labelled as a *daihitto*, then it was possible to see the film gathering momentum. It was only after its first month of release that *Princess Mononoke*'s advertising began to reflect its box office strength in Japan, as its studio became willing to credit it with the power to compete with Hollywood's biggest film products. From that point onwards the language used in the advertising campaign took on added significance, and *Princess Mononoke* will be shown to have succeeded because its advertising played specifically to the film's domestic audience.

Going back briefly to Wyatt and Vlesmas's assertion about the journalistic impulse to focus on a blockbuster film's record-breaking potential, this investigation will show that box office records are an aspect of journalistic culture that feeds directly into advertising culture in Japan. *Princess Mononoke* was not just labelled as a *daihitto*; rather, this idea was supported in its advertising with evidence from audience figures. This tends to be one of the three ways in which blockbuster status is conferred on a film in the Japanese market (and often elsewhere). First, cost, in the form of budgets, marks the blockbuster as it goes through production. Then, enormous box office receipts become a marker of the successful blockbuster. The other marker of the blockbuster tends to be audience figures. These circulate more frequently around non-American blockbusters, and frequently appear in journalistic *and* academic discourse. For instance, in his discussion of *Shiri* (South Korea, 1999), Chris Berry comments on audience figures: '*Titanic*'s Korean box office record of 4.7 million viewers was swiftly overcome by the local 1999 action blockbuster, *Shiri*, which attracted 5.78 million viewers.'[14] Here Berry implicitly recognises a major divergence from the blockbuster culture of Hollywood and that of other national film industries. The blockbusters of Asia and elsewhere, dependent as they tend to be on local, or regional, language-specific audiences for the majority of their box office revenues, seem to pay close attention to their audience figures.

The post-release phase of *Princess Mononoke*'s promotion is heavily implicated in making direct addresses to potential audience members. In doing so, it employs surprisingly obsequious language. One example in particular illustrates this trend well (see Figure 1).

This third of a page advertisement appeared in *Asahi Shimbun* in early August 1997. In prominent letters across the top of the advertisement, it announces that *Princess Mononoke* is celebrating the fact that it is showing to capacity-filled theatres. In between those large symbols (*Manin Gorei*, each symbol relating to half a word) runs a diagonally placed thank you to audiences which reads: 'It has surpassed Japan's biggest records ... Continuing new audience records ... Thanks to you, 4.7 million people!' The *okagesamade* or 'thanks to you' included

Figure 1. Advertisement taken from the *Asahi Shimbun*, appearing 8 August 1997

here is a set phrase in Japanese and appears commonly in conjunction with the audience figures provided for *Princess Mononoke* throughout the campaign. The use of this set phrase, and the formal language employed to describe *Princess Mononoke*'s capacity-filled theatres, indicates how traditional aspects of Japanese language are utilised in the campaign to distinguish this film from other, namely American, *daihitto* films on offer. These set phrases stand in stark contrast to the fusion language exemplified in the *daihitto* itself, and found in the rest of *Princess Mononoke*'s campaign.[15] The traditional phrases work as specific appeals to indigenous audiences, and the fact that they utilise the language of celebration and thanks, helps to reinforce the film's dependent *daihitto* status: its reliance on its audience. The use of these phrases represents a calculated attempt to key into the nationalistic elements of the film's success, appealing directly to patriotic sentiment within potential Japanese audiences.

Concentration on the national success and importance of the film can also be seen elsewhere in this advertisement for *Princess Mononoke*. In the lower left-hand corner of Figure 1, directly underneath the photo-negative smear containing the word '*daihitto!*', is the claim that '"The *Princess Mononoke* Phenomenon" has Conquered these Islands!'. The use of 'these Islands' or *rettou* (literally meaning 'archipelago') forms an additional geographic and nationally specific reference to Japan that incorporates all parts of the nation. The thanksgiving banner and this reference to a *Mononoke* phenomenon were the only differences between this and earlier advertising for *Princess Mononoke*. The fact that both are culturally, nationally and geographically specific to Japan demonstrates an associative trend in *Princess Mononoke*'s advertising that attempted to link audiences to discourses on national community and patriotism. Although it may be slightly overstating the case based on this single advertisement, there is an apparent determination here and across the campaign to manipulate the Japanese viewing public into seeing this film for patriotic (sweeping across the nation/conquering the islands) or even cultural (*okagesamade* – thanks to you) reasons. This is important when considering *Princess Mononoke* as a *daihitto* because such nation-based appeals gave the film-makers access to the widest possible 'niche' market for this Japanese film – a generalised 'Japanese' audience.

The constant references across *Princess Mononoke*'s advertising campaign to running audience figure totals are perhaps the strongest way in which blockbuster-style appeals were made. In these audience figures, which start to appear five days after the release of *Princess Mononoke* and continue for the next 19 weeks (albeit somewhat sporadically), millions of Japanese people were implicated in the success of *Princess Mononoke*. The sense of collectivity, of community, fostered by these figures, may well betoken why they became an advertising focus rather than the film's box office gross earnings. The notion of community remains vital in Japanese culture and the notion of community spirit was certainly mobilised in the advertising for this *daihitto* film, in a manner that suggests the term carries far more meanings than just 'big hit'. Such appeals to a large collective (over 12.5 million people by late November 1997) may therefore have had a significant impact on the *Princess Mononoke*'s popularity in its domestic milieu, and on perceptions of its 'phenomenal' status.

Publicity: The Japanese *Daihitto* and the American Blockbuster

Concurrent with the advertising that promoted *Princess Mononoke*, several newspaper and magazine articles appeared which acted as publicity for the film. Though coverage of *Princess Mononoke* was expansive, particularly across the magazines owned by producers Tokuma Shoten Publishing, there were also articles in newspapers unaffiliated to it. Some of these will be examined here, ranging in temporal terms from the first week of the film's release through to its breaking of all Japanese box office records in late October 1997. A variety of newspapers are included in this sample in an attempt to articulate the differing stances from which *Princess Mononoke*'s success was approached in Japan. It is

hoped that these articles will provide further enrichment of the contexts of *Princess Mononoke*'s release and the discourses in Japanese
popular culture that surrounded it. These will help bridge the
intention-reception gap evident between the advertising for the film
and media responses to it. Consequently, these articles will also be
analysed to illustrate the points at which *Princess Mononoke*'s advertising jarred with even the earliest stages of its reception, and what the
film-makers sought to do to combat unauthorised responses to their
film.

The first newspaper response to *Princess Mononoke* was also the one
which most fully described the contexts under which it was released.
Only a few days after *Princess Mononoke* opened to the public, the
Yomiuri Shimbun included the film in a review of forthcoming summer
features.[16] The article outlines the crowded summer film marketplace
in Japan, including everything from American blockbusters to art house
and European films in perceived order of descending box office potential. *Princess Mononoke* appears in this list in direct comparison with
Spielberg's *The Lost World*. The reviewer states:

> Big hit [*daihitto*] film sequel *The Lost World* (director Steven Spielberg)
> has doubled its appeal, increasing the scale and also the variety and
> number of its dinosaurs. It does not disappoint this summer's biggest
> genre film expectations. In opposition, Japan's example is master artist
> Miyazaki's five-year big project anime *Princess Mononoke*. Staged in the
> Muromachi period, the battle between humans and nature incarnated is
> drawn on a grandiose scale. It is a film that is its artist's gem, full of
> deeper meaning, and it will no doubt resound deep in our hearts.[17]

The reviewer positions Miyazaki's film through the use of sophisticated
oppositional techniques. Where *The Lost World* is bigger and therefore
better than its predecessor, *Princess Mononoke* is deeper, more artistic
and more meaningful than its American rival. The clear description of
The Lost World as *daihitto* and *Princess Mononoke* as 'Japan's example'
further points to *Princess Mononoke*'s positioning as an alternative to
The Lost World. *Princess Mononoke* is also set apart by reference to its
'newness' through plot summarisation. Whereas *The Lost World* is a
sequel and therefore part of a blockbuster franchise of films, *Princess
Mononoke*'s blockbuster status requires explanation here both in terms
of its 'grandiose' nature and the 'five-year' length of the project. Thus,
mixed in with these relatively simple descriptions of these two films,
are a series of discourses designed to purposely put the films 'in opposition' to one another, particularly in terms of size and quality.

A preference for Japanese film over foreign film in this article is another way in which the national film product was distinguished and preferred in comparison to non-domestic films. At a basic level, descriptions of Japanese films here tend to be lengthier than those for their foreign counterparts (as can be seen in the example above). In two paragraphs on children's cinema, for example, foreign films including Disney's *Hercules* rate a total of only two sentence clauses that read: 'Disney's anime *Hercules* using materials from Greek mythology, *Elmo's Adventure* an adaptation of a story belonging to dream-filled children's literature.'[18] These rather nebulous descriptions are bracketed on either side by more concrete analyses of Japanese anime such as '*Jungle King*, Osamu Tezuka's most famous film'. That Disney's *Hercules* is described not as an animated feature film, but as an anime, also indicates a subversive repositioning of this film under domestic generic auspices, placing it into a category of films already highly competitive in Japan.

The review article, through its careful positioning of *Princess Mononoke* as an alternative blockbuster, belies somewhat the film's advertising during this period. Here *Princess Mononoke* is not placed alongside anime films or art house ones (although a list of these appears at the end of the article) as it is in its advertising campaign. Instead, it emerges as a blockbuster, and one of greater importance than the majority of the American films surrounding it in the Japanese market. This is not to suggest, however, that these American blockbuster films were not accorded importance. *The Lost World* 'does not disappoint' and *Speed 2: Cruise Control* (US, 1997) and *Batman and Robin* are also mentioned. However, it is again telling that while those two latter American films receive only cursory plot synopses, the Japanese film *School Ghost Story 3* is commented upon in more detailed and critical fashion, for example: 'although seasoned with love and friendship, it is truly frightening'.[19] The critical emphases and omissions in this review work to disguise a preference for Japanese film over American and other foreign films. What the review provides, in addition, is a detailed appraisal of the Japanese film market that includes not only local and foreign products in an uneasy balance, but also clear evidence of a complex programming and counter-programming system of exhibition.

Princess Mononoke acts as a counter-programme to *The Lost World* in this review. Similarly, the sequel or franchise film market is not only balanced between local and foreign film, but also provides alternatives to the top layer of domestic *daihitto* films represented by *Princess Mononoke*. The children's niche market and the art house niche market are also provided as counter-programming alternatives to the summer's big films. This is evidence of the sophistication of the Japanese market, a sophistication marked not only by issues of relative size, but also genres, niches and language. The advertising surveyed in this chapter suggests as much, but this reviewer's hierarchy-construction adds more weight to claims for the complexity of the Japanese film marketplace.

Further positioning of *Princess Mononoke* takes place across the remaining articles. As the film continues to break records, changes become apparent in the filmic frames of reference applied to it. For example, there is mention in another early *Yomiuri Shimbun* article of both *South Pole Story* (Japan, 1983) and Disney more generally.[20] *South Pole Story* (sometimes titled *Antarctica* in English) was the previous domestic box office record holder, surpassed by *Princess Mononoke*'s gross earnings in September 1997, which were nearing ¥ 60 billion. References to domestic box office records here implicate this article in the project of promoting *Princess Mononoke* as a blockbuster film. That it also mentions *Princess Mononoke*'s record-breaking compounds its implication that this film is not only significantly popular, but that it is even better than the popular Japanese films that preceded it. However, situating the film between Disney, whose advertising tends to avoid reference to the blockbuster, and to another domestic hit implies some level of reluctance on the part of the journalist to align *Princess Mononoke* wholeheartedly with its live action American blockbuster cousins.

This domestic frame of reference changed though after *Princess Mononoke* beat the overall Japanese box office record set by *E.T. The Extra Terrestrial* (US, 1982), late in October 1997. This mirrors the move already seen in the film's advertising, which, building up to and moving beyond the breaking of this record, had begun to position *Princess Mononoke* wholeheartedly within the same category as American blockbusters. However, in the *Mainichi Shimbun* article titled '*E.T.* Outdone by *Princess Mononoke*', Miyazaki's film is termed a '*daihitto* anime'.[21] *Daihitto* anime as a term has two ramifications in this context. Firstly, it differentiates *Princess Mononoke* from the live-action blockbuster *E.T.* Secondly, however, the additional term, anime, though descriptive, may have actually been intended to qualify the phrase *daihitto*. Put another way, it may have been used here to indicate either particularity or 'Japaneseness'. Given the rarity of this level of success among anime films, either is likely, but it may have also been used to diminish potential American associations and expectations for *Princess Mononoke*. An anime blockbuster would necessarily be a very different kind of film to an American live-action blockbuster and, hence, might not be expected to perform in quite the same way.

Echoing the use of the qualified *daihitto*, the rest of the article contains attempts by Miyazaki and others to distance themselves from *Princess Mononoke*'s success. For example, Miyazaki states explicitly here that 'I really don't understand why this has happened', when quizzed on the film's success, despite his involvement in its pre-release promotion.[22] Miyazaki's role as a promoter for his film is also clear from his statement that 'the money is one thing separate from appreciation of the text', in response to which the author of the article comments that 'he is keeping his distance from the film, which goes on alone'.[23] This movement to separate *Princess Mononoke*'s text from its contextual economic achievements is similar in a way to the differences mentioned between the film's and other blockbusters' advertising. Working to counteract the hype around *Princess Mononoke*, Miyazaki's comment forces focus back onto the film, thus encouraging further potential audiences to ignore the hype and see it for themselves. This is not a new tactic in blockbuster promotion. James Cameron's comments about *Titanic*'s budget similarly acted to control errant media speculations about his blockbuster film.[24] That these directors become conduits for communication passing from the studios to the press should not be altogether surprising, given their importance to the initial project of selling their blockbuster films. Rather, Miyazaki and Cameron's star status makes them the useful vehicles for this kind of media manipulation.

Another point of similarity between *Princess Mononoke* and American blockbusters, which began to be discussed in the latter part of its promotion, was its merchandising. When *Princess Mononoke* broke *E.T.*'s box office record, Katsuda Tomomi was quick to express that its profits were not limited to gross earnings:

> For Tokuma Shoten, the *Princess Mononoke* hit is in related goods as well, selling around 2.5 million publications like explanatory books and comics, making around ¥ 1.5 billion. It is said that they have also sold 90,000 copies of the theme song and other CDs.[25]

Interestingly, Katsuda mentions Tokuma Shoten's tie-ins to *Princess Mononoke* and not Studio Ghibli's extensive merchandising for it. Nor does she mention that the arm of Tokuma that published the film's music was a joint venture between the publisher and the film's studio. This again deflects attention away from the corporate nature of *Princess Mononoke*'s producing studio, and also away from Studio Ghibli's direct attempts to capitalise on and commercialise their film product. Therefore, even when journalists seem to have tapped into 'unauthorised' or unsanctioned aspects of *Princess Mononoke*, it is clear that such views have themselves been, potentially at least, guided by the film's various producers.

Conclusions

What emerges from the publicity generated during *Princess Mononoke*'s promotion is a view of the film that shares much with marketing culture the world over; attempting to persuade the viewing public to see *Princess Mononoke* using hyperbole, and appealing to the film's quality and 'Japaneseness'. As *Princess Mononoke* becomes more clearly identified with the blockbuster through reference to its record-breaking box office, the print media responded by likening it increasingly to its American blockbuster counterparts. However, the evidence suggests that the film-makers attempted to combat such straightforward comparisons through a variety of methods, distancing themselves from the film as phenomenon and attempting to refocus attention back onto the film text rather than on the blockbuster phenomenon it was becoming. Studio Ghibli's relative success in this matter helped to create *Princess Mononoke*, in the Japanese media at least, as an alternative form of blockbuster film.

As the examples here have shown, Japanese film product is not isolated in its market. On the contrary, Japanese films are constantly juxtaposed with films from all over the globe. The result being that film-makers and studios in Japan have sometimes found unusual methods of marketing that enable their products to find audiences. Similar film types appear to cluster, in this instance, around film-making modes like animation, and around scale and success of products in previous markets.

The blockbuster film does therefore exist in the Japanese film market. As the *daihitto*, it is visible in Hollywood's films on offer there and equally in Japan's domestic film products. However, as has been explored here, the blockbuster in Japan is perhaps even more diverse and complicated a notion than it is when applied to the study of Hollywood's biggest films. For it is mobilised not only in similar industrial and critical frameworks as those found in America, but in this case the term was further utilised and denied by those who wished to position *Princess Mononoke* and other Japanese films in opposition to those same Hollywood blockbusters. This added layer of meaning and complication does not preclude the usefulness of blockbuster or *daihitto* as a frame of reference in which we can understand the meanings of a film like *Princess Mononoke*. Instead, the appropriation of the term by Japan's film industry, film-makers and film commentators is evidence of how vital understanding these films as blockbusters can be.

The way that *daihitto* is used does differ somewhat from the uses generally made of the term blockbuster. Examples from this study show that the term is not endlessly elastic, but that it is used superlatively to bolster impressions of success. The term *daihitto* is also especially important when used in relation to Japanese films, particularly prestige productions with large budgets such as *Princess Mononoke*, but also *School Ghost Story 3*, itself part of a franchise of Japanese films. Furthermore, because of the combination of film and exhibition advertising, the term *daihitto* becomes attached even to those blockbusters, like *Hercules*, that would never be described as such in their home markets. Again, much more work is needed in this area, and not only in relation to Japan, but to the whole of East Asia. Until we understand how films are promoted, traded, exhibited and consumed in this region, we will have no framework for discussing them as cultural objects.

The language of the blockbuster should, in conclusion, not be seen as a discourse originating solely from, and describing only, the product of American film-making. It can equally be found in other national film-making cultures, including Japan. More than location, however, the language of the blockbuster must be understood as culturally specific and as one of perpetual negotiation. Applied to film texts with proven box office records, to aspirational texts desiring hit status, used generically and adjectivally and, finally, mobilised in Japan to describe not one nation's films but seemingly the products of all national industries, the *daihitto* is a term of inclusion. A word in a marketing language that gives meaning to films as their place in film history continues to be negotiated.

Acknowledgement

I would like to thank the Arts and Humanities Research Council for funding this research, and Mark Jancovich and Sachiko Shikoda for their help in shaping the materials.

References

1   Stringer, Julian, 'Introduction' in Stringer (ed), *Movie Blockbusters* (London and New York: Routledge, 2003), pp.1–14; James Naremore, *More Than Night: Film Noir in its Contexts* (Berkeley, CA, London: University of California Press, 1998).

2   Barker, Martin and Brooks, Kate, *Judge Dredd: Its Friends, Fans and Foes* (Luton: University of Luton Press, 1998), p.185.

3   Stringer: 'Introduction'.

4   Stringer: 'Introduction', p.3.

5   Wyatt, Justin and Vlesmas, Katherine, 'The Drama of Recoupment: On the Mass Media Negotiation of *Titanic*' in Sandler and Studlar (eds), *Titanic: Anatomy of a Blockbuster*, p.29.

6   Perren, Alisa, 'Sex, Lies and Marketing', *Film Quarterly* 55/2 (2001), p.30. Exceptions include: Neale, Steve, 'Art Cinema as Institution', *Screen* 22/1 (1981), pp.11–39.

7   Wyatt and Vlesmas: 'The Drama of Recoupment', p.38.

8   Klinger, Barbara, 'Film History Terminable and Interminable: Recovering the Past in Reception Studies', *Screen* 3/2 (Summer 1997), pp.107–28.

9   This equates roughly to US $20 million. Budget information taken from the Internet Movie Database, <http://us.imdb.com/Business?0119698> accessed 2 March 2003.

10   *Shimbun* is the Japanese for 'newspaper'; all newspapers will be given by their Japanese titles thereafter.

11   *Hercules*, advertisement, *Asahi Shimbun*, 22 August 1997, sec.2:6.

12   Neale, Steve, 'Hollywood Blockbusters: Historical Dimensions' in Stringer (ed), *Movie Blockbusters*, p.54.

13   *Trainspotting*, advertisement, *Mainichi Shimbun*, 4 July 1997, sec.2:11.

14   Berry, Chris, 'What's Big about the Big Film?: "De-Westernising" the Blockbuster in Korea and China' in Stringer (ed), *Movie Blockbusters*, p.224.

15   Fusion language is used here to refer to the kind of mixing of Japanese and loan words commonly found in the campaign. *Daihitto* is a good example of this, with *dai* taken originally from Chinese and *hitto* referring to the English, 'hit'.

16   'Summer Holiday Films: We Recommend These!' *Yomiuri Shimbun*, 19 July 1997, sec.2:5.

17   *Yomiuri Shimbun*: 'Summer Holiday Films'.

18   *Yomiuri Shimbun*: 'Summer Holiday Films'.

19   *Yomiuri Shimbun*: 'Summer Holiday Films'.

20 'Record Breaking Hit: The *Princess Mononoke* Phenomenon', *Yomiuri Shimbun*, 24 July 1997, sec.14:30.

21 Katsuda Tomomo, '*E.T.* Outdone by *Princess Mononoke*', *Mainichi Shimbun*, 31 October 1997, sec.14:30.

22 Katsuda: '*E.T.* Outdone by *Princess Mononoke*'.

23 'The *Princess Mononoke* Phenomenon which has Surpassed New Records in Grosses and Audience Mobilisation', *Asahi Shimbun*, 31 October 1997, sec.2:7.

24 Wyatt and Vlesmas: 'The Drama of Recoupment', p.35.

25 Katsuda: '*E.T.* Outdone by *Princess Mononoke*'.

PART THREE

MADE IN TRANSLATION –
TRANSNATIONAL IDENTITIES

8

Adam Knee

Suriyothai Becomes *Legend*: National Identity as Global Currency

Suriyothai (Thailand, 2001), an historical epic directed by a member of the Thai royal family and reportedly the most expensive film in Thai history (until the same director's three-part epic follow-up *Naresuan* in 2007), plainly functions as an expression of traditional Thai values within modern times (and through a modern medium), a self-conscious attempt to reassert what Thai identity means in the face of contemporary global, cultural and political flows. In its focus on a legendary sixteenth-century queen who sacrifices her life on the battlefield in support of husband and nation, the film is also concerned more specifically with the status of womanhood within Thai history and culture. The expression of Thainess within such an eminently global medium (and with such an enormous investment of capital) clearly suggests an understanding that the likely audience would not be merely a local one. It is no small irony, however, that the version of this film eventually prepared for export (*The Legend of Suriyothai*, 2003) was subject to the editorial contributions of a foreigner, Francis Ford Coppola, and that, this essay will argue, this version mutes or erases some of the more important cultural meanings present in the earlier Thai release. This essay will be concerned initially with highlighting some of the key Thai values *Suriyothai* appears to emphasise and its textual means for articulating them; it will then go on to look at the nature of the changes that were made in the international release version and the implications of these changes for nationally specific meanings. It will argue, finally, that the fate of *Suriyothai* in its altered format provides an object lesson in the potential vulnerability of a culturally specific text removed from its initial contexts.

That the *Suriyothai* project was self-consciously concerned with widening awareness of Thailand's history (or at least one particular version of said history) was clear from its very inception: the project was initiated by the queen, with the professed goal of improving Thai knowledge of Thai history, and bankrolled by the royal family. Suriyothai was an attractive choice for subject matter in part because she is a widely known figure who had already entered strongly into popular legend. The selection of Prince Chatrichalerm Yukol to direct was certainly also a natural one for a project of this scale and prestige, even beyond the most obvious reason of his relation to the queen: Yukol (often referred to in Thailand with the honorific *Than Mui*) has since the 1970s consistently been one of the few internationally recognised Thai directors, and by virtue of his royal status he could be said to have somewhat freer rein in his ability to represent other royals, a highly sensitive issue in Thailand, where charges of lese-majesty are not unheard of. And although Yukol's filmography had not previously included period pieces or epics, his work had shown a consistent affinity for dealing with topical and controversial issues, a penchant he was singularly well-placed to pursue owing to his singular social status among directors. Yukol was also a logical choice given the aim of reaching international audiences, a necessity even aside from purposes of disseminating information about Thai history, in that a budget of this size could not be made up from Thai box office returns alone. He had had film training abroad (at UCLA, where Coppola is a fellow alumnus), had worked in the Hollywood industry (as an intern to the producer Merian C. Cooper), and had subsequently shown a familiarity with Western generic and stylistic vocabularies in his own work, such as the realistic social problem dramas for which he was probably best known. Indeed, in the lushness of its spectacle (its elaborate camerawork, mise-en-scène and period costuming) and the expansive and provocative scope of its narrative, *Suriyothai* arguably recalls the 'golden age' of the Hollywood-produced historical epics of the late 1950s and early 1960s. The choice of an 'international' style for the project was also evident from early on in the hiring of a Czech cinematographer and a British composer.[1] Additionally, an American post-production facility (American Zoetrope) was eventually used for audio post-production.

In its look to foreign markets, *Suriyothai* is by no means out of sync with the Thai film industry of its time. During the years of *Suriyothai*'s production, Thai film-making was very gradually beginning to achieve a new momentum (one which has grown further since), predicated in part upon both growing international success of Thai art films (especially on the film festival circuit) and growing local interest in more commercially oriented Thai films (notably horror, comedy and romance). This increasing activity, moreover, was beginning to have greater synergy with another phenomenon starting to gain momentum: an increasing Asian presence on the world film stage in terms of successful feature exports, the purchase of Asian properties for Western remakes, new levels of aesthetic influence, migrations of creative personnel, and so on.

Suriyothai's self-consciousness about issues of national identity is also not entirely unique among this new crop of globally visible Asian films, as indeed, national specificity is often what is being 'sold' as a distinguishing quality in any film being offered for export to a world market. The film's degree of emphasis and self-consciousness on matters of national specificity, though, may be exceptional: *Suriyothai* is, after all, a royally-conceived, royally-backed production, focusing on highly popular historical figures and on sometimes contentious historical events pertaining to the evolution of the nation and its interrelationship to both the region and the world. Moreover, the project evinces not just a local but a global engagement with such issues from its inception, an awareness of a foreign gaze. This can be surmised not only from the aforementioned efforts toward a globalised style, but also from the use of Western (specifically Portuguese) sources in the film's construction of its historical events and an initial plan to include a Portuguese narrator.

A practical awareness of this international audience is what eventually leads to the altered international release version of the film (referred to in the following as *Legend*), which at one point was going to include the addition of a foreign observer of Thai historical events, to be played by Harvey Keitel.[2] Certainly, the release of international versions of films for distribution abroad – typically with some alterations to the soundtrack and/or the addition or deletion of a handful of scenes – is not that unusual. However, the degree of adjustment in the instance of this film, as well as the public nature of that adjustment (with the addition of Coppola's globally recognised imprimatur and a change in the film's title), are in fact uncommon. *Legend* in effect becomes a kind of cross-cultural remaking or adaptation of *Suriyothai*, in some sense along the lines of, and with many of the same purposes as, Hollywood's more literal remaking of a range of recent popular Asian films (mostly in the horror genre). Given the earlier version's preoccupation with issues of national identity, however, the question arises as to what extent the film's discourses about Thai-ness are altered in the international 'remake', and, more broadly, to what extent local cultural meanings can be sustained within the global realm. Indeed, in these terms, we can understand the doubled versions of *Suriyothai* as enacting in tandem, at intra-, inter- and extra-textual levels, a drama regarding the inter-relationships of Thai culture with the rest of the world, at the same time as it also offers a case study of the kind of 'de-nationalisation' of film texts which tends to be obtained in the current globalisation of Asian film industries.[3]

National Identity

A number of scholars have commented upon some of the nationally specific implications or meanings of *Suriyothai*; in the English language literature, perhaps most notably Amporn Jirattikorn, Glen Lewis and Hong Lysa, from the disciplines of anthropology, media studies and history respectively.[4] Although employing different methods and having different emphases, all three make the case that the film needs to be understood as not just about distant past history, but also about the status of national identity in the context of the film's production. More specifically, all three view the film's evident nationalism as consonant with a rhetoric of self-sufficiency that arises in the wake of Thailand's transnationally fuelled economic boom and its subsequent post-1997 crisis. They also see the film as concerned with the contemporary status of Thai womanhood, Amporn noting the film's conservative bent in this regard. While I am in agreement with the general sentiment of these readings, it is my aim here to add to this conversation a further examination of some of the nuances that arise in the positioning of the titular figure in particular, largely through more extended employment of textual analysis. It is important to do this, I would argue, in that the film is hardly so pat in its messages about what constitutes Thai identity/nation; that it takes a very broad view and figures this identity as involving a complex and ongoing dynamic, a negotiation between varying forces the parameters of which it is the film's project to lay out.

On a most literal level, this negotiation is figured as continuous struggle between the rulers in Ayuthaya (and those affiliated with them) and various neighbouring powers. The film's most central battles are those with the Burmese, but the plot also makes repeated allusion to concerns over the allegiances of neighbouring factions in the north (Chiang Mai) and in the northeast (Laos). From the southeast, Khmer make their presence felt in the form of hired assassins who appear in one sequence of the film. These struggles are not merely a backdrop to a drama of royal life, but are rather a central, recurrent feature of the film's highly episodic narrative structure, an inescapable component of

Thai existence as it is figured in *Suriyothai*. These external struggles operate in tandem with equally virulent internal ones – struggles for control amongst different siblings, family branches and lineages. The film makes a point of characterising these struggles, both internally and externally, as fluid and continually shifting, often marked by subterfuge or downright treachery, and only possible to win by creating effective alliances.

It does not require much of a reach to see similar struggles functioning in *Suriyothai*'s historical context of production.[5] A number of contemporary Thai film productions have caused diplomatic flare-ups with Burma and Laos for their perceived negative representations of those countries, while a reported insult by a Thai actress against Cambodia (false as it turned out) resulted in wide rioting against Thai businesses in that country (and a subsequent antipathy toward Thai film and television productions). In terms of internal struggles, Thailand's long-standing attempts to bring its various regional ethnic groupings (Muslim (southern), Isaan (northeastern), etc.) together under a central Thai umbrella have continued to run into trouble (most recently, with heightened violence in the south). And Thai audiences would be readily able to perceive, in the film's depiction of administrative corruption, favouritism and intrigue, an analogue for a range of like problems plaguing many modern Thai government administrations – including, quite notably, the one in power at the time of *Suriyothai*'s initial release, though it has since been forced out by a military junta using the justification of (among other things) widespread corruption.

Suriyothai (at least in its initial form) makes reference to interaction with more distant neighbours as well, especially in the context of international commerce, and the contemporary resonances in this aspect are even more self-evident. We see a Chinese merchant use his money to buy himself both preferential trade treatment and a naturalised Thai status and Thai name, only to then wield his influence to control local commodity trading; much as naturalised Sino-Thai do in fact stand as a central part of Thai trade. The West is present in the person of Portuguese mercenaries and a Portuguese doctor, as well as in the form of Portuguese liquor, armour and weaponry (the latter also supplied by China). These factors also seem to have strong present-day analogues: a strong Thai cooperation with Western (specifically US) military forces since the 1950s and a Thai dependence on foreign research and technology, a phenomenon often decried by critics preaching greater Thai self-sufficiency. Simply the very fact of the widespread presence of non-Thais within Thailand in the narrative has its correspondence to the country's contemporary real-world position as a key international tourist destination.

Heroism in *Suriyothai* appears linked to an ability to negotiate with or stave off these threats, internal or external, as well as a willingness to fully sublimate personal desires in favour of one's duty to support the nation. It is in her singular demonstration of such traits that Suriyothai arguably becomes the film's most significant protagonist. While it may be her husband Prince Tien (later the king) who formally holds power and who literally goes out into battle (though Suriyothai ultimately joins in this as well), it is Suriyothai who acutely observes potential internal enemies and skilfully develops internal alliances to ensure her family is safe from treachery. It is Suriyothai, too, who actively pushes her husband to take decisive, judicious action to stave off adversaries internal and external and who shows far more ambition regarding her husband gaining the crown – not, the film makes clear, out of her own desire for personal gain, but out of her knowledge that his leadership is what would best ensure the future of the Thai nation.

Clearly, however, while the film offers up its title character as a model and emblem of Thai values and behaviour, her qualities are not gender-neutral: Suriyothai is positioned not just as an exemplary Thai, but, more specifically, as a paragon of Thai womanhood, properly fulfilling her various roles as Thai daughter, wife, mother and, finally, queen. Suriyothai is revealed to be skilful and wise, a great military strategist with sharp intuition, and a remarkable coalition builder; but this is specifically in support of her husband and in turn Thailand. And while she often appears more wise and more driven than her husband, the film makes it clear that she nevertheless knows her place as a woman in Thai society, and that while she will sternly and vigorously disagree with him and attempt to sway his opinions when need be, she remains loyal to a fault, never directly disobeying him.

The film's need to focus on this particular image of (contained) femininity suggests yet another set of tensions and negotiations in the constitution of the Thai nation – one which also has contemporary repercussions – that regarding the status of women. Indeed, the status of women in Thai society has long been a paradoxical one: women have historically held authority within the household, even if external polit-ical power has been male. In contemporary Thai society, in contrast to those of many other Asian nations, women hold positions of power and authority in quite a number of arenas (e.g. a number of university pres-idents), even if top positions in other realms (e.g. government) remain closed off to them. The contemporary tensions regarding the status of Thai womanhood are, moreover, linked on multiple levels with those

regarding Thai identity in a global age more broadly: shifts in traditional Thai female roles and codes of behaviour are often viewed as in
large measure a function of a modern increase in foreign commerce and
global cultural influence. Although operating (safely) within a distant
historical past, it is precisely these kinds of negotiations of female identity that Suriyothai must work through: striking the proper balance
between obeisance and initiative, tradition and pragmatism, in an age
(the sixteenth century) when foreign influences can no longer realisti-
cally be ignored, and when internal social stability is also under stress.

Central to the film's representation of Suriyothai as a model of Thai
femininity in uncertain times is its detailing of her ability to absolutely
forgo her own personal desire for the greater good of the nation. Early
in the film she is portrayed as a wilful, uppity teenager, fully prepared
to go against rules of royal decorum in order to pursue Piren, the object
of her romantic desire. When subsequently courted by the highly
placed Tien, she objects (against her father's wishes); but she decides
to relent and marry the man when she learns that her refusal might
cause a rift between royal families and in turn threaten instability to the
nation. It is at this defining juncture, the moment of her apprehension
of her own responsibilities to the welfare of the nation, that Suriyothai
literally becomes someone else. In the next scene she is married, and
shortly after that she is replaced by another, older actress, who portrays
her for the remainder of the film. And while some might find the neo-
phyte actress Piyapas Bhirombhakdi's portrayal of the adult Suriyothai
cold and distant, I would argue she is a felicitous choice. Her sombre,
sometimes scowling demeanour, the extreme paucity of any expression
of tenderness towards Tien, makes clear that the capricious, romantic
youth has completely disappeared, to be replaced by someone whose
goals are, before all else, the preservation of Thailand's interests and
her husband's, which she understands to be one and the same. The
repression of Suriyothai's desire is also literalised in the extreme
de-emphasis on her physical person, the distinctive de-eroticisation of
her body in comparison to those of other female characters (including
her teenage self), made especially evident in the form-disguising battle
garments she wears in later sequences of the film. Significantly, in
diametrical opposition to Suriyothai's need to forego the fulfilment
of romantic desire, Piren's male prerogative *is* to have his desire eventually fulfilled, as a reward for his loyalty to the nation. In appreciation
for his unwavering support of Suriyothai in a time of crisis, he is
granted a marriage to her daughter, portrayed (lest the logic of exchange
be overlooked) by the very same actress who portrays the teen
Suriyothai.

The film makes eminently clear, moreover, that Suriyothai's difference from other women is not merely a matter of moral and behavioural
predilection, it is a matter of national consequence. Women who behave
in a manner other than Suriyothai are consistently responsible for
events which threaten the stability and integrity of the nation. At the
polar opposite to Suriyothai in terms of bodily representation (and, by
association, in terms of moral/national stature) is a young courtesan
who is seen (to the shock of Thai audiences) bare-breasted (something
rare for both Thai films and Thai actresses); and it is no coincidence
that King Athitaya's desire for her leads to a number of decisions on
his part (granting her father a certain influence, insisting their young
son replace him on the throne) which threaten the stability and welfare
of the kingdom. The demise of this king with a weakness for the flesh
is itself presented as an event of bodily weakness and excess, as he dies
in the throes of smallpox, his body grotesquely rendered for the screen.

Suriyothai's eventual nemesis Srisudachan, the woman who almost
successfully orchestrates a passing of the Thai royal lineage from
Suriyothai's dynasty to her own, is also distinctly contrasted with
Suriyothai, not only in terms of lack of loyalty to the man she serves
(first as courtesan and then as wife and queen), but, again, in terms of
sexuality. Her impulse toward treachery is represented firstly as an
erotic impulse, and only subsequently as an impulse to wrest power for
her own family line. More specifically, when she first sees the fellow
member of her dynasty whom she will eventually draw into her plot as
a collaborator, the film shows us the erotic fantasy that arises in her
mind's eye – a subjective intimacy, it could be added, unlike anything
offered in association with Suriyothai (save, perhaps, for one nightmare
sequence), whose own personal emotions, after the opening sequences,
are always kept at arm's distance, hidden deep behind her armour.

What is indeed suggested at several levels in the film is not just a gender anxiety, but a sexual panic, a sense that sexual license is a threat to
the State, that lack of sexual control, lack of corporeal restraint, will
lead to national calamity. Significant in this regard is that one of the
clearest villains of the piece, Srisudachan's 'muscle' as it were, her assistant Preekh, is figured as a butch, murderous lesbian – one who simultaneously transgresses sexual norms and national ideals. In one of the
film's most lurid sequences, Lord Mahasena, a minister perceived to be
disloyal, is locked into Srisudachan's palace grounds and then surrounded by a group of young, spear-wielding women under Preekh's
command; the women incapacitate him with stabs from the spears
before Preekh steps up to slit his throat, casually twirling her knife as
she walks away from the scene. This linkage between non-normative

sexuality and national peril is echoed in the representation of another key antagonist, Burma's King Hongsa. Even if his heavy make-up, jewellery, practised gestures, soft voice and close intimacy with his male advisors (in the absence of any evident queen) are in fact historically accurate, their figuration here clearly evokes 'queerness' for contemporary audiences (including the American students with whom I shared this film). Sexual license more broadly is thematically linked, moreover, with a sense of contagion, of a (national) danger that can spread: Srisudachan draws the man of her dynasty into her plot by way of seduction (also a factor in her successful hiding of her intentions from her husband Chai Raja), while the aforementioned king with a weakness for young flesh ends up succumbing to a literally contagious ailment, in which the body grotesquely exceeds regulation, both in the appearance of skin eruptions and in the loss of motor control. The sense of bodily excess articulated there is engaged once again with the introduction of a character who poses far more peril for the State: the dynastic matriarch who gives suggestions to Srisudachan for her treachery is likewise figured as grotesque in appearance, with a skin ailment recalling the symptoms of smallpox.

The above account describes only a few of the film's many instances showing the potential power of women, and the importance of a distinctive regulation of that power, the denial of female personal desire and ambition, in ensuring the welfare of the nation. For this film, Suriyothai becomes a heroine both in this self-denial, and, as mentioned, her distinctive ability to politically support her husband by building alliances and strategising; and also finally (but only in the film's penultimate moment) by literally going into battle for the nation herself.

In focusing on these particular dimensions of Suriyothai's importance, in figuring her with these particular qualities, it is logical that much of the original film dwells on things other than the physical battles, the visible actions, which help determine Thailand's history, that it focuses at length, rather, on its title character's often subtle interactions with those in her world. This tendency puts the original film somewhat at odds with classical Hollywood's kinetic, cause-and-effect drive, something the executive producer of the international version, Kim Aubry, indicated outright: '[The film] is a tough sell because American audiences have a difficult time with films that aren't driven by simple narrative or action sequences. This is more like "Masterpiece Theatre" meets "Ran".'[6]

Suriyothai's International Makeover

It was in an effort to produce a film in which the narrative through-line, the causal chain of events so central to the classical Hollywood style, was more heavily emphasised that a range of alterations to *Suriyothai* were carried out to meet the aim, as Coppola describes it, of making it 'more clear to Western audiences'.[7] What was performed under the supervision of executive producers Aubry and Coppola, therefore, was not (as it has sometimes been described) a re-editing of the original film (in fact, the editing in the original version is quite polished and did not call for 'fixing'), but a series of adjustments and additions to help ensure narrative transparency and entertainment value. *Legend* is thus not so much a condensed 'Reader's Digest version', as Yukol at one point jokingly described it (although it is about 25 minutes shorter),[8] as it is an annotated version designed both to give requisite background knowledge to those not familiar with the film's original context and to more readily hold the attention of those most comfortable with the Hollywood mode.

To this end, then, *Legend* has added to it various maps, titles and passages of explanatory voice-over narration not in *Suriyothai*. Subtitles, too, are reworked to help clarify details that would be confusing to a non-Thai audience. For example, while many of the characters are called by several names (in part a function of shifting social status) over the course of the film, and while *Suriyothai*'s English subtitling keeps most of these shifts intact, *Legend*'s subtitles reduce such shifts to a minimum; and along similar lines opts for geographical terminology that is more likely to be recognisable for an international audience. Moreover, in the last third of the film, a number of scenes of military planning and battle are removed in order to allow the narrative to progress more swiftly (and perhaps to lessen the accumulation of minute historical details, with ever more names and places being added). In addition to these kinds of adjustments, there are even a few scenes added, and a few others re-ordered, to help ensure narrative clarity. Most immediately, while *Suriyothai* begins by briefly showing the death of the title character in 1548, operating under the assumption that the local audience is already well aware of this event having occurred, before returning to the start of the plot in 1528, *Legend* withholds this narrative information until the film's conclusion, and even then makes a few adjustments to its presentation in order to characterise its momentousness (the sense of a turning point in a classical narrative). In both films, Suriyothai is shown falling from her elephant after being mortally wounded in battle, but while in the former film her helmet stays on during this fall, in the latter film the helmet flies off in a slow-motion special effects close-up, the woman warrior's long, dark hair now flowing out in all directions.

These shifts arguably do indeed, for the most part, improve narrative legibility (although some of the shuffles in temporal order produce their own causal illogicalities), especially for the international audience. But in putting a new emphasis on narrative action, I would argue, Coppola and Aubry undermine some key signifying systems of the earlier text, de-emphasising precisely what is, I have suggested, most central to its local cultural meanings in an effort to create a more globally saleable product. At a most fundamental level, *Legend* removes much of the ambiguity and nuance which makes *Suriyothai* so fascinating to observe; this is so both in terms of the earlier film's general view of history and its more specific view of the character of Suriyothai. The earlier film offers a strikingly dispassionate perspective, casting a cold eye on the tumultuous succession of dynasties that characterises this particular period in Thai history (and many others as well). This expansive view, one which demands viewer reflection upon the nature of historical happenstance, arguably puts *Suriyothai* in a league with some of the most accomplished of historical epics. *Legend*, on the other hand, strips *Suriyothai* of much of its moral ambiguity, offering clearer clues as to how to 'read' the nature of events and thus fitting more comfortably into the Hollywood entertainment mould.

A few examples will help demonstrate this tendency to efface the earlier film's ambiguity or openness. A very simple instance involves the difference in the two films' representations of poisonings which occur as part of Srisudachan's efforts to gain power. *Legend* tends to concretely show the logistical details of such poisonings, while *Suriyothai* is more likely to leave such details to the imagination. This has the effect, in *Legend*, of not only removing a measure of plot ambiguity, but also of lessening the level of moral and emotional nuance in the representation of those involved. Another example of this effacement of ambiguity is in a scene where Suriyothai's husband Prince Tien must drink to show allegiance to his cousin Chai Raja, newly installed as king, although he has some misgivings about this accession. While in *Suriyothai*, viewers are invited to read Tien's complicated mix of emotions through his facial expressions and bodily comportment as he pauses before taking the drink, in *Legend* this hesitation is accompanied by a voice-over from Suriyothai which spells the issues out in black and white: 'However bitter, you must drink your allegiance to the King.'

One further, more complex, but also more pivotal, instance of this anchoring of meanings will serve to illustrate to what extent such subtle adjustments work to shape our readings of the film. The scene in question occurs relatively early on in *Suriyothai* (at 25 minutes) and helps establish the parameters of the title character's relationship with her family. It is preceded directly by a scene in which Suriyothai's former love interest Piren refuses to socialise with her because of her new higher social status (which renders it inappropriate); and presumably also because of his hurt feelings. After a quick fade out, we fade in on a domestic scene of Suriyothai doing some handiwork with flower blossoms, surrounded by her maids. Upon hearing the sound of a baby's cry, she looks up with a typically sombre expression on her face, as the camera tracks in to a close-up. A point-of-view shot reveals that Tien is sitting some distance from her, caring for a baby. Another reverse shot details Suriyothai's face as she responds to the scene, smiling slightly. Tien notices that she is now making her way over to him, and a close-up shows his expression quickly becoming more serious. Tien hands the baby over to a servant so he can focus his attention on Suriyothai, who places her hand on his as she sits by him. He gives her a somewhat concerned look, as he in turn places his other hand on hers. However, she now smiles reassuringly, and his face in turn becomes somewhat more relaxed. The scene, then, is mounted entirely without dialogue, built upon the alternation of shots and reaction shots, and the subtle play of facial expressions; but it manages to inform us, nevertheless, that the couple have had at least one child, that Suriyothai is accepting of a marriage based upon a sense of duty, that Tien is concerned about her possible feelings of frustration or dissatisfaction, and that Suriyothai wants to reassure him about such concern. It tells us this, and yet it also retains a productive measure of ambiguity regarding the characters' emotions, which requires us to continue to observe them to understand their perspectives.

In contrast, in *Legend*, the scene is preceded by a transitional montage accompanied by a voice-over (which continues over the start of the scene) that explicitly lays out most of the narrative and dramatic information derivable from the scene itself, and forces us to accept a certain reading:

> The waning moon and waxing sun transpired into countless nights and days. The seasons came and went. The years passed and Princess Suriyothai grew into womanhood. Although her marriage with Prince Tien was blessed with children and happiness there was something missing in her heart.

Visually, the scene then proceeds in the same fashion as in the earlier film; however, at the close-up of Tien's hand clasping Suriyothai's, added to the soundtrack is his utterance of 'My Suriyothai', which, again, has the effect of anchoring the meaning of the otherwise silent looks and actions and removing most ambiguity, telling us that Tien has his wife firmly in hand.

It is in fact perhaps in the loss of detail and subtlety in the portrayal of Suriyothai's character that *Legend* suffers the most. As suggested earlier, in opting for a globally saleable narrative form, *Legend* puts the emphasis on certain codes of action, at the expense of precisely those kinds of events which are eloquent of Suriyothai's culturally specific qualities. Suriyothai excels not so much in taking or causing direct action in order to solve problems (except for her penultimate sacrifice at the close of the film), but in her skill and nuance in interaction and negotiation and compromise with diverse people, in her ability to foster confidence and forge alliances, in her resourcefulness at keeping order in a royal household under adverse conditions, all of these in turn in large measure owing to her own embodiment of loyalty and personal integrity. The scenes that suggest these qualities tend to be scenes more concerned with character development and dialogue-driven drama than with forwarding the causal chain of the narrative, and hence they tend to get short shrift in *Legend*.

To offer but a few examples of this: a scene where Suriyothai quickly analyses and comes up with a solution for the financial difficulties of her household is gone, a scene where she interacts with an ally from another dynasty who pledges support for her and warns her about Srisudachan is gone, and the scene where she skilfully gains the support and trust of an important ally in Srisudachan's household (Lord Mahasena) is shortened. Gone as well is a significant scene where Suriyothai discusses with her husband's army captain the relative merits of the Thai bow and arrow and the Western rifle. She exhibits at one and the same time the precision of the local weapon and her own skill at using it, as she hits a watermelon target with the arrow dead on. The captain makes clear, however, that despite the accuracy of the traditional weapon, the new weapons are necessary because they 'have five, ten times the power'. He demonstrates this colourfully and definitively by taking aim at the same melon with a rifle and blowing it to bits. The scene is important not only in suggesting once again Suriyothai's association with precision and nuance, and in narratively establishing her skill in weaponry (which becomes important to the plot later on), but also in providing one of the film's very few explicit articulations of the kinds of distinction which exist between Thailand and the West, wonderfully metaphorised as the contrast between the piercing from the Thai arrow (traditional, clean, skilled) and the explosion from the Western bullet (modern, messy, powerful).

Legend's own emphasis upon a Western approach, and its attendant de-emphasis on certain local cultural values within the text, paradoxically result in a reshaped film which many Western critics, too, feel is in some ways lacking, a number of them questioning why the title places focus on the queen, where the reorganised film does not. For example, David Rooney, reviewing for the industry in *Variety*, complains:

> Film's title is misleading, in that Suriyothai barely registers as its subject for much of the action, particularly in the long central stretch. She later resurfaces to restore the rightful monarch, going on to meet a warrior's death, but her absence from much of the action makes her resourcefulness and valor, not to mention physical fighting skill, seem to come almost out of nowhere.[9]

Several other reviewers (even appreciative ones) likewise comment on lack of clear characterization; typical is Geoff Pevere's comment that the film is 'Heavy on pageant and incident but light on character and motivation'.[10]

Such comments would appear to re-confirm the perils of 'Hollywoodising' or 'de-nationalising' culturally specific non-Hollywood films. As the coherence of original textual systems is undermined, local significations come under threat of erasure. In this case, both the film and the character with the name 'Suriyothai' are stripped of a significant measure of integrity owing to efforts to force them into more standard Hollywood form. This is nicely emblematised in the aforementioned addition of newly flowing hair in Suriyothai's death scene. While the earlier film gives the character the dignity of retaining, even in death, the unwavering *composure* (both in emotion and appearance) which has defined her, the later *Legend of Suriyothai*, seemingly under the sway of Hollywood's drive for romantic resolution through heteronormative coupling, insists upon making her in some way more accessible than her conscious character would allow, indeed more 'feminine', more conventionally attractive precisely at the moment of her most heroic sacrifice.

References

1   On these choices, see Pimpaka Towira, 'A queen's sacrifice', *The Nation* (Thailand), Focus section, 18 May 1999; and Atiya Achakulwisut, 'Making history', *Bangkok Post*, 27 May 1999.

2   Elley, Derek, 'Review of *Suriyothai*', *Daily Variety*, 2 January 2002, p.14.

3   For an overview of this trend toward de-nationalisation, see Klein, Christina, 'Martial arts and the globalization of US and Asian film industries', *Comparative American Studies* 2/3 (2004), pp.360–84.

4   Amporn Jirattikorn, 'Suriyothai: hybridizing Thai national identity through film', *Inter-Asia Cultural Studies* 4/2 (2003), p.305; Lewis, Glen, 'The Thai movie revival and Thai national identity', *Continuum: Journal of Media & Cultural Studies* 17/1 (2003), pp.69–78; Hong, Lysa, 'Does Popular History in Thailand Need Historians?', *Thai Khadi Journal* 1/2 (2004), pp.31–66.

5   The queen's lady-in-waiting suggested as much in an interview published around the time of the film's initial Bangkok release. Gearing, Julian, 'Webfiles: A movie to the rescue', *Asiaweek*, 20 August 2001, <http://www.asiaweek.com/asiaweek/daily/foc/0,8773,171432,00.html>

6   Page, Janice, 'A history of Siam gets royal treatment: Thai prince and filmmaker aims for a broad audience with *Suriyothai*', *Boston Globe*, 22 June 2003, third ed., p.N11.

7   Quoted in 'The Making of *Suriyothai*', featurette included on *Suriyothai* DVD, Sony Pictures Classics, 2003.

8   Page: 'A history of Siam'. *Suriyothai* runs 185 minutes, while *Legend* runs 142 minutes. A five-hour version of the film was subsequently also released on DVD in Thailand.

9   Rooney, David, 'Review of *The Legend of Suriyothai*', *Variety*, 7 October 2002, p.26.

10 Pevere, Geoff, 'Long on detail, short on story', *Toronto Star*, 18 July 2003, p.D03.

9

Brian Ruh

Last Life in the Universe: Nationality, Technology, Authorship

What does it mean when we say we have watched a film? Even though the claim to have seen a 'film' seems to imply a format specificity suggesting a certain viewing practice, in discussions about cinema we seldom make reference to how we were exposed to the text. For example, when someone asks me if I have seen a particular film it usually matters little to them whether I saw it in its original theatrical run or on a rented DVD copy at home: primacy is placed on the experience of the film's diegetic world. Similarly, in academic discourse when one refers to a film, the conditions under which the author experienced the film are rarely mentioned. However, this is a significant omission as different versions of a film can leave the viewer with different impressions of it. As Charles R. Acland writes: 'The film performance varies across time and across consumption contexts and carries a degree of unpredictability with it. *No two screenings are absolutely identical.*'[1] Watching a film in a theatre is not the same experience as watching it at home. Even saying that one has watched a film on DVD brings up a myriad of questions: was the DVD the widescreen or fullscreen version?; was it the original release or the newly remastered special edition with Dolby 5.1 sound?; was it the theatrical version or the director's cut?; and from which region was the disc? For example, when confronted with the Hong Kong version of the DVD for *Days of Being Wild* (Wong Kar-wai, Hong Kong, 1991) in an interview, cinematographer Christopher Doyle suggested that the interviewer obtained the Japanese DVD of the film, saying: 'The colour is wrong on this one. It's not green enough. It was all green, but then they kind of "corrected" it when I wasn't there. They took away the green because they thought I didn't know what I was doing.'[2] Thus the version of a film a person is watching can have a serious impact on one's reception of it.

The film *Last Life in the Universe* (Pen-Ek Ratanaruang,[3] Thailand, 2003) presents an intriguing case study through which to examine the experience of contemporary transnational Asian cinema. Although technically a Thai film (it was Thailand's submission for Best Foreign Language Film to the 76th Academy Awards), the national identity of *Last Life* is complicated by the varying backgrounds of its cast, crew and producers. The film details the story of Kenji (played by Asano Tadanobu), an obsessively tidy Japanese librarian working in Bangkok who is often overcome by suicidal feelings. At the beginning of the film, he is visited by his gangster brother Yukio (Matsushige Yutaka), who we later learn is on the run from his gang boss back in Japan. At work one day, Kenji is entranced by Nid (Laila Boonyasak), a young Thai woman in a Japanese-style sailor suit. Kenji goes to a bridge to contemplate suicide again where Nid, who is walking in the street after having an argument with her sister Noi (Sinitta Boonyasak), sees him, pauses, and is struck and killed by a passing car. Returning home, Kenji ends up killing Takashi (Takeuchi Riki), another Japanese gangster, in self-defence after Takashi kills Yukio on the orders of Yukio's boss. Noi visits Kenji at his work, after which the two have dinner and Kenji asks if he can spend some time at her house (he does not tell her at first that the reason why he does not want to return home is that he has two dead bodies hidden in his apartment). The remainder of the film is about the relationship that develops between Kenji and Noi, as well as the cultural and linguistic differences that separate them: Noi is learning Japanese and Kenji knows a little Thai, and they are able to supplement their meagre linguistic abilities by communicating in English. At the end of the film, as Noi prepares to leave for a new job in Japan, Kenji's life is interrupted by the arrival of more gangsters from Japan (headed by film director Miike Takashi in a cameo role).

Although the above summary presents an example of a film that crosses the boundaries of nation and culture, a viewer's understanding of the film encompasses more than just plot and narrative. The reception of a film like *Last Life* is shaped by the conditions under which it is viewed, which are increasingly taking place not in theatres but rather in the home through the proliferation of consumer technologies like the Digital Video Disc (DVD). Because DVDs can vary in terms of how truthful they are to the original film prints of a movie, as anecdotally mentioned above by Christopher Doyle, it is important to be aware of the ways in which viewing a movie on DVD can alter one's perception of the film. An awareness of the characteristics of DVDs is important because many of them have additional features that can vary from region to region, such as interviews, featurettes, commentaries and the like, which can also impact on one's interpretation of a particular film.

In this essay, I weave together the three threads of nationality, technology and authorship, in order to better understand the position of *Last Life in the Universe* within the context of global cinema, to illustrate the transnational connections present in many contemporary films, and to examine how such connections come together to complicate a notion of the film as a discrete and stable text. In the first thread I examine the relation of *Last Life in the Universe* to other national cinemas – specifically those of Japan (through the casting of Asano and Miike) and Hong Kong (through the work of Christopher Doyle). In the second thread I look at the film's relation to consumer technologies, focusing on the DVD. Through this viewpoint, I go beyond the film text itself to detail the different ways in which the film can be understood through its release in different consumer formats. Specifically, I examine how the US and UK DVD releases may encourage certain readings of the film by examining some of the special features on the DVDs, such as interviews with the director, commentary tracks by the cinematographer, and other bonus materials. The third thread running through the essay examines how the director, cinematographer and actors contribute to different ways of being able to understand a film, and how these understandings complicate notions of authorship, especially given the film's transnational production and the differing viewpoints enabled by the various DVD releases of the film. By examining these threads, we can begin to get a better grasp of the complicated intertextuality of modern films and see how such complications lessen the ability for a strictly auteurist reading of *Last Life in the Universe*.

The different readings enabled by multiple DVD releases are a factor in how DVD technology came about. Work began on the DVD format in 1993, with players and content first coming out in Japan at the end of 1996. The format was introduced to the US in 1997 and to Europe in 1998. Unlike previous media formats like laserdiscs and videotapes, DVDs were given specific region codes based on where they were being sold. In general, DVDs from one region cannot play in DVD players from another region. (However, many players can be modified to ignore this region coding.) This system was set up in order for movie producers to maximise profits by releasing their titles in different formats in each region. The companies were afraid that 'without region codes, people in other countries could simply import DVDs of the latest films from the US, which would hurt profits from the film's international theatrical release'.[4] Region coding is made even more complicated because not all countries use the same television standards. This means that, for example, a DVD from the UK may not play in a DVD player in Japan, even though both countries use Region 2 discs, because the UK DVD is coded for PAL playback and the Japanese televisions are NTSC.

The audience response to the special features commonly found on DVD has been somewhat contradictory. It has been suggested that in the early days of the format, producers would try to put anything they could find on the disc, even if it was only marginally related, in order to make the list of extras look more impressive. The additional pieces of information one gets in a DVD have become so commonplace that they are an expected presence on the DVD and, even if unwatched, make consumers feel as if they are getting their money's worth. It should be noted, then, that the present discussion of the way DVD extras affect the viewing experience of a film could be said to apply to only a specific segment of the viewing population. Even those who are creating the extras seem to be aware of this fact. However, even unviewed extras can contribute to the overall discourse of a film. For example, the knowledge of the presence of a commentary track by the film's director can lead to a higher estimation of the director, promulgating a form of auteurism.

The audience response to the special features found on DVDs has been somewhat contradictory. On the National Public Radio show *All Things Considered*, Art Silverman opined that interesting DVD extras can make a 'bad' movie worth seeing. However, Silverman's interviewees in the DVD creation industry say that most of the people they know never listen to the commentaries or watch the extras. However, one of the interviewees said that there is a 'vocal but commercially significant minority' of people who watch and buy such products.[5] The accusation that DVD producers inflated the extras on DVDs to make them look more impressive suggests that there is not necessarily a contradiction between the belief that extras and special editions drive DVD sales and the perception that people do not often watch such extras. There is not even a necessary connection between the purchase of a DVD and the watching of it. As philosopher and sociologist Slavoj Žižek has quipped: 'Videos and DVDs have ruined movies for me ... Instead of seeing the movie, I buy it, and then I have it, so why should I watch it?'[6]

In their analysis of the *Fight Club* DVD, Robert Alan Brookey and Robert Westerfelhaus[7] draw on John Fiske's[8] idea of 'primary texts' (the film or, in Fiske's case, television programme under discussion) and 'secondary texts' (writings about the programme). In order to more accurately describe the presence of supplemental materials on DVDs, Brookey and Westerfelhaus posit the term 'extra texts' because 'the material resides outside of, and in addition to, the cinematic text as traditionally defined by film criticism – i.e., the parameters of the theatrical release. Although extra-text materials function in a way similar to secondary texts, we do not believe the term "secondary" fully conveys the signifying relationship they have with the primary-cinematic text'.[9] Although I believe that Brookey and Westerfelhaus are correct in thinking about DVD content as falling outside of the strict primary/secondary text dichotomy, I do not think that the term 'extra texts' does the job they intend of making the connection with the primary text. The word 'extra' by itself implies that the DVD content exists in addition to, can be separated from, and possibly even stand apart from the primary text. However, this is not necessarily the way in which viewers experience the film. One generally will become aware of the disc's packaging, artwork and menus before even being able to play the movie. All of these elements bring with them certain characteristics and help to structure one's viewing experience; they are an inseparable part of the domestic consumption of many films. The DVD can be conceptualised as containing (generally) a single primary text and (possibly one or more) associated texts necessarily in relationship with one another by virtue of their physical connectedness. Therefore, I will slightly modify Brookey and Westerfelhaus's idea and call the additional DVD content 'extra-primary texts'; I believe this term more fully emphasises the links between the DVD material and the primary filmic texts by more explicitly linking the two classes of texts.

Thread One: Nationality – Contextualisation and Intertextuality

Early in the commentary track on the US DVD of *Last Life in the Universe*, cinematographer Christopher Doyle remarks that this is 'my first Thai film ... purely Thai except for me and the main actor, Asano'. This is quite an intriguing statement which suggests to the viewer that one should approach the film as a native Thai creation. The reality is of course not nearly this simple, and Doyle's comment obfuscates the fact that the film is the product of a web of collaboration that draws on resources from across the globe. Although it is only recently that we have begun to write about topics like 'transnational cinema', the international and border-crossing aspects of a film like *Last Life* really date back to the medium's inception. One might wish to argue that this makes all film, regardless of national origin, a strictly Western phenomenon. However, a convincing argument is made by Japanese film scholar Eric Cazdyn, who argues against the idea that film-making 'still leaves traces of the West on every print that is made', explaining that film as a medium 'may well be contingent on modernization, and modernization may well have happened in the West first, but modernization is part of a world structure that seems infinitely more productive to understand as having no firsts, only dependencies'.[10]

Transnational cinema is not a new phenomenon, and this is particularly true of Thai cinema. In addition to the fact that the technology of movie-making came from abroad, from the very beginning of film in Thailand there were foreign influences. For example, the first permanent exhibition space for films in Thailand was built by a Japanese promoter in 1905, and '[b]ecause of his success, *nang farang* ["western shadow theatre," the previous Thai term for cinema] gradually came to be known as *nang yipun* (Japanese shadow theatre) among Siamese audiences'.[11] Also, the first feature-length film made in Thailand, *Nang Sao Suwan*, was filmed in 1922 by Hollywood film-maker Henry A. MacRae. In their book *A Century of Thai Cinema*, Dome Sukwong and Sawasdi Suwannapak write that even though it 'was an American film, since it was made by an American, Thai people at the time regarded it as the first Thai film'.[12] *Nang Sao Suwan* was not unique in this regard, though. In his brief history of Thai cinema, Boonrak Boonyaketmala writes that during the early part of the twentieth century the Thai government cooperated with Western (mostly American) producers to make 'about one dozen' films dealing with Thailand.[13]

Last Life in the Universe carries on this theme of cinema connectivity. The international dimension of the film can be gleaned in part from an examination of the credits. Two of the film's three producers are from Thailand-based Cinemasia, whose goal, according to the company website, is 'to make Thai films and expand to international viewers ... [which] will contribute the world immeasurable culture value and mutual appreciation [sic]'.[14] The third producer is from Netherlands-based Fortissimo Films. The credits also list American company Bohemian Films as a co-producer along with Five Star Production, which calls itself 'one of Thailand's oldest and most famous production and distribution houses', and says that *Last Life* was the company's 'biggest co-production'.[15] Money to create *Last Life* came in part from the Hubert Bals Fund, which, according to their website, 'is designed to bring remarkable or urgent feature film and feature length creative documentaries by innovative and talented film-makers from the developing countries closer to fulfillment'.[16] The capital for this fund is supplied by the Dutch Foreign Affairs Ministry, as well as other Dutch organisations. From this brief account, it seems evident that simply calling *Last Life* a 'Thai' film is a problematic assertion from a production standpoint.

The transnationalism of *Last Life* can be seen through Pen-Ek's cast and crew, which positions the film as one that is in dialogue with other contemporary Asian films through his choice of collaborators. Cinematographer Christopher Doyle, actor Asano Tadanobu and actor/director Miike Takashi had all worked together before coming together on *Last Life*, each one bringing something unique to this ostensibly Thai film. It should be noted that Pen-Ek and scriptwriter Prabda Yoon also bring an international perspective to their art, as both men worked in New York for a number of years before returning to Thailand.

Christopher Doyle is particularly emblematic of the transnationalism inherent in modern cinema. Born in Australia, Doyle left home at an early age for miscellaneous jobs around the world before ending up in Taiwan in the 1970s, where he cut his teeth on documentary films for television. Since then, Doyle has come to be one of the best-known cinematographers working in contemporary Asian cinema. He is probably best known for his many collaborations with Hong Kong director Wong Kar-wai. Doyle has also shot films the nationality of which can be classified as Australian (*Rabbit Proof Fence*, 2002), American (*Psycho*, 1998), Taiwanese (*That Day, On the Beach*, 1983) and South Korean (*Motel Cactus*, 1997).

Doyle has said that the land of his birth should not be indicative of the cultural life he has come to lead. He seems to embrace the flexibility and fluidity that modern travel can give to one's sense of belonging to a specific national or cultural group. Doyle has written: 'Don't call me a Westerner just because I'm white! It's like expecting Wayne Wang to make a film about Beijing instead of the Brooklyn he really films well and seems to care so much more about. In both our cases our skin tone is deceptive, a patently fake résumé. It's our films that show what we really think and care about.'[17] Doyle's own directorial debut *Away with Words* (1999) is emblematic of this philosophy. Similar in concept to the pan-Asian mix of *Last Life*, the film stars Asano Tadanobu in the lead role (providing a previous connection between the star and cinematographer of *Last Life*) as a Japanese man in Hong Kong who develops a relationship with a woman from Singapore (Mavis Xu). Doyle has also stepped out from behind the camera on occasion and has acted in a couple of Asian films, including Miike Takashi's pop cyber-thriller *Andromedia* (Japan, 1998).

Since the early 1990s, Miike Takashi has directed over 60 films and has acted in over ten. Although there cannot be said to be a 'typical' Miike film, he is mainly known for his work in the horror and yakuza (Japanese gangster) genres. Although Miike's character in *Last Life* does not appear until the very end, his work casts a shadow over the entire film; for example, the report about *Last Life* from the 2003 Venice Film Festival, which ran in *Film Comment*, read simply 'in-between days of wonder, plus a Takashi Miike cameo'.[18] Early in the film, Kenji's brother is talking in a bar with Takashi, one of his yakuza friends, who tells him: 'You've seen too many gangster movies.' There is then a cut to a tracking shot across a poster for the film *Ichi the Killer* (Japan, 2001), hanging in the library in which Kenji works. Not only was *Ichi* a gangster movie directed by Miike, but it stars Asano Tadanobu. Takashi's comment takes on added meaning because he is played by Takeuchi Riki, who has built a career around playing gangsters and tough guys and who has been described as the 'undisputed king and master thespian of Japanese V-cinema [straight-to-video film]'.[19] Appearing alongside Miike is Sato Sakichi, who wrote the script for *Ichi the Killer*, and Tanaka Yoji, who acted alongside Asano in *Shark Skin Man and Peach Hip Girl* (Ishii Katsuhito, Japan, 1998). Incidentally, Sato and Tanaka also appeared in another cross-cultural gangster film in the same year as *Last Life*: Quentin Tarantino's *Kill Bill Volume 1* (2003). Thus through the casting choices, *Last Life in the Universe* makes conscious reference to the contemporary Japanese yakuza cinema, creating another layer of international intertextuality.

This discussion brings to mind the varying ways in which *Last Life* can be understood. Is it a Pen-Ek Ratanaruang film because he directed it, or can it be considered to be a Christopher Doyle film because it has more in common visually with the cinematographer's previous work than it does with that of Pen-Ek? What does this mean in terms of the film's nationality? Since it was in his commentary on the US DVD of *Last Life* that Doyle asserted that the film was 'purely Thai', it is useful to turn to an examination of the DVDs themselves and their extra-primary texts.

Thread Two: Technology – The DVDs

For this study I compared two different versions of the *Last Life in the Universe* DVD – the US Region 1 (NTSC), released 15 February 2005, and the UK Region 2 (PAL), released 22 November 2004.[20] As each version of the film brings different visual factors and extra-primary texts into play, the ways in which film can be understood may differ significantly.

The US DVD of *Last Life* is the only version of the film that includes a commentary track. As mentioned before, the commentator is not the film's director but rather the cinematographer. Doyle begins with a direct address to the viewer, saying: 'I think the thing I'm most proud of [in] this film is [that] it is Thai ... It's my Thailand, and I hope as we go along, it becomes your Thailand.' This may be a colloquial way of speaking, but it is interesting because in saying this, Doyle is encouraging further viewer identification with the people and the land he is filming – we are encouraged to share in the experience Doyle has already received of somehow 'owning' these images. Thus Doyle begins by drawing attention to the setting of *Last Life* specifically as Thailand rather than a nameless exotic 'Other', but this has a different effect than if director Pen-Ek (who incidentally speaks excellent English) had given the commentary. Doyle's Thailand is certainly different from the Thailand of a native of the country, and as such the encouraged view is close to that of a tourist, always coasting along the surface. Throughout other parts of the commentary, Doyle discusses cinematography in general, how to film emotions, and how the choice of location can influence the style of a film. In doing so, Doyle prioritises certain aspects of the film. For example, he encourages the viewer to focus on the mise-en-scène when he calls Noi's house 'the third major character of the film' and states that 'without this house, this film would be only half of what it could have been'. Although this is Doyle's personal interpretation, it is a privileged one and therefore carries some impact. Doyle's commentary also emphasises some of the intertextual aspects discussed above when he states 'I think in many ways this film is our homage to Miike, believe it or not'.

One of the interesting things highlighted by Christopher Doyle's comments on the US DVDs of *Last Life* is the spirit of collaboration he had with the director. He mentions a brief part in the middle of the film when the deceased Nid reappears to Kenji in the place of her sister Noi. On the commentary, Doyle says that the change of Noi and Nid came out of a conversation he and Pen-Ek had while sitting around their hotel pool one evening. The two men had noticed that the energy on the set had been flagging as the shoot went on, so they devised a plan to bring back the actress Laila Boonyasak to inject some liveliness into the filming. Thus, what seems at first like an inquiry into guilt and metaphysics (because Kenji felt partially responsible for Nid's death) is revealed to have much more prosaic roots. But this also reveals a way of working that is intensively collaborative, with a great deal of

give-and-take between the director and his crew. Doyle's statement on
the method used to create *Last Life in the Universe* echoes something
he wrote a few years earlier:

> I'm often asked where an image or idea or certain effect came from.
> Whose idea was it? I usually honestly don't know. It's like a good date
> to me: You say 'Let's try some seafood', and things evolve to a point
> where you could be doing things to each other with live seafood in bed!
> Ideas are points of departure; you take them where or as far as you can.
> If I say 'Let's try this angle', it may suggest to you another. If you ask,
> 'What if I say it this way?' it may become Hamlet's soliloquy![21]

Similarly, Doyle emphasises the role that others had in the production
of the film, mentioning that the scenes with Miike and his entourage
were crafted by Miike himself: 'He basically came off the airport [sic]
already in character, in costumes that he designed himself or he had
made himself. We had no idea what was going to happen.'

Another feature unique to the US *Last Life* DVD is the art gallery it
contains. 'The Art of Chris Doyle' is an extra featuring photo collages,
presumably taken and assembled by cinematographer Christopher
Doyle while filming *Last Life in the Universe*. There is no text accom-
panying the artwork. In addition to photos of actors and locations,
Doyle incorporates into his collages what look to be clippings from
magazines, as well as sections of the English script for the film. The
photo collages do not illuminate anything about the story of the film
itself, but rather might serve as Doyle's comment on what it was like to
be working on *Last Life* in Thailand. Although one should be careful
not to read too much into the artwork, as an extra-primary text they
serve to reinforce the idea that Christopher Doyle was one of the key
creative forces on the film, downplaying the contributions of director
Pen-Ek. A possible explanation for this emphasis is that Pen-Ek is a
relatively unknown director in the West (or at least he was before he
made *Last Life*), while Doyle's reputation has been well established. As
Adam Knee wrote in an article on the pre-*Last Life* films of Pen-Ek:
'Thai cinema is not yet a "known quantity" with an established
draw, [so] distributors are hesitant to take a risk on it – which means
that Thai cinema remains unknown.'[22] The foregrounding of
Christopher Doyle's efforts may be one way of trying to minimise the
'unknown quantities' of the film. In this respect, the US DVD seems
to be positioning Doyle as the main creative force of *Last Life in the
Universe*, an idea that is lacking from the UK DVD version of the
film.

One extra-primary text the US and UK DVDs share is that they both feature interviews. However, in the US version, there is only a single interview segment with Pen-Ek, while the UK disc is more wide-ranging, featuring two different interviews with Pen-Ek as well as interviews with Japanese male lead Asano Tadanobu, Thai female leads Sinitta and Laila Boonyasak, one of the producers, and the production designer. All of the interviews on the disc, save one of the two with Pen-Ek and the interview with Asano, are in Thai.[23] Through the ways the interviews are deployed on the different discs, the viewer gets a different impression of the film. The single interview in the US version implies an idea of directorial control, which stands in sharp contrast to the highlighting of Christopher Doyle's work that appears elsewhere on the disc. On the other hand, the multiple interviews on the UK disc remind the viewer of all of the different talents that went into creating the film, illustrating that such a film cannot be the sole work of one or two unique individuals. Such extra-primary texts perhaps lessen the chance of an auteurist reading of the film.

Thread Three: Authorship – Understanding the Artist

Echoing Christopher Doyle's sentiment that 'It's our films that show what we really think and care about', Pen-Ek has said: 'Movies shouldn't always be catalogued by the passports of the film-makers … There are more important things to discuss than whether this is qualified as "Thai cinema" or not.'[24] In their comments about the film, both Doyle and Pen-Ek play down the notion of nation and nationality. However, the concept of nationhood does provide some ways of understanding the film as well as how we can discuss the text's authorship, and how this is constructed through the additional DVD features.

The extra-primary texts on a DVD, however, do not necessarily reach everyone who views the film. Accessing these elements that build on the primary text is up to the individual viewer. Parker and Parker quote an industry insider who has worked to create DVD commentary tracks as noting that directors often ask: 'Who is going to listen to this except a bunch of film students?'[25] On the *Last Life* DVD, Doyle expresses his own version of this, saying: 'I guess if you're listening to this DVD then you have a certain attention span [laughs]. Or you've turned it off earlier. Which means perhaps you do expect more from films. I hope we expect more from films. Otherwise why don't we go into real estate … ?' Who indeed accesses the extra-primary texts on a DVD? It seems like the video industry is not even sure who is watching.

However, there are a number of writers who are obviously interested in these DVD features. Writing in the online magazine *PopMatters.com*, Cynthia Fuchs begins her review by focusing on Doyle, quoting from the commentary track.[26] Throughout the review, she keeps referring back to things Doyle said and even ends by quoting him. Thus, for some viewers the extra-primary textual material obviously shapes the reception of the film, as it is an integral part of the review. A post on the movie weblog *Twitch* also illustrates how the extras can shape perception of a film. The writer lists the details of the then-upcoming *Last Life* US DVD and punctuates the inclusion of a Christopher Doyle commentary track with an exclamation mark, stating:

> Now, not only is Doyle one of the very best cinematographers
> in the world, he's also one mighty fine interview and I can't
> wait to hear what he's got to say about this ... he's a funny, sarcastic,
> bitingly intelligent man and I'm betting he's got a story or two to tell
> about Tadanobu Asano, Takashi Miike and Riki Takeuchi ... [27]

Interestingly, the original post contains no mention of director Pen-Ek by name or the interview with him on the DVD. Through such writings, people are encouraged to read the film as a Christopher Doyle film, which might place it in a general 'transnational Asian' category, rather than as a Pen-Ek Ratanaruang film, which could mark it as a specifically Thai film.

Pen-Ek has tried to position his films as both Thai and as appealing to a wider audience. According to an article in the *Bangkok Post*, Pen-Ek's films are 'more popular abroad than at home'.[28] Even in his first film, *Fun Bar Karaoke* (Thailand, 1997), Pen-Ek tried to cross over into relatively unknown territory by screening the film with English subtitles, described as 'clearly part of a self-conscious effort to position the work as an "art film", and to include Bangkok's large expatriate community in its implied audience, as well as to foster its partaking of a global art-film economy'.[29] This way of creating and marketing films goes against much of Thai film-making that has come before; as anthropologist Annette Hamilton writes: 'Thai films are seldom if ever made with the eye of an alien Other in mind.'[30] If Hamilton is correct in her assertion, then Pen-Ek's films seem to be created in a different mindset than many of the films made in Thailand.

Conclusion

As of this writing, Pen-Ek Ratanaruang's follow-up to *Last Life in the Universe*, titled *Invisible Waves*, is making the rounds of the festival circuit. The new film is again a collaboration with Christopher Doyle and Asano Tadanobu, and it was filmed in a wide range of locales, including Bangkok, Phuket, Macau and Hong Kong. Interestingly, the crew decided to film much more of the film than had originally been planned in Phuket following the disastrous tsunami that hit the region on 26 December 2004. According to Thailand's tourist agency, the film will 'publicize the beauty of the island to Thais and foreigners alike' and 'restore tourist confidence that Phuket is still safe'.[31] Even more so than *Last Life in the Universe*, *Invisible Waves* seems to be made with the gaze of an international audience in mind. Also, in another example of the transnational flow of filmic ideas, there are currently plans for a Hollywood remake of *6ixtynin9* (Thailand, 1999), one of Pen-Ek's previous films, to be directed by Jim Fall, who most recently helmed *The Lizzie McGuire Movie* (US, 2003). As many of *6ixtynin9*'s elements stem from Thailand's socioeconomic downturn of the late 1990s, it remains to be seen how well the film will translate into a US context.

Last Life in the Universe is just one of many pan-Asian films in existence. However, an analysis of this single film can serve as a case study to better understand the currents circulating around transnational Asian film more generally. By examining the details of the film in terms of production, acting and home video distribution, one can begin to see how such films can be received. Such transnational films will continue to be created and puzzled over. Although previous writings on the DVD have suggested that the format will lead to a rise in auteurist analysis,[32] through my present analysis I hope to have shown that this is not necessarily the case. By examining the different versions of DVDs of the same film, the auteurist conception of the director may be complicated and even somewhat lessened.

References

1 Acland, Charles A., *Screen Traffic: Movies, Multiplexes, and Global Culture* (Durham, NC: Duke University Press, 2003), p.47; emphasis in original.

2 Axmaker, Sean, '"The strangest cinematographer in the world": Christopher Doyle', *GreenCine.com*, 29 November 2004, <http://www. greencine.com/article?action=view&articleID=168> accessed 28 February 2005.

3   The names in this article follow Thai and Japanese naming conventions. In Thai, the given name precedes the family name, as in the West, but on subsequent references a person is generally referred to by his or her given name rather than the family name. In Japanese the family name precedes the given name, and a person is referred to on subsequent references by his or her family name.

4   Hunt, Bill and Doogan, Todd, *The Digital Bits: Insider's Guide to DVD* (New York: McGraw-Hill, 2004), p.51.

5   Silverman, Art, 'Surveying the Extras on DVD,' *All Things Considered*, National Public Radio, 25 February 2005, accessed online at <http://www.npr.org/templates/story/story.php?storyId=4514032>

6   Mead, Rebecca, 'The Marx Brother', *The New Yorker* (5 May 2003), p.42.

7   Brookey, Robert Alan and Westerfelhaus, Robert, 'Hiding Homoeroticism in Plain View: The *Fight Club* DVD as Digital Closet', *Critical Studies in Mass Communication* 19/1 (2002), pp.21–43.

8   Fiske, John, *Television Culture* (New York: Routledge, 1987).

9   Brookey and Westerfelhaus: 'Hiding Homoeroticism', p.23.

10 Cazdyn, Eric, *The Flash of Capital: Film and Geopolitics in Japan* (Durham, NC: Duke University Press, 2002), p.3.

11 Sukwong, Dome and Suwannapak, Sawasdi, *A Century of Thai Cinema*, trans. David Smith (London, Thames and Hudson, 2001), p.6.

12 Sukwong and Suwannapak: *A Century of Thai Cinema*, p.33.

13 Boonyaketmala, Boonrak, 'The Rise and Fall of the Film Industry in Thailand, 1897–1992', *East-West Film Journal* 6/2 (1992), p.63.

14 'About Us', *Cinemasia* website, last modified 28 September 2004, <http://www.cinemasia.co.th/aboutus.htm> accessed 2 May 2005.

15 'Five Star Production – Company Profile', *Fivestarent.com*, <http://www.fivestarent.com/aboutus/index.asp> accessed 18 April 2005.

16 'Hubert Bals Fund: Realizing Dreams', *FilmFestivalRotterdam.com*, <http://www.filmfestivalrotterdam.com/en/hubertbalsfund/article/33790.html> last modified 18 March 2005, accessed 18 April 2005.

17 Doyle, Christopher, *A Cloud in Trousers* (Santa Monica, CA: Smart Art Press, 1998), p.42.

18 Moller, Olaf, 'A Specter Called Knowledge', *Film Comment* 39/6 (Nov./Dec. 2003), p.62.

19 Macias, Patrick, *TokyoScope: The Japanese Cult Film Companion* (San Francisco: Cadence Books, 2001), p.230.

20 Please note that this is not a comprehensive list of all of the *Last Life* DVDs available; for instance, it does not take into account the Japanese Region 2 (NTSC), the Thai Region 3 (PAL), or the Hong Kong Region 3 (NTSC) discs.

21 Doyle: *A Cloud in Trousers*, p.37.

22   Knee, Adam, 'Gendering the Thai Economic Crisis: The Films of Pen-Ek Ratanaruang', *Asian Cinema* 14/2 (Fall/Winter 2003), p.102.

23   Asano's interview is in Japanese, subtitled in English and Thai, although there is also a brief on-set scene that shows Asano taking direction from Pen-Ek in English.

24   Rithdee, Kong, 'Strange Cruise', *Bangkok Post*, 8 April 2005, <http://www.bangkokpost.com/en/Realtime/08Apr2005_real62.php> accessed 27 April 2005.

25   Parker, Deborah and Parker, Mark, 'Directors and DVD Commentary: The Specifics of Intention', *The Journal of Aesthetics and Art Criticism*, 62/1 (2004), p.15.

26   Fuchs, Cynthia, 'Last Life in the Universe', *PopMatters.com*, 14 April 2005, <http://popmatters.com/film/reviews/l/last-life-in-the-universe-dvd.shtml> accessed 22 April 2005.

27   Brown, Todd, 'Last Life in the Universe DVD Specs!', *Twitchfilm.net*, 22 November 2004, <http://www.twitchfilm.net/archives/2004/11/last_life_in_th.html> accessed 22 April 2005.

28   Rithdee: 'Strange Cruise'.

29   Knee: 'Gendering the Thai Economic Crisis', p.107.

30   Hamilton, Annette, 'Cinema and Nation: Dilemmas of Representation in Thailand', *East-West Film Journal* 7/1 (1993), p.102.

31   'Movie to be Shot Almost Entirely in Phuket', *PhuketIndex.com*, 2 April 2005, <http://www.phuketindex.com/phuket-news/2005-04/phuket-news-2005-04-02-01.htm> accessed 2 May 2005.

32   Brookey and Westerfelhaus: 'Hiding Homoeroticism', and Barlow, Aaron, *The DVD Revolution: Movies, Culture, and Technology* (Westport, CT: Praeger, 2005).

10

David Scott Diffrient

From *Three Godfathers* to *Tokyo Godfathers*: Signifying Social Change in a Transnational Context

Having earned worldwide acclaim for his cerebral pop-thriller *Perfect Blue* (Japan, 1997) and his postmodernist mock-biopic *Millennium Actress* (Japan, 2002), Kon Satoshi is today recognised as one of the most visionary film-makers in Japan, an anime auteur whose penchant for narrative reflexivity, chronotopic complexity and generic hybridity puts his work on a par with that of Miyazaki Hayao, Takahata Isao, Oshii Mamoru and Ōtomo Katsuhiro. Kon's follow-up to those critically lauded films, *Tokyo Godfathers* (2003) is his most accessible feature to date, a heartwarming tale of three homeless vagabonds who individually undergo psychological transformations and collectively achieve a kind of emotional catharsis after finding and nurturing an abandoned baby in the days between Christmas and New Year's Eve. Indeed, this allegorical picaresque, which sweeps us along with its unconventional heroes through shadowy districts of snow-covered Tokyo, appeals to connoisseurs of the genre as well as anime neophytes, drawn more to story development and character depth than to fetishistic displays of cyber-technology and misogynistic representations of female sexuality.

While *Tokyo Godfathers* certainly satisfies in terms of its realistic yet sometimes fantastical depiction of finely wrought characters, equally remarkable is the film's intertextual density. Although the writer-director has stated in interviews that his ideas come from the quotidian world in which he lives, even a cursory glance at Kon's oeuvre reveals a thickly tangled network of cross-cultural references – antecedent texts that suggest a truly transnational array of audiovisual material drawn from Asian, European and American contexts. *Tokyo Godfathers* alone includes direct references to literary icons like John Donne and Fyodor Dostoevsky, as well as musical compositions such as Rodgers and Hammerstein's *The Sound of Music*, Salvatore Adamo's *Mauvais Garcon*, Handel's *Hallelujah Chorus* and Beethoven's *Ninth Symphony*, the latter rendered in a reggae style by sound designer Suzuki Keiichi. It also indirectly alludes to earlier Japanese films such as Yamanaka Sadao's *Priest of Darkness* (1936), a Hara Sestuko vehicle set in the yakuza-filled underworld of Tokyo, which was itself inspired by John Ford's *Three Bad Men* (US, 1926) and Misumi Kenji's *Fight, Zatoichi, Fight* (Japan, 1964), the eighth entry in the perennial chambara series and starring Katsu Shintaro as the blind swordsman who rescues a baby after its mother has been killed.

This essay explores the intertextual dynamics between a group of Hollywood films based on Peter B. Kyne's 1913 western novel *The Three Godfathers* and Kon Satoshi's animated recycling of that oft-adapted literary property. Concerning a trio of outlaws who find a newborn baby in the desert, Kyne's book was the source of no fewer than six stateside cinematic adaptations, including William Wyler's *Hell's Heroes* (US, 1930) and, most famously, John Ford's *Three Godfathers* (US, 1948). Each of these renderings is steeped in Christian symbolism, with prayers frequently passing across parched lips and the town of New Jerusalem conveniently serving as a locus of racial homogeneity and moral redemption. If it lacks the cross-shaped cacti and Wild West iconography found in its American predecessors, *Tokyo Godfathers* nevertheless retains strong religious overtones, sending its destitute characters down a providential path of chance encounters and *deus ex machina* coincidences. After attending a Christmas nativity play at a soup kitchen, the film's three 'magi substitutes' – Gin (a grizzled dipsomaniac who left his family due to gambling debts), Hana (a towering ex-drag queen who always wanted to be a mother), and Miyuki (a 16-year-old runaway whose policeman father has been tracking her whereabouts) – find an abandoned infant in a Shinjuku dumpster. The baby girl, whom Hana christens 'Kiyoko', is referred to as a 'messenger of God'. She, along with the singing of 'Silent Night' and the sudden appearance of Hispanic immigrants, are just a few of the many elements in the Japanese text that gesture toward Kyne's novel.

Despite its status as a cross-cultural remake, *Tokyo Godfathers* is not simply a secondary text paying homage to a canonical 'original', but rather a re-conceptualised update of a literary property that shifts the syntactical operations of its basic plot into new settings peopled with significantly different characters. By replacing the American film's original milieus (the Mojave Desert and Death Valley) and trio of bank robbers with a contemporary, snow-covered metropolis filled with downtrodden and demoralised individuals who undergo dramatic changes, this animated rendering illustrates the inherently trans-formative nature of the remake at diegetic and extradiegetic levels. Much like the way in which the three main 'dumpster divers' in *Tokyo Godfathers* transform into responsible human beings attentive to the welfare of the newborn baby, Kyne's tale of western outlaws can be said to have 'matured' thanks to Kon's more progressive film. A western saga with religious overtones, *The Three Godfathers* has grown from a hermetic depiction of antiquated race relations and gender politics into a sensitive portrayal of marginalised people, in the process transform-ing from a national tale set in the Old West to a *transnational* narrative that collapses temporal and spatial coordinates, while blending genres and genders in a promiscuous way.

A mixture of social commentary, whimsical comedy and melodra-matic pathos, the film – as a 'true' yet 'disguised' remake[1] – thus uproots the semantic fixity of the Old West and relocates Kyne's story of pater-nalism, self-sacrifice and surrogate families in a more discursive field of cultural production and reception; one in which gender slippage, the representation of gays and lesbians, transnational mobility, and the social conditions and public apathy faced by the Japanese underclass figure prominently. In addition to its focus on both traditional and non-traditional family units, *Tokyo Godfathers'* emphasis on such themes as abandonment, protection, possession and recycling suggests that there are also textual solutions to the question of film adaptation, itself a form of inheritance requiring a degree of care, dedication and devotion not unlike that expressed by the film's three central characters. In a simi-lar vein, media scholars may take a similar journey in their hunt for the 'real' parents of this film – those antecedent texts like *Hell's Heroes* and *Three Godfathers* that likewise provide an intertextual bridge between Japan and the US.

What follows, then, is a brief assessment of the half-dozen or so thematically overlapping narratives spun out from Kyne's story, culmi-nating with a critical exploration of *Tokyo Godfathers*, a film that invites us not only to ruminate on the 'family resemblances' between texts that are *about* surrogate families, but also to speculate on the potentially lib-erating yet still limited sociopolitical outcomes of so much cultural mixing in terms of transnational East Asian cinema's ability to either cross, erase, or re-inscribe borders. Should this film in particular and Asian cultural productions in general be conceived of as the offspring of 'parental' texts from the West (a problematic concept to begin with)?

Or might the gender-specific term 'godfather' actually problematise such imperialistic notions by virtue of its ability to connote both proximity and distance, spiritual inheritance and creative appropriation?

More specifically, as individuals who are neither biological parents nor distant relatives, might the god*parents* (both male *and* female) in Kon's film, who frequently utilise English loan words (like 'homeless') to describe their situation, at least partially personify the obligatory aspects of adoption built into the process of adaptation, wherein narratives about radically transformed characters are seen as the principle means for adducing cultural distinctions based on the latter's willingness to take on new challenges (as caretakers for an abandoned infant), yet settle into socially defined roles (as mother, as father, as daughter, etc.)? Does *adaptation*, as a reworking of an antecedent text, automatically imply *adoption*, or the acceptance and implementation of certain normative codes, tropes and motivic elements? Or can that process be 'queered', so to speak, through the addition of new narrative elements, the likes of which have rarely been seen in animated films from Japan, much less live action westerns made during Hollywood's studio system era?

'I Want to Be Reborn!': Adapting to Animation, Animated Adaptations

Throughout the history of Hollywood, remakes have provided film-makers as well as the studios that employ them with a pragmatic means of exploiting new technological breakthroughs and screen practices. Profit-oriented film companies privilege the economic side of this 'industrial and economic genre', one that is capable of generating revenue from still-viable properties that have been acquired inexpensively. Certainly, this logic filtered into the rationale behind the making of John Ford's *Three Godfathers*, a film which gave John Ford his first opportunity to utilise 3-strip Technicolor, thus differentiating it from earlier big-screen versions of Peter Kyne's novel. While profit motives are a central component of the genre, other factors should be taken into consideration; first and foremost the interpretative aspects that connect film-makers, audiences and critics in a triadic relationship not unlike that between the three leads in all of the films, who each endeavour to make sense of the events which have thrust them into their roles as godfathers.

Such a relationship, I argue, extends even further into the extra-diegetic realm to connote 'the triangular notion of intertextuality' that

Thomas Leitch and other critics posit as the primary means of differentiating 'true remakes' from mere updates, homages and re-adaptations.[2] That is, while these latter varieties typically renounce 'any claim to be better than [the] original', the true remake 'deal[s] with the contradictory claims of all remakes – that they are just like their originals *only better*' [emphasis added]. As Leitch explains, 'since their rhetorical strategy depends on ascribing their value to a classic earlier text ... and protecting that value by invoking a second earlier [film] text as betraying it',[3] true remakes like *Tokyo Godfathers* engage in a complex dialogue with at least two pre-existing works – the literary property itself and an earlier adaptation. However, triangulating the relationship between Kyne's novel, Ford's film and Kon's revisionist take on their main themes proves to be difficult due to his use of animation, as well as the presence of several other texts – earlier adaptations and remakes that may 'compete directly and without legal or economic compensation with other versions of the same property'.[4] It is to those earlier versions that I now turn.

Kyne's novel, *The Three Godfathers*, provided the literary basis for several stateside adaptations, beginning with a same-titled *Bluebird Photoplays* production released in 1916. Written and directed by Edward J. Le Saint, this first feature-length cinematic imagining of Kyne's novel starred Harry Carey as Bob Sangster, a charismatic horse-thief-turned-bank-robber who makes up one-third of a trio of desperados that is transformed into an unlikely group of Good Samaritans after saving a baby from certain death in the desert. Three years later, Carey and co-star Winifred Westover appeared in another silent adaptation, *Marked Men* (US, 1919), directed by John (then known as Jack) Ford. This too revolved around such themes as crime, childbirth, ersatz families, self-sacrifice and redemption. Although basically playing the same character from the earlier version, Carey's jailbird is now named Cheyenne Harry. This five-reeler starred Carey as an escaped convict who meets up with two other outlaws at a mining camp. Together, the three eventually stage a bank robbery and find a dying mother and her child in the Mojave Desert, whom they 'adopt' and eventually carry back to 'civilization'.

Another Ford-directed motion picture, *Three Bad Men*, was theatrically released in 1926, and eventually inspired film-maker Yamanaka Sadao to make *Priest of Darkness* ten years later. Despite its title, *Three Bad Men* is based not on Kyne's story but rather on Herman Whitaker's 1917 novel *Over the Border*, although it too explores the themes of surrogate families brought together by unfortunate circumstances. One year after the release of *Three Bad Men* came an unacknowledged

adaptation, Frank Capra's *For the Love of Mike* (US, 1927), which borrowed only a few elements from Kyne's story (the three modern-day
godfathers come from different ethnic and religious backgrounds:
Jewish, Irish and German).

Two more versions of Kyne's novel would roll off the Hollywood
assembly line during the Great Depression – William Wyler's stark
Hell's Heroes (US, 1930) and Richard Boleslawski's equally austere *The
Three Godfathers* (aka *Miracle in the Sand*, US, 1936) – before Ford
returned to Kyne's story in 1948, making what is undoubtedly the best
remembered adaptation: *Three Godfathers*. This film stars John Wayne,
Harry Carey Jr. and Pedro Gregorio Armendáriz as bank-robbers who,
by carrying the infant to safety despite innumerable odds, learn valuable life lessons through self-sacrifice and are ultimately redeemed in
the eyes of the law. As stated above, all of the above mentioned renderings brim with religious symbolism and cater to an audience sympathetic to Judeo-Christian values and precepts. Each film also hinges
upon an act of theft – the robbing of a bank – that lays the foundation
upon which the outlaws' moral redemption can be formulated and
measured in relation to their inglorious pasts.

Of all of the adaptations and remakes made prior to *Tokyo
Godfathers*, however, Wyler's 1930 version and Ford's 1948 version
have best stood the test of time. *Hell's Heroes* in particular is remarkable for its technical virtuosity, as a compendium of deep-focus shots,
crane shots, tracking shots, whip-tilts and dissolves. After the camera
pans across the vast desert in the opening scene and settles on a sign
outside the town of New Jerusalem (reading 'A Bad Town for Bad
Men'), we are introduced to the main characters of the film: Bob
Sangster (Charles Bickford), 'Barbwire' Tom Gibbons (Raymond
Hatton) and 'Wild Bill' Kearney (Fred Kohler). José (José De La Cruz),
the fourth member of the bunch, dies early in the story, before having
a chance to become a godfather to the baby. After agreeing to take care
of the baby, whom they name William Robert Thomas Jr., they one by
one succumb to dehydration and death. After drinking arsenic-laced
water, Bob, the last of the men to die, does manage to amble back to
town during a Christmas Day church service. This final scene, showing him join the all-white congregation to the sound of church bells
ringing and 'Amen' being sung, is the most overtly religious scene
in a film filled with references to Jesus, Moses and other Biblical
figures.

Shot in and around the same areas where *Hell's Heroes* was filmed
(primarily Red Rock Canyon and Death Valley, California), *Three
Godfathers* is very different from Wyler's film, although both pivot on

such themes as family, paternity, personal redemption and community. Whereas *Hell's Heroes* is a pre-Hays Code film with intimations of sexual violence and desperate acts of suicide, culminating with an ironic yet sentimental coda (showing Bob drop dead in the middle of a church service), the 1948 version of the story features more sympathetic characters, including one (John Wayne's Bob) who actually survives at the end. And only in this more lighthearted version does the Mexican character Pedro 'Pete' Fuerte assist in delivering the baby, whom they collectively name 'Robert William Pedro Hightower'.

As might be expected of a film voted one of the '100 best conservative movies' by the *National Review*,[5] *Three Godfathers* adheres to certain normative conceptions of 'traditional family values'. Harry Carey's son, Harry Carey Jr., plays a character called 'The Abilene Kid', the first of the men to die. But before his death, he is seen reading not from the books of high literature owned by the doctor of philosophy in the 1936 version, but rather from two far more instrumental texts necessary for the 'proper' upbringing of the child: the Bible and a *Care for the Baby* book authored by Doc Meecham (both of which are referenced in the 1930 version as well). From the Bible he recounts the story of the 'infant in the manger' and the 'three wise men [who] came from the East'. Despite being made by an Irish Catholic director prone to sentimental narratives filled with miraculous events (like the sudden appearance of two mules toward the end that will carry Bob back to New Jerusalem), *Three Godfathers* is closer in spirit to *Tokyo Godfathers* than any of the other remakes and adaptations, and it is to this latter version of Kyne's story – a truly transformative yet equally quirky version *from the East* – that I now turn.

As stated earlier, *Tokyo Godfathers* kicks off with the singing of a yuletide favourite, 'Silent Night', which is also performed in the final scene of *Three Godfathers*. Kon's inclusion of this popular Christmas carol not only sets the stage for subsequent expressions of seemingly antiquated religious or spiritual devotion, but also gestures back toward both Ford's and Wyler's films, and, in doing so, foregrounds the cross-cultural, intertextual dimensions of the film. Actually, that musical number – sung in Japanese – is immediately preceded by a nativity play being performed on an outdoor stage by children, who announce: 'We have seen a star in the east. It told us the Son of God is born.' Directed toward the group of homeless people who have gathered in front of the stage, those words are then followed by a Christmas Eve church service, during which the pulpit-pounding preacher promises God's 'salvation to those who have nowhere to go'.

In a scene that recalls a similar moment at the beginning of John Ford's *Three Godfathers* (when Perley Sweet and his obliging wife provide hot coffee to the titular outlaws they have just met), soup kitchen volunteers feed the hungry men and women in attendance. Among those present are the three protagonists of the film: Gin, a bedraggled ex-cyclist who struggled to stay awake during the kids' performance; Hana, a talkative cross-dresser flummoxed by Gin's bad manners; and Miyuki, a sullen teenager who joined them on skid row six months ago, and who appears to have a combative relationship with her two older, more experienced companions.

Miyuki's mounting anger and dissatisfaction with her station in life are expressed in the next scene of the film, which shows her standing atop a tall building, looking out over the nocturnal cityscape, and spitting on the pedestrians below. This is her rather futile way of breaking free from the rigid hierarchy (*keigo*) that posits homeless people as the bottom-feeders of society, individuals to be looked down upon, pitied or scorned. By ascending to such heights, Miyuki momentarily inhabits a different field of social relations, an imaginary zone of temporary emancipation, and treats the well-to-do holiday shoppers below her with the same contempt that she has been dealt in her day-to-day encounters with fellow city-dwellers. The image of Miyuki emitting spittle while standing heroically on top of an office tower is juxtaposed with the billboard advertisement on the building's facade, one featuring an angel whose smile is like a beacon in the night. Together, these two shots simultaneously collapse and solidify distinctions between the earthy and the transcendent, the physical and the metaphysical, thereby inscribing an uncanny dialectic that will continue to haunt the film's realistic yet fantastical representations of homelessness and destitution.

This tension between high and low becomes even more pronounced in the scene that follows, featuring all three of the protagonists rummaging through trash bins for Christmas gifts. Among the loot they root out is a Dostoevsky novel and a set of World Literature for Children books. Although many of the Hollywood westerns adapted from Kyne's novel include references to literature and philosophy, only *Tokyo Godfathers* makes such explicit overtures toward 'high art' a means for interrogating and collapsing cultural distinctions, a slippage that furthermore spills over into the realm of gender. For it is during these same pre-credit moments of the film, prior to the trio's discovery of the baby in the trash bin, when Miyuki is forced to declare 'I am a woman!' This self-defensive declaration comes after Hana, a flamboyant, male-bodied cross-dresser, has told the tomboyish girl to close her legs while sitting and 'act like a lady'. Miyuki's angry response – that she *is* a woman (albeit a young and inexperienced one) – is met with feigned disbelief and actual sarcasm from Gin, who gropes her breasts in a nonsexual yet humiliating way. Ironically, these initial anxieties related to the public performance and successful maintenance of socially defined gender roles are the foundation upon which the three-some come to comprise a family of sorts, one that is challenged yet strengthened by the addition of a new member. That addition, of course, is the baby girl whom they find while digging through the trash.

Apparently abandoned by her biological mother, the infant, whom Hana christens Kiyoko (because *kiyo*, or *kiyoshi*, means 'pure'), is crying but in good health. She is also the last thing these homeless people need in their lives: another mouth to feed. However, the purity of the child will positively affect these three 'godparents', who are each seeking some sort of redemption related to their own biological families. Buried in her swaddling clothes is a handwritten message: 'Care for this child'. This command plus the mysterious key they find among the baby's things (including a birth certificate) suggest that Kiyoko will be the means for unlocking the secrets of their pasts and opening doors to their future, when they will be reunited with their loved ones and per-haps no longer seen as 'burdens on society'. The newborn child is thus not strictly a 'MacGuffin' or an interchangeable plot device, but rather a prime mover of the diegesis, driving the three godparents deeper into the underbelly of the city and ensuring the arrival of a cathartic end-ing that brings together missing family members and long-lost loves. Moreover, Kiyoko comes to embody the idea that remakes and adapta-tions, as the 'progeny' of pre-existing texts, require fostering from those who have come into a kind of inheritance and who are expected to abide by certain guidelines (like those put forth in a baby's manual that Miyuki finds) lest their attempts be deemed failures.

The uplifting finale, which unites missing family members and caps *Tokyo Godfathers* with a *Clockwork Orange*-inspired musical fanfare, has furthermore been anticipated by the film's opening credits, which arrive nearly five minutes into the narrative, just after the trio has found the baby. With the names of the film's crew members printed on the facades of commercial buildings and on the sides of city buses, this upbeat credit sequence sets a quirky tone for the otherwise discom-bobulating film, which seems to delight in undermining audience expectations as it swerves from pathos to Dickensian satire, from mor-bid melodrama to action adventure. Although shot through with heart-warming optimism and mystical whimsy, *Tokyo Godfathers* is quite sobering, indeed, harrowing, in its depiction of the social ostracism (*mura hachibu*) faced by Japan's increasingly visible 'silent minority' of homeless people, drifters, immigrant workers, bar girls (*hosutesu*), homosexuals (pejoratively known as *okama*) and other stigmatised groups. While the film does not delve very deeply into the politics of exclusion or the reasons why public apathy remains widespread in an era of neo-liberalism and multicultural awareness, it nevertheless makes a crucial intervention in contemporary debates about the status of so-called *rojo seikatsusha* (poverty-stricken street dwellers), shedding light on a side of urban life in modern Japan that is all-too-frequently left in the shadows, ignored or forgotten by most cultural producers. Although it is not the first anime film to treat the homeless in a respectful way,[6] *Tokyo Godfathers* still manages to go further than most earlier works in sensitively illustrating some of the unfortunate circumstances that might lead people to either a life of crime or destitution, all the while juxtaposing the extraordinary and the ordinary, the magical and the mundane, through a style that is rich in intertextual allusions.

Hana's earlier naming of the girl is just one of many imbedded references to John Ford's 1948 version, which not only similarly hinges upon the interwoven themes of possession, paternalism and self-sacrifice, but also highlights how the variety of appellations attached to individual characters (such as 'Brick-top' and 'The Abilene Kid' for the youngest member of the outlaws, William Kearney) might create anxieties about one's identity, especially for those who either strive to fit into certain socially defined gender roles or struggle to imitate their elders. Gin may call Hana 'a homeless homo', but he ultimately fails to fasten his transvestite companion to any one gendered designation that might delimit agency. In addition, the act of naming underscores Hana's own professed desire to 'feel like a mother', and by extension lends greater authority to Gin and Miyuki's assumed roles as 'father' and 'child' throughout the film, thus emphasising their status as a surrogate family.

However, their failure to emulate the 'perfect' middle-class family pictured inside the baby manual that Miyuki finds (a text reminiscent of Doc Meechum's instructional child-raising book in *Three Godfathers*) is a source of frustration compounded by the fact that the entire city is festooned with signs, posters and billboards celebrating bourgeois notions of domesticity and consumption. Indeed, the trio's many inadequacies and inability to successfully imitate a heteronormative ideal are mentioned on several occasions throughout the film, particularly during a moment when the foul smelling, physically unfit Gin admits that he is 'not an action movie hero', just a 'homeless bum'. This seems to be a coded message about the status of this Japanese remake, which opts to take creative departures from Kyne's original tale rather than being strictly imitative of a western film starring that most prototypically 'American' of action movie stars, John Wayne.

Yet another intertextual inscription can be found in the film's stylised opening credits, when Hana, holding the baby, stands in the middle of a street outside a video store (obliviously causing a traffic accident). Audiences familiar with Kon Satoshi's two earlier feature-length films, *Perfect Blue* and *Millennium Actress*, might catch fleeting glimpses of posters for these two animated motion pictures plastered on the store's windows behind Hana. Much like Alfred Hitchcock's cameo walk throughs in his own films, the inclusion of these poster images, not to mention the appearance of Kon's name on the trailer of a stalled truck (at the end of the opening credits), foregrounds an ironic detachment on the part of the auteur, who is at once acknowledging his own centrality to the project yet also undermining it by situating himself and his works in the world of commodities, which are 'owned' less by film-makers than by companies and consumers, or rather fans who take possession of the text in imaginative ways.

Not every fan, though, is expected to make sense of the many inter-textual allusions sprinkled throughout this film: references to 'high' literature and popular culture, as well as cinematic precursors that test an audience's familiarity with said texts. The key that is found alongside Kiyoko in the garbage bin (and which takes them to a storage locker at a train station where they find a photo of the mother and father) would thus seem to serve both narrative and hermeneutic purposes, allowing the film's protagonists to discover additional clues about the identity of the abandoned child's biological parents, while reminding us that our own storehouse of accumulated cultural knowledge is required to make sense of those clues, which often hinge upon one's recognition and understanding of intertextual allusions. While the sources for many references are fairly obvious, such as Hana's ostentatious performance of 'Climb Every Mountain' (from *The Sound of Music*) while trudging through the snow toward a cemetery, other moments are more subtly encoded and thus speak to a considerably smaller audience. Images of the trio putting a diaper on Kiyoko before feeding her allude to a few of the earlier Hollywood films based on Kyne's novel, especially Ford's version, which shows the three outlaws not only doing their best to save milk for the baby, but also smearing the boy with grease from a stage-coach axle (in lieu of olive oil). By momentarily focusing on the trio's footprints in the snow as they make their way to a graveyard, *Tokyo Godfathers* subtly suggests that motion pictures too can be seen as following a path already cleared by earlier productions, in this case

Three Godfathers (which features similar shots of tracks in the desert sand).

The key motif alone provides numerous opportunities to move beyond the 'primary text' into surrounding narratives, such as Kon's sophomore film *Millennium Actress*, which features similar iconography related to the unlocking and opening of doors. The key in *Tokyo Godfathers*, however, bears the number 1225, a marker of the Christmas holiday and a numeric inscription that re-emerges at certain junctures throughout the film. Given the preponderance throughout this prayer-filled film of Christian numerology and iconography (such as blonde-haired angels and nativity scenes), it might seem odd that other religious practices and spiritual motifs proliferate as well, including passing references to Buddhism and fleeting glimpses of Shinto architecture. However, not unlike the small yet prominent, bindi-like birthmark on Kiyoko's forehead, which might remind viewers of the Bodhisattva dot that symbolises wisdom and inner vision, the many seemingly contradictory references to both Western and Eastern philosophies and religions are rendered in an ornamental style, and thus, like so much pastiche, emptied of their *intended* meanings. They are surface signifiers, as artificial and depthless as the plastic baby Jesus doll used in the nativity scene and the tropical island imagery adorning the lockers at the train station, as well as the inside of Gin's makeshift *danboru*.

This is not to say, however, that such images are meaningless; rather, they take on *new* meanings that only begin to make sense once we learn that the 'mother' and 'father' whom the trio is searching for are *imposters*, no more real as parents than Gin, Hana and Miyuki, who may believe in 'Christmas miracles' and behave in ways that recall the three wise men from the New Testament, but who nevertheless reject social codes of 'proper' behaviour. Indeed, the trio's trek to a cemetery results not in any cathartic release of the emotions through mourning or ritual. It is simply another place in the city where they can scavenge through other people's things, the ancestral offerings left in memory of the dead that might be put to better use by these three, including bottles of milk (which they pilfer for the baby) and sake (which Gin takes for himself from a nearby gravesite).

From the cemetery they make their way to an entirely different place, Club Swirl, the upscale venue where a young bride-to-be (notably named Kiyoko) is being feted by her father, a mob boss whom the wandering trio had managed to rescue earlier. Due to an unfortunate series of events, the overweight crime lord, Kinschino, had been trapped under his own automobile as it began rolling backwards on an

icy incline. Because they saved him, Gin, Hana and Miyuki are invited
to a yakuza-filled wedding reception that introduces new genre elements into the film. Gangster iconography comes to the fore during the
film's most unexpected departure from Kyne's original story, a subplot
that beckons toward the aforementioned 1936 melodrama, *Priest of
Darkness*, yet also seems to belong in the macabre hit-man flicks made
by Kitano Takeshi. In this scene, after learning that the woman in the
picture is named Nishizawa Sachiko, and that her hostess name had
been Midori before she quit that job due to her pregnancy, the trio wit-
nesses a vendetta-style shooting. One of the waitresses serving cocktails
at the club fires a gun at the fat mob boss, whose life is spared thanks
to the brave bridegroom, Hiruta Mitsuo, who leapt into the path of the
three bullets. In the ensuing chaos, the waitress, a Latino wearing a wig
and maid's uniform, flees the scene, taking Miyuki and the baby with
him as human shields or hostages.

The Spanish-speaking 'assassin' eventually dumps the teenager off
at a nearby tenement flat, where a Latina sits nursing her own baby. She
has enough milk for two, though, and is shown feeding little Kiyoko
from her other breast. This shot is certainly loaded with allegorical sug-
gestiveness, reminding us that Kyne's original story has produced more
than one adaptation over the years, that it has indeed been the source
of nourishment for several works produced in different cultural and
national contexts. It is quickly revealed that this unnamed immigrant
woman has something in common with Miyuki. Both of them have
fathers who are policemen. This connection between the two young
women illustrates the many links that can be uncovered between very
different films – *Tokyo Godfathers*, *Three Godfathers*, and any of the
other versions of Kyne's tale. For example, in both the American and
Japanese versions, Latin Americans may be peripheralised, yet they
play pivotal roles in transmitting the theme of otherness, which defines
the outlaws' or outsiders' relationship to the larger community. Their
difference is made prominent primarily through language, much of
which goes un-translated or un-subtitled. Such intertextual links are
furthermore visually echoed in the image of two skyscrapers looming
above Tokyo. The shot of the twin towers, each joined to the other by
an elevated bridge, is therefore indicative of the double motif found
throughout *Tokyo Godfathers* (the two Kiyokos; the two lottery
winners; the mythological Red Devil and Blue Devil whose stories are
recounted by Hana; the Latina wet nurse and Gin's daughter, a hospital nurse, etc.), which contributes to the many parallels between otherwise disparate individuals. Moreover, because one of the conjoined
skyscrapers is slightly taller than the other, this frequently repeated

image suggests that a remake may stand next to an original, but often fails to measure up to it. *Tokyo Godfathers*, however, bucks that trend, and in many ways surpasses the cinematic and literary texts on which it is based, standing tall as a sign of Kon Satoshi's sophisticated treatment of serious themes and adult subject matter.

Thanks to the size of the skyscrapers, which Gin, Hana and Miyuki finally see during their search for the missing parents, the trio manages to find the former residence of Sachiko and her husband, pictured in the photograph they found in the locker. However, the photo of the family (showing the twin towers visible in the distance) does not match the current state of things, for all that is left of their house are the foundations and bits of rubble. Now a construction zone, the residence has been torn down and reduced to a pile of concrete and plywood, home to stray cats and little else. More details about Sachiko's troubled life are provided in this scene, which features a group of gossiping women explaining that the woman had to pay off her frequently inebriated husband's gambling debts, leading to the city's seizure of their house. This important piece of information, which had thus far been withheld, allows the audience to draw comparisons not only between Sachiko's story and Gin's own personal history of gambling (which contributed to the break-up of his family), but also between *Tokyo Godfathers* and the 1936 version of Kyne's novel, which includes a poker-playing scene that leads to financial ruin for one character.

By this time in the narrative, Gin has begun to spiral downward into self pity. Although Gin had earlier comforted a dying stranger in his temporary shelter, telling the old man that he is not trash, the alcoholic protagonist believes himself to be beyond redemption. Thinking that no one would care if he died in the gutter, Gin even states outright that he feels like 'living trash' – a sentiment that is seconded by a group of baseball bat-wielding punks. These teenaged hoodlums, who get their kicks (literally) by beating up the homeless, proudly announce 'Time for New Year's Eve clean up!' This emphasis on trash is later reiterated just after the midpoint of the film, when Gin finally encounters his estranged daughter, now a 21-year-old woman about to be married and working as a nurse at the hospital where Hana is being tended to. Attempting to explain his current profession to her, Gin states: 'I'm in recycling'.

For all of his failings, though, Gin becomes brave and resilient in the face of danger, switching into 'action movie hero' mode as he peddles a bicycle through Tokyo in pursuit of Sachiko, the woman who only pretended to be the baby's biological mother and who is, in his words, a 'fake'. This action sequence, which shows Gin on a stolen bike pursuing a truck containing the woman and the child, is slightly reminiscent of an early scene in *Three Godfathers*, when the Marshal's posse pursues the three robbers on horseback into the sun-baked desert. The nighttime chase in *Tokyo Godfathers*, though, culminates with the truck crashing through the window of a commercial building in the ward of Shinagawa, a moment that recalls an earlier scene in the film (when an out-of-control ambulance nearly killed Hana, Gin and Miyuki as it drove into a convenience store). Still carrying the baby, Sachiko climbs several flights of stairs to the top of the building, with all three of our heroes in hot pursuit. 'The baby is mine', she exclaims to Miyuki, the first to make it to the top. However, it is revealed during these penultimate moments that Sachiko's own baby died during childbirth, resulting in the emotionally distraught woman's theft of Kiyoko. 'I want to be reborn', she cries, stepping toward the ledge out of desperation. She stops short of falling, though, when she catches sight of her husband, who has just won 100,000 yen in the lottery.

A mixture of coincidence and contrivance, this revelation anticipates Gin's own impending discovery that he too is a lottery winner. Serendipity spreads throughout the film, and the 'meteorological miracle' (as one critic has described it) that intervenes when the baby falls from Sachiko's arms is just one of the many moments of magical realism which differentiate *Tokyo Godfathers* from its cinematic antecedents. After Hana saves the falling baby thanks to a blast of wind, a brief coda shows Kiyoko being returned to her rightful parents, a middle-class couple who have gathered at the hospital. Miyuki too reunites with her parents, who have seen the recent events play out on a televised news report. This cathartic, if implausible, ending of the film, which suggests that a 'benevolent deity' has been watching over the characters, recalls the denouement that brings *Three Godfathers* to a close: Bob, the only one to make it out of the desert alive with the baby, stumbles into the town of Welcome, Arizona, and is given a light sentence by the Marshal and his wife, who agree to look after the infant.

'A child never forgets its parents'. These words, spoken by Hana much earlier in the film, suggest that the film-makers who remake earlier texts are not likely to forget those things that drew them to the subject in the first place. Presumably, Kon Satoshi pursued this third feature-length film project not out of a desire to base his work on pre-tested material. It is more likely that he was drawn to the idea of a surrogate family brought together in times of desperation, a trio of individuals unlike any other characters ever seen in Japanese animation. Hana's allegorical words thus take on new meaning in light of the film's final scene, which shows Kiyoko purring in the arms of her *true* biological parents. Hana had 'always dreamed of being a mother to a little girl', remarking at one point: 'If the Virgin Mary was able to get pregnant, why not a transvestite?' Yet the ex-cabaret performer is willing to concede that maternal role to the girl's 'real' mother, a middle-class woman who appears with her husband in the final scene. The handover of the child to a more conventional family unit sits uncomfortably with the film's sympathetic yet frequently caricatured depiction of transvestite performances and queer identities. Indeed, the somewhat clichéd representation of Hana's histrionic outbursts of profanity and tears risks turning her more nurturing maternal instincts, not to mention her proclivity to compose haiku, into just another mode of performance.

And yet, for all of the film's possible shortcomings, not to mention Gin's casual usage of such potentially upsetting epithets as 'faggot' and 'homo' when mocking Hana's maternal instincts (recalling Bob's derision of the Marshal's 'right pretty name' Perley B. Sweet in Ford's 1948 film), *Tokyo Godfathers* still surpasses earlier versions of the story in terms of its sociopolitical awareness of marginalised communities. What had been mere subtext in the earlier adaptations and remakes of Kyne's story, or what had seemed like textual anomalies (as when, in *Hell's Heroes*, the newly crippled 'Barbwire' Tom states: 'I ain't interested in no woman, not now I ain't!'), are brought to light in a decisive, perhaps subversive, way in Kon's film. Although gender slippage is very much a central component in all of these tales, which force men to adopt a more maternal attitude toward child-rearing, only through this latest, Japanese version can we retroactively extrapolate from such moments a sign of things to come.

In the 1936 *Three Godfathers*, Walter Brennan's illiterate character Gus initially refers to the male baby as a 'she'. In changing the sex of the child from male to female, Kon has inherited Gus's tendency to mix up gendered identities while taking such apparently innocent confusions to another level, one where it seems completely reasonable for a gruff old man like Gin to be tended to (like a baby) by a group of transsexuals after his violent run-in with juvenile delinquents. While playing with the constructed nature of such socially defined terms as 'masculine' and 'feminine', Kon is able to cast light on Japanese culture's ambivalent attitudes toward those who flit between the two, inhabiting a liminal zone not unlike that occupied by the three main protagonists in *Tokyo Godfathers*.

In both the 1916 and 1919 silent versions of Kyne's story, Harry Carey's protagonist is the only member of a three-man group who manages to survive the desert heat and make his way to town with the baby, where he finds an initially unsympathetic sheriff waiting for him, ready to put the outlaw back behind bars. However, each film ends not only with the romantic reunion of the hero and his sweetheart, a former dance-hall hostess named Ruby Merrill, but also with the lawman bestowing his gratitude upon Carey's character. Having realised that the dead woman in the desert was his sister, the sheriff thanks him for saving his nephew and obtains a pardon from the governor, thus ensuring the reconstitution of a heterosexual couple. In contrast, the 1936 version of the story ends not with the image of a couple holding the baby, but instead with a medium shot of a woman named Molly being given the child from Bob as he finally succumbs to death in the middle of a church. This image of one person passing the baby to another person (who, in this case, walks toward the camera holding the infant until it takes up the bulk of the frame in close-up) resonates with the idea that Kon has inherited a literary property that has been nurtured by several earlier godparents.

In this way, the interwoven themes of life and death assume extra-diegetic meaning, insofar as something old must pass away in order for something new to rise up and take its place. Just as the old man being looked after by Gin during an early scene in *Tokyo Godfathers* takes a final swig of alcohol and bids 'Sayonara' only to 'return from the dead' (if only temporarily), Kyne's story keeps coming back to life, albeit in different generic guises and cultural contexts. In this latest version, sandstorms have become snowstorms; dance-hall girls have been replaced by drag queens; discussions of the zodiac and horoscope have given way to conversations about AIDS. These and other 'surface' modifications are not merely examples of cosmetic surgery: they are textual transformations that reflect social and geopolitical shifts in an era of transnational flows. The remake is therefore a significant type of cultural praxis that generates questions about such things by way of juxtapositions and comparisons. Are certain texts and social values untranslatable? Does cultural hybridisation naturally result from a remake that pulls together vastly different narrative elements and generic codes? Where does creative invention end and parodic imitation begin? How does one distinguish between these and other acts of cultural appropriation, such as transculturation, when meanings – like movies – are in continuous flux, defined only in relation to historical contexts that are themselves shifting due to critical reevaluations, as well as new consumption patterns resulting from the flow of material goods across the Pacific?

Of course, transcultural flows are not unidirectional. In the past two decades, Japanese anime has become increasingly popular in Europe and North America, where diverse audiences eagerly consume such feature-length motion pictures as Ōtomo Katsuhiro's *Akira* (Japan, 1988), Takahata Isao's *Only Yesterday* (Japan, 1991), Oshii Mamoru's *Ghost in the Shell* (Japan, 1995), and Miyazaki Hayao's *Spirited Away* (Japan, 2001). Although this recent phenomenon might be linked to earlier manifestations of Japanophilia in European and American contexts, centred around Western fans' fondness for the *Godzilla* or *Zatoichi* series of films produced in the 1950s and 1960s (and later the vogue for such things as sushi bars and karaoke clubs in the 1980s and beyond), I am inclined to read it as further indication that East Asian cinema transcends 'geographical, cultural and theoretical boundaries', while challenging 'existing conceptions ... such as textuality, authorship, Hollywood domination, third cinema and national allegory' (to quote the editors of this volume).

Slightly modifying John Donne's famous adage, I wish to close by saying that no film is an island, entire of itself. Every motion picture is a piece of the larger, ever growing continent of cultural productions that simultaneously resist essentialist or reductive analysis, and provoke a transnational imaginary and intertextual unconscious. Donne's actual words – 'No man is an island' – provide us with a simple expression that speaks volumes about our intrinsically linked lives, regardless of geographical distance or cultural barriers. It should come as no surprise, then, that Hana, the haiku-composing transsexual character in *Tokyo Godfathers*, invokes the spirit of this seventeenth-century English poet during a moment of epiphany. As a cross-cultural remake of several pre-existing texts, *Tokyo Godfathers* can be situated both inside and outside the overlapping spheres of Japanese manga and anime production and consumption. Perhaps even more so than the above mentioned films by Ōtomo, Oshii and Miyazaki, *Tokyo Godfathers* provides audiences with the analytical tools necessary to extract meanings from the 'fabulous mix of culture' that currently defines the relationship between East and West, even as that binary is proving to be less an actual or even discernible thing than an imaginary construct, like something in a movie.

References

1   Druxman, Michael B., *Make it Again, Sam: A Survey of Movie Remakes* (South Brunswick: A.S. Barnes, 1975).
2   Leitch, Thomas, 'Twice-Told Tales: The Rhetoric of the Remake', *Literature/Film Quarterly* 18/3 (July 1990), p.147.

3   Leitch: 'Twice-Told Tales', p.147.
4   Verevis, Constantine, 'Re-viewing Remakes', *Film Criticism* 21/3 (Spring 1997), p.5.
5   *National Review*, 46/20 (24 October 1994), p.53.
6   For instance, Studio Ghibli auteur Takahata Isao's *Grave of Fireflies* (Japan, 1988) features a scene in which one particularly unlikeable character muses: 'It is disgusting having these bums around'.

11

Theresa L. Geller

Transnational Noir: Style and Substance in Hayashi Kaizo's *The Most Terrible Time in My Life*

On the cover of the recently released *Kino* DVD of Hayashi Kaizo's film, *The Most Terrible Time in My Life* (1994), is a black and white photograph of Japanese star Nagase Masatoshi standing in front of a movie theatre, with a hand covering one eye and above him a neon sign attached to the theatre that beams 'CinemaScope' high over his head. Filmed in glossy black and white, the movie is both a homage to and critical revision of the American film noir of the 1940s as well as a tribute to its epigone, the French New Wave. This appropriation of noir sensibilities moves beyond surface encoding to naming its detective protagonist Hama Maiku; 'my real name', as the character states in each instalment of the Hama trilogy. This parodic citation of Mickey Spillane's Mike Hammer sets in motion a simulacral world where the style and substance of 'B' movies have gone global. The political impulse to recast noir motifs, such as the hard-boiled detective, corrupt police and the chaotic underworld of crime that eludes the law, in contemporary Yokohama grounds the narrative in the wake of cultural and economic changes wrought by the Second World War. This undercurrent of social nihilism, from the loss of the war, the West's enforced reconstructions of Japanese society, and the traumatising impact of the atomic bombs dropped on Hiroshima and Nagasaki haunts Hayashi's noir sensibility. Yet, by centring the narrative on the ultimately doomed friendship between the Japanese detective and the Taiwanese 'gangster', a complex history of cultural affinities, colonial antagonisms and shifting international power relations are set in motion that are anything but black and white.

Its focus on the bond between the hip detective Hama and the Taiwanese 'illegal' immigrant and gang member, Yang Hai Ping, whom he befriends, translates the couple of 1940s noir into an allegory of postmodern geopolitical tension. The film's citational practices – significantly placing Hama's office in a movie theatre – underscore cinema as a privileged forum for the aesthetic mediation of epistemological crisis in modern Japan, a Japan, as the commentary on the DVD package makes plain, 'with vanishing borders'. The fascination with American style – not just in Hollywood's glossy, wide-screen genre films, but the generalised Westernisation of Japanese culture that followed the loss of the war – becomes inseparable from the substance of transnational violence and loss of 'brotherhood' the film represents. Such contradictions resonate in the image of the neon 'CinemaScope' sign, signalling a moment in Hollywood history when films were meant to be 'larger than life', that is dwarfed by the giant red title, 'The Most Terrible Time in My Life'. Nagase Masatoshi's covered eye, then, suggests a monocular vision that characterises Japan's ambivalent modes of national and cultural representation. Film noir's stylistic elements of oblique lines, chiaroscuro lighting, compositional tension, and obtuse framing and point-of-view, highlight the irreducible tensions and conflicts that are the stuff of contemporary transnationalism.

Despite their bleak and increasingly surreal themes, Hayashi's films were quite popular in Japan, and led to a television series. The trilogy's popularity, however, is less surprising when compared to the fame of other Japanese films, exemplified by the unsurpassed success of Miyazaki Hayao's *Princess Mononoke* (1997), which refuse to 'provide a happy form of closure'.[1] Hayashi's Hama series falls in line with other films that reject a conventional approach to Japanese history and stand as 'contrast to the idealized myths of harmony, progress, and unproblematic homogeneous Japanese people (*minzoku*) ruled by a patriarchal elite that held sway in Japanese textbooks and postwar Japanese history'.[2] Hayashi's films, though a very different type of genre film from the animated quest-romance of *Mononoke*, echo its 'vision of cultural dissonance ... (b)y confronting and even subverting traditional notions of the past ... to provide a provocative, heterogeneous, and often bleaker view than the conventional vision of Japanese history and identity'.[3] Although set in Yokohama's historical present, *Terrible Time's* stylisation evokes the past to stress the historical underpinnings that inform the present day scenario, a scenario of explicit cultural dissonance in which the history of Japanese colonisation is confronted. *Terrible Time* centres on the belated return of the postcolonial, which exposes the limits of Japan's post-war cultural mythologies. Indeed, the film presents several Taiwanese characters: Yang, his brother De Jian, and Hama's first and unrelated client Kim. The proliferation of the nation's 'Others' implies the endless 'repetition or return of the postcolonial migrant', whose very presence works 'to alienate the holism of history'.[4] In that the substance of Hayashi's film concerns Japan's own 'history that happened elsewhere, overseas', the presence of Taiwanese immigrants in Japan 'does not evoke a harmonious patchwork of cultures, but articulates the narrative of cultural difference which can never let the national history look at itself narcissistically in the eye'.[5]

At first, the film appears as a celebration of style – a hip nostalgia for the 'cool' aesthetic of noir. The Hama trilogy has in fact been explicitly marketed as simple postmodern pastiche, as the back of the second DVD puts it: 'a dazzling crime film dripping with retro gloss and irreverent post-modern cheek'. Yet, each film's unique affective intensity quickly unseats the cool detachment the films, at first, seem to exhibit. In other words, these films move from (and through) both parody and pastiche to *refiguration*:

> refiguration takes formal elements of past styles and brings them
> forward into a contemporary context, resulting in a sometimes
> disquieting synthesis of past form and present context. At work is a
> process of refiguration, or conversion: the past form is converted into a
> sign of the present, while the present is historicized through its
> containment within a formal element taken from the past.[6]

Terrible Time refigures post-war cinema's 'world of existential, epistemological, and axiological uncertainty' to reflect on the disorientation of contemporary geopolitics.[7]

The film begins above and behind a man, who is walking through the 'Western Japanese Cinema Center', the sign for which is framed in the establishing shot as he passes beneath it. This spatial designation takes on deeper meaning than simple geographical demarcation, as the conjunction of 'Western' and 'Japanese' names the fungible boundary between the East and West that the film examines. This boundary is ironically signalled as the man passes Hama's Nash Rambler parked in front of the theatre. Further underscoring the hybridisation between the West and the East, the man – who we now see to be a nervous Chinese man – is told by the ticket taker: 'Today's movie is an American film.' He enters the chiaroscuro-lit office abutting the projectionist's booth, introducing himself as 'Kim'. Kim explains that he has turned to Hama because 'the police are cold to foreigners'. In response, Hama enters the frame in a two-shot, which appears to be lit from a single source except for the strobe effect of the projector bleeding into Hama's office, and offers Kim a cigarette, leaning in close to light both cigarettes. This intimate gesture recalls heightened film noir moments in which the protagonist is drawn in by the femme fatale. Because their intimacy is based on an economic exchange that grants the detective a cool detachment, the scene is citational rather than critical. Hama's position as a paid detective defines 'his role as cultural go-between, of an individual willing to bridge the ideological chasm between the civilized and the criminal for whoever can pay his [fifty thousand yen a day]'.[8] However, the film juxtaposes this scene to the relationship with Yang to stress that Hama's 'role as cultural go-between' is not founded on economic exchange, but rather is in the tradition of 'the hard-boiled detective [who] ... solves his cases with the personal commitment of somebody fulfilling an ethical mission'.[9] Significantly, this act of intimacy with Kim becomes a placeholder for the ethical commitments Hama will come to represent.

As Tom Conley has suggested: 'When neo-noir alludes to the past, whether innocuously or obsequiously, unlike commemorative genres, it invites a critical and interpretive relation.'[10] It is this critical or interpretive relation that motivates transnational noir. *Terrible Time* at first appears to be obsequious in its self-conscious engagement with film noir, replicating 'the clearest manifestation of American Expressionism ... the successful marriage of the *film noir* style and the widely popular hard-boiled detective story'.[11] Indeed, the film's debt to both generic and stylistic elements is overtly acknowledged in the photos hanging in Hama's office. As Kim enters Hama's office, which is too darkly lit to make out the decor, much less its period, the single source light that encircles Kim also lights three framed pictures on Hama's wall: an image of Humphrey Bogart, signed 'Sam Spade'; a sketch of Shishido Jô (who himself uses the symbol of the spade as a character for his anglicised name); and a still of Jeanne Moreau from *Elevator to the Gallows* (France, 1957). Although each image indexes a noir form – American Expressionism, French New Wave and Japanese crime drama – taken together, they suggest the pre-existing internationalism of noir's generic and visual language. The film exploits the implicit hybridity of noir to establish a critical relation to it.

The film restages film noir's classic scenario of the client engaging the detective to set this historical relation against the determinants of the present. That this scene with Kim in the office is a prologue is underscored by the fact that it precedes the title and its single credit. Opposed to the winking, self-reflexive tone of the prologue, what follows the title sequence is a critical revision of film noir to reflect contemporary transnational politics. The scene following Kim's office visit is in effect the start of the plot – at the mah-jong parlour set clearly in today's Yokohama. Hama is gambling with his friends when he meets Yang Hai Ping, who is a waiter there. Yang takes their order, having trouble with the Japanese. The kindness of Hama's friends in simplifying their order, and encouraging applause when Yang eventually gets the order correct, is inversely reflected in the other occupied table's response to Yang's trouble with the language. As Hama's table looks on, the Japanese man (who is later revealed to be a yakuza member) at the other table stands up from his table to confront Yang, threatening him, demanding: 'You're in Japan; learn Japanese.' Hama's friends comment that 'things are heating up ... better stay out of it', as the yakuza slaps Yang. When Hama catches a glimpse of a hidden gun in Yang's waistband for which he appears to be reaching in response to the yakuza's escalating threats, he immediately jumps in between the men to stop Yang from using the gun, only to turn around and have his pinky finger sliced off. The quick-paced editing stops, brought to a halt by the stilled shot of the fallen finger lying on the floor, which is followed by what appears to be a jump cut to a shot of a panting but unmoving dog. Following the dog who has ran off with the finger down to street level, the friends are filmed from the dog's perspective as they coax the dog to drop the finger with a piece of meat. The scene ends with the sound of the dog barking.

This scene sets the tone of the film as one which pinballs between tense violence and black humour, between homage and parody. Indeed, the castration metaphor of the cut-off finger has such blatant psychosexual implications that they seem to invite a level of parodic self-mocking. However, there is a notable resignification of psychosexual imagery inherited from film noir, in which the circuit of desire initiated by the appearance of the femme fatale is reworked as transnational Otherness. The scene in the parlour plays on fundamental noir tropes; Yang is to all appearances the victim in need of rescuing by the detective hero. Yet, Yang, like so many gun-toting femmes fatales before him, is 'armed', his demureness and subservience a screen for his phallic power. The hard-boiled detective is in turn castrated in the attempt to 'rescue' the supposed victim. The sexual anxieties manifest in film noir are tied to the ideological wake of the war: 'whether considered a genre or a style, the films circumscribed as noir are seen as playing out negative dramas of postwar masculine trauma and gender anxiety brought on by wartime destabilization of the culture's domestic economy'.[12] By invoking these, *Terrible Time* traces contemporary anxieties about Japan's porous borders to the traumatic impact of the Second World

War that continues to haunt Japan and its 'friends'. Central to the film's critical noir strategies is this reworking of the femme noire as post-colonial Other, in relation to the detective as a culturally-coded dyad; replacing the gender anxieties of classical noir is the Otherness of cultural and national difference.

The relationship between Yang and Hama is overdetermined by the relationship between Taiwan and Japan, a relationship acknowledged throughout the film. The historical affinity between the two countries is grounded in 'a shared history, which began when Taiwan became the first colony of Japan; common values; economic ties; strategic alignment; and political and social networks'.[13] The film's narrative arc is built around the characters' burgeoning friendship against the wishes of those aligned with the national interests, either the corrupt Japanese police or the Chinese gang members who warn Yang, 'friendship ... can be dangerous'. Throughout the film, Hama's closest companions ask 'why do you care so much?' and 'why are you so taken with this Taiwan guy?', to which Hama responds: 'there's something about him'. Indeed, this bond at the centre of the film reflects a strengthening of transnational ties, particularly in the 1990s; the 'friendship associations ... between Japanese and Taiwanese parliamentarians strengthened despite protest from Beijing'.[14] That this film was made in cooperation with the government of Taiwan lends some credence to the film as political allegory. Although the film is set in the 1990s, its noir style links its narrative to the years between 1945 and 1958, in which a dramatic restructuring of Asia took place.

Situating this friendship in the bleak and fatalistic tones of film noir, particularly as a refiguration of the desire and ambivalence that draw the hard-boiled detective to the femme fatale, suggests the complicated and troubled relationship between the two countries. By transposing sexual anxieties with transnational tensions in its neo-noir context, *Terrible Time* does not simply reflect but rewrites the historical past in the present. Homi Bhabha argues:

> the enunciation of cultural difference problematizes the binary division of past and present, tradition and modernity, at the level of cultural representation and its authoritative address. It is a problem of how, in signifying the present, something comes to be repeated, relocated and translated in the name of tradition, in the guise of a pastness that is not necessarily a faithful sign of historical memory but a strategy of representing authority in terms of the artifice of the archaic.[15]

This artifice is highlighted in the film's noir stylisations, while the substance of its narrative is set in the present. What I am suggesting is that the structure of noir symbolisation appropriated by the film works to translate and rehistoricise its signs in order to fit the contours of cultural difference. Specifically, the film refuses to be faithful to the power relations that gird classic film noir by rearranging the subjective qualities associated with noir's cast of characters and, in doing so, subvert the ideological assumptions on which the genre relies. The detective is no longer so hard-boiled and his constitutive partner is no longer his Other as much as his *brother*, whose criminal transgressions are seen from a much more sympathetic standpoint.

Yang is both narratively and visually coded in ways quite similar to noir's original femme fatale. Hama officially meets Yang outside the doctor's office, after having his finger reattached. They are filmed close together while Hama reassures Yang that it was not his fault, but warns him against using his 'little toy' and taps Yang's gun, still hidden under his belt. By brushing off the danger of Yang's little toy, he is placed in a feminised relation to Hama. This is underscored by the closing shots: when Yang asks his name, Hama looks directly into the camera in a shot-return-shot sequence that sutures the audience into Yang's position, strengthening the empathy already established from his victimisation in the previous scene. The return shot frames Yang's smiling face in close-up and soft key lighting. The perfectly symmetrical framing of Yang is used only one other time, significantly in the narrative flashback of De Jian's meeting of his wife, Huang Bai Lan, at the brothel. In his relationship with Yang, Hama 'loses the distance that would enable him to analyze the false scene and to dispel its charm; he becomes the active hero confronted with the chaotic, corrupt world, the more he intervenes in it, the more involved in its wicked ways he becomes'.[16] But what makes the film a critical revision of the noir form is its indictment of the historical origins of the 'corrupt world' rather than personify it in an individual.

Neither brother is demonised, despite the fact that the film shows their violence, because Hayashi's film places their actions in a larger context. It does so by setting two of film noir's genres in dialogic relation – the hard-boiled detective and the gangster film. Because the film utilises most, if not all, of the features of film noir, from flashback and voice over, to investigative structure and femme fatale, we are provided a proliferation of points of view that indicate a complex social context that is both cross-cultural and trans-historical.[17] The film implements multiple framing devices to refigure noir thematics in terms of the post-war restructuring of East Asia. In fact, the chronological and ideological middle of the film speaks to this directly. In Hama's search, a story of 'yakuza', 'illegal aliens' and violent crime is articulated, reflecting the ideological terminology of the nation state. Against this is the brothers' narrative, which is literally cast as the negative of the official story. When Yang meets with his contacts and is told to kill his brother, De Jian, there is a close-up on his face and the film image fades to a negative still, reversing the black and white contrast. This cuts to an image of the countryside of Taiwan, where two young boys are shown hungrily eating food that they apparently stole. This is followed by another silent scene of the adult brothers, returning from a clearly more violent crime, fading out with an image of Yang remorsefully washing blood from his hands. This flashback aligns the brothers with Taiwan itself in contrast to Hama's own synecdochic relationship to Yokohama. The fusion of the Yakuza gangster film with the hardboiled detective genre articulates the ways in which global monetary circuits have deterritorialised national and cultural borders.

Yet, it is for love and not money that De Jian switches gang allegiances, allowing him to become Yamamoto-san, 'the family man'. De Jian's doubled name, one Taiwanese, one Japanese, is one of the several signifiers of hybridity the film presents. Although De Jian's gang is referred to as the 'Black Dogs', they call themselves the 'New Japs', because it is made up of Chinese and South Korean immigrants naturalised as Japanese citizens. Unknown to Hama, Yang is a member of the Dragon Union, come to assassinate his own brother for 'turning his back on China', as his contact describes it. After Hama is brutally beaten by the 'New Japs', he is lectured by his 'mentor', Shishido Jô (the famous Japanese actor who goes by his real name in the film). Shishido informs him that Kano, the South Korean leader of the 'New Japs', has ordered the hit on their own assassin, De Jian, in order to 'restructure Asia', in effect starting a gang war between the Black Dogs and the Dragon Union. This intricate plot structure suggests the equally complex historical restructuring of Asia following the war. Underscoring the historical underpinnings of the film's conceit, the scene in which Shishido provides the central exposition frames the concern with the 'restructuring of Asia' as a generational issue. Shishido, himself an icon of early post-war Japanese crime films, tells Hama that 'I am too old to play Dad', and warns Hama not to get involved. Hama angrily replies that he does not 'need permission'. The two embody Japanese generational positions with regards to Taiwan. The scene ends with Shishido taking his leave, with a military salute with his cane. He represents the post-war position informed by the pacifism institutionalised in the country's 1947 Fundamental Law of Education, and influences Japan's position of non-interference between Taipei and Beijing, a relationship implied when De Jian mentions he would like to visit Beijing, and a fellow gang member tells him he can now visit as a naturalised Japanese citizen.

It is the concept of citizenship that underpins Hama's relationship to Yang, making the detective and the gangster 'brothers'. The detective's ethical mission reflects Japan's ethical debt to its former colony. In the bar scene, Yang tells Hama that his only family is De Jian, and Hama says that all he has is his sister: 'parents dead, same as you'. Yang corrects him: 'No not the same', proceeding to tell him that his parents are not dead but rather abandoned the brothers because of poverty, insinuating the traumatic history of compounded colonialisms. Yang's abandonment is not so much a metaphor for Japan's decolonisation as it is metonymic of the colonial effects of Japan's occupation, which aimed at providing an 'agricultural surplus', but did so 'in ways that destroyed traditional social bonds'.[18] That noir does not simply 'reflect' historical material, but articulates its affective impact on a cultural psyche, begins to explain its appropriateness to cross-cultural translation. The parodic and pastiche returns to film noir in the form of neo-noir has made it all too clear that noir was never simply a reflection of historical events, and that history's impact on the genre was never direct as once thought. Rather, 'film noir's relations to its historical and social context can be best described not as metaphoric but as synecdochic and hyperbolic'.[19] The film utilises the synecdochic qualities of noir to suggest the war's long-term effects in rearranging geographical and political space.

Hama is metonymic of Yokohama itself – his name literally part of the whole – which is expressed in the first voice-over, as he states 'I am a Yokohama detective', and reinforced through continual deep-focus shots that place Hama within, and equal to, the urban cityscape.[20] At first, Hama is aligned with Japan generally, as in the mah-jong parlour, in which his comment on 'changed' behaviour – i.e. hesitance to fight – reflects Japan's own former aggressive behaviour, of which its colonisation of Taiwan was a part. Yet, he is referred to more than once as a 'stray dog' – the same term used to describe both Yang brothers – and, outside the immigration office, Lt. Nakayama scoffs at Hama referring to himself as a 'citizen'. His metonymic relationship to Yokohama connects him to its own hybrid history of occupation as far back as the nineteenth century when American warships arrived there, demanding that Japan open several ports for commerce. Yokohama's historical internationalism, though, is the history of invasion and occupation, exemplified by its massive destruction in the Great Yokohama Air Raid, and its subsequent

American occupation after the loss of the war. The history of the city does not require explicit reference but rather haunts the narrative, implied in the film's visuals of the city against which Hama takes his meaning. As Vivian Sobchack argues: 'the baroque qualities of noir's visual style, the particularities of its narrative thematics and structure, emerge as an intensified form of selection, foregrounding, and conse-quent exaggeration of actual cultural spaces charged with contingent temporal experience'.[21] The cultural space of the city is particularly charged in classic film noir because it spatially operates as the alienating Other to the idea of home for which America supposedly fought, a dichotomy particulary acute for the hard-boiled detective: 'For the detective, the ideal social order is denied by the urban reality around him. The ideal represents not simply a promise, but a broken promise.'[22]

The broken promise of classic noir, underscored by the city setting and the non-reproductive couple of the detective and femme fatale, is the (denied) myth of home. *Terrible Time* returns to noir to comment upon this broken promise, translating it to fit 'the perplexity of the unhomely, intrapersonal world'.[23] *Terrible Time* transnationalises noir by revisiting this central conceit of the loss of home: 'both wartime and the home front together come to form a remembered idyllic national time-space of phenomenological integrity and plenitude', forming a 'mythological chronotope' within the national imaginary.[24] Hayashi's film summons noir's time-space or chronotope to interrogate the con-tinuing geo-political affects of this mythology. Notably, the film returns to noir's chronotope dialogically from the present to connect the *time* of the noir to an altogether different *space,* i.e. to the space of Asia/ Pacific: 'the space of Asia/Pacific cinema is the space of translation ... In ... the queer [sic] sights, the anachronistic temporality, and the inconclusive visions of the past and the present, films from the Asia/Pacific continue to disturb specularity'.[25] The disturbing transla-tion of American film noir's chronotope 'captures something of the estranging sense of the relocation of the home and the world – the unhomeliness – that is the condition of extra-territorial and cross-cultural initiations'.[26] Asian/Pacific spaces such as the serially colonised Taiwan and the forcibly internationalised Yokohama exemplify such unhomely initiations.

Hayashi's film references noir's mythological chronotope only to reverse it, exposing its underside. Although the film is set in the pres-ent day, it is intertextually presented as, literally, the flipside of *The Best Years of Our Lives* (1946), William Wyler's Oscar-winning social realist depiction of post-war life for the returning US soldiers.[27] The title sequence consists of a close-up on the movie theatre's sign displaying *The Best Years of Our Lives,* but after a beat, the sign flips over to reveal the title of the film we are actually watching. Hayashi's film is literally and figuratively the underside of *Best Years:* 'the United States emerged from World War II with its industry intact, its political influence paramount in every corner of the world, and its economic weight felt in shattered nations from Japan to France. The sense of nearly limitless opportunity runs through *Best Years* and serves as a balance to the otherwise bleak tone of the film'.[28] *Best Years* works as a counterpoint to and historical frame of reference for *Terrible Time,* presenting a dialogic relation between the films that turn on the transnational and transhistorical effects of the war on Asia/Pacific – the obverse of 'limitless opportunity'.

In *Terrible Time's* postmodern return to noir in general, and specifically referencing *Best Years,* in which 'the atomic theme appears several times', Hayashi's film cites the stylised effects of noir to confront what the original form would not confront – that the dropping of the bombs on Japan were *the* broken promise of an ideal global order.[29] In this way, transnational noir is not defined by taking noir abroad, but rather by the excavation of the form's own global unconscious: 'in the background, underlining each of the world's political and economic troubles, was the new force that had been released over Hiroshima in August 1945'.[30] Although never articulated in the substance of its content, the horror of atomic devastation is the historical undertow of film noir. Indeed, it has been argued that the film noir cycle ends with *Kiss Me Deadly* (1955), what Paul Schrader has argued to be 'the masterpiece of film noir', a film that comes closest to facing 'the inhumanity and meaninglessness of the [American] hero', notably Mike Hammer, who, in the end, is himself destroyed by the 'great whatsit': the return of noir's repressed.[31] Spillane's Hammer personifies the ambivalence that troubles the authoritative history of the West and the violent ends to which it went to consolidate its power against the East. *Terrible Time* is less homage than 'mimicry' of American noir; it speaks back to the West, exposing 'the mote in the eye of history', the blind spot of classic post-war film noir that informed its bleak fatalism and hopeless mood, though never directly addressed.[32]

The atom's threat of annihilation begins to explain why 'a certain mode of hysteria and overwroughtness becomes the norm of ... noir's everyday life'.[33] Yet, it too is synecdochic of a larger social thematic that makes the film style of noir a popularly revisited form. Historically, the stylistic qualities of noir emerged before the atom was split; Thomas Schatz acknowledges film noir as 'American Expressionism', to reference the direct influence of the German Expressionism of the

1920s on the cinematic style of the 1940s in the US. Generally speaking, cinematic expressionism emerged as an aesthetic response to the German national crisis following the devastation of the First World War, then American Expressionism appeared in the wake of the Second World War, French New Wave came to fruition, and openly referenced, international conflicts with Indochina and Algiers, and the neo-noir of the 1970s has been perceived as a nihilistic reaction to the Vietnam War. Film expressionism, in other words, surfaces in the history of a nation when it is forced to confront its own liminality. The style and substance of expressionism in film, like world literature, as Goethe once suggested, 'arises from the cultural confusion wrought by terrible wars and mutual conflicts'.[34]

It is this very cultural confusion that is revisited in neo-noir, arising in the 1970s but coming to fruition in the 1990s. However, discussions of neo-noir have been marked by a Euro-American bias that has neglected to comment on neo-noir's profound transnationalism. Hayashi Kaizo is among the school of neo-noir directors, including John Woo and Quentin Tarentino (with whom Hayashi shares not only film references, such as Suzuki Seijun, but actors as well), who were 'cognizant of the noir heritage, but utilized it in new and revealing ways'.[35] I want to conclude by sketching out a different approach to neo-noir that provides a 'new way' to conceptualise it as a transnational aesthetic, based on an interpretive model for world literature that reflects the fact that 'the very concepts of homogeneous national cultures, the consensual or contiguous transmission of historical traditions, or "organic" ethnic communities − *as the grounds for a cultural comparativism* − are in a profound process of redefinition'.[36] Contemporary film studies need to come to terms with this redefinition, rethinking its categorisations restricted by national borderlines. I would suggest that neo-noir's historical roots as a form that dealt with the anxieties produced by newly emancipated others, women specifically, makes it an ideal forum for the articulation of decolonisation and other shifting terrains of power and identity. For this reason, neo-noir can be framed as a stylistic category of world cinema, 'concerned with a form of cultural dissensus and alterity, where non-consensual terms of affiliation may be established on the grounds of historical trauma. The study of world [cinema] might be the study of the way in which cultures recognize themselves through their projections of "otherness"'.[37] By centring my analysis on a non-Western text, the implicit hybridity of neo-noir is foregrounded, yet this hybridity is eminent to the postmodern return that is itself a translation of (and intervention into) a historically situated transnational form of aesthetic refiguration.

Like other noirs that deal explicitly with 'cultural confusion' such as
Chinatown (US, 1974) and *Touch of Evil* (US, 1958), *Terrible Time* ends
tragically, with consequences outside the detective's control: his client-
brother, in the place of the lover, 'finally is killed and the villain [Kano]
gains control over the community' in the role of leader of the 'New
Japs'.[38] Yet, unlike Polanski's neo-noir, Hayashi's film refuses to turn
its back on the alterity China(town) represents. Cawelti makes the argument that 'The present significance of generic transformation as a creative mode reflects the feeling that not only the traditional genres but
the cultural myths they once embodied are no longer fully adequate to
the imaginative needs of our time.'[39] *Terrible Time* critiques the very
cultural myths that inform it by framing Hama's last interaction with
Yang against the backdrop of cinema itself. Played out in Hama's office
as the sounds of an American western movie play in the background,
he draws a gun on Yang to stop him from killing his brother. The two
friends end up with guns aimed at each other as the recognisable sounds
of a 'cowboy and Indian' shoot-out bleeds into the office from the film
being projected. The intertextual framing presents a critical distancing
from the inherited mythologies of the West that mystify its imperialist
history of violent conflict in the face of cultural difference. By acknowledging the cinematic transformation of this (film) mythology, the movie
theatre becomes 'the split-space of enunciation ... conceptualizing an
*inter*national culture, based not on exoticism of multiculturalism or the
diversity of cultures, but on the inscription and articulation of culture's
hybridity'.[40] The film stresses this hybridity by emphasising its status
as a film, particularly at the climax when Yang is finally killed by his
'countryman' (if not his brother), and the glossy black and white image
is washed over with red in a non-diegetic visual effect that arrests the
flow of the narrative.

   This effect is one of several the film uses in its self-aware neo-noir
repertoire: 'symptomatic of neo-noir ... is a Baroque self-consciousness
imbuing it with an allusive force of citation ... As a consequence the
evocative force of the new movement can be said to depend on its capacity to sift out degrees of cinematic consciousness among the viewing
public'.[41] We know we are watching a film to which we purchased a
ticket; the film's prologue has told us so – as Kim leaves the theatre, the
ticket taker says to no one in particular: 'to come to a movie and not
watch it ... if you can't take the time to watch a movie, why bother?'.
This metatextual commentary is echoed in Hama's voice-over following the title in which he breaks the fourth wall, addressing the audience
directly. By self-consciously referencing the movie as a movie, *Terrible
Time* substitutes film noir's master chronotope, what Sobchack names

'lounge time', with the chronotope of 'cinema time'. Lounge time is 'the spatial and temporal phenomeno-logic that, in the 1940s, grounds the meaning of the world for the uprooted, the unemployed, the loose, the existentially paralyzed'.[42] As a master chronotope of film noir, lounge time is the obverse of the mythological chronotope of the home discussed above. Yet, if 'chronotopes are not merely descriptive but rather constitutive of what we apprehend as genre', then I suggest that 'cinema time' names neo-noir's generic chronotope.[43] In its cinematic self-awareness, neo-noir displaces 'lounge time' with 'cinema time', but in doing so, reverses the meanings ascribed to noir's dialectic – lounge/home.

The home is still absent in neo-noir, but it has taken on larger meanings – to be unhomed in the world. Cinema time can be understood as the concretisation of the 'unhomely moment': 'the unhomely moment relates the traumatic ambivalences of a personal, psychic history [*my life*] to the wider disjunctions of political existence'.[44] In the postmodern return to film noir, the felicitous chronotope of home is now conflated with the alienating temporality of the nation-state, that 'strange forgetting of the history of the nation's past: the violence involved in the nation's writ ... the anteriority of the nation, signified in the will to forget'.[45] In Japan's will to forget the past is the makings of the 'most terrible time', emblemised in the violent and tragic deaths of the 'uprooted' Taiwanese brothers. Opposed to this is cinema time, that spatiotemporal structure which allows for incommensurable narratives and a hybridity of histories. Cinema time 'speaks to the "unhomely" condition of the modern world' through narratives of identification and images of cultural translation.[46] In this way, the film ends with a crane shot through the Western Japanese Cinema Center, book-ending the opening, to dolly in once again on the movie theatre. Significantly, lounge time once named the 'dark and perverse' spaces of the 'unfamilial, unfamiliar, and anonymous' city of film noir.[47] In transnational noir's shift from lounge time to cinema time, the city and its representative spaces, such as the movie theatre and the mah-jong parlour, are no longer 'cold to foreigners'; rather, 'it is the city which provides the space [and spaces] in which emergent identifications and new social movements of the people are played out'.[48] To this end, the plot of *Terrible Time* concludes with cuts between images of the movie theatre, Hama's empty office, and Hama himself walking through the city streets of Taiwan to the brothers' 'home', where he looks out over Taiwan and across the ocean. Cinema, the film suggests, allows us to see through the other's eyes, to 'un-home' ourselves through the process of 'taking the time to watch a movie'.

References

1   Napier, Susan J., 'Confronting master narratives: history as vision in Miyazaki Hayao's cinema of de-assurance', *Positions: East Asia Cultures Critique* 9/2 (Fall 2001), p.477.
2   Napier, Susan J., 'Confronting', pp.476–7.
3   Napier: 'Confronting', p.478.
4   Bhabha, Homi, *The Location of Culture* (London: Routledge, 1994), p.168.
5   Bhabha: *Location*, p.168.
6   Barbiero, Daniel, '"Dark art" into allegory: from transfiguration to refiguration', *M/E/A/N/I/N/G* 8 (1990), p.11.
7   Sobchack, Vivian, 'Lounge time: postwar crises and the chronotope of film noir' in Nick Browne (ed), *Refiguring Film Genres: Theory and History* (Berkeley: University of California Press, 1998), p.133.
8   Schatz, Thomas, *Hollywood Genres: Formulas, Filmmaking, and the Studio System* (New York: Random House, 1981), pp.128–9.
9   Žižek, Slavoj, *Looking Awry: An Introduction to Jacques Lacan Through Popular Culture, An October Book* (Cambridge: MIT Press, 1991), p.60.
10 Conley, Tom, 'Noir in the red and the nineties in the black' in Wheeler Winston Dixon (ed), *Film Genre 2000: New Critical Essays* (Albany: SUNY Press, 2000), p.196.
11 Schatz: *Hollywood Genres*, p.112.
12 Sobchack: 'Lounge time', p.130.
13 Lam, Peng-er and Ja, Ian Chong, 'Japan-Taiwan relations: between affinity and reality', *Asian Affairs: An American Review* 30/4 (Winter 2004), p.250.
14 Lam and Chong: 'Japan-Taiwan relations', pp.256, 253. Notably, the deregulation of Japanese imports that occurred in the 1990s created an influx of Japanese movies and television melodramas to Taiwan.
15 Bhabha: *Location*, p.35.
16 Zizek: *Looking Awry*, p.60.
17 Schatz: *Hollywood Genres*, p.114: 'that sultry seductress who ... functioned to manipulate ... the male lead'.
18 Armes, Roy, *Third World Film Making and the West* (Berkeley: University of California Press, 1987), p.155.
19 Sobchack: 'Lounge time', p.146.
20 In the television series, he is simply referred to as 'Maiku Yokohama'.
21 Sobchack: 'Lounge time', p.148.
22 Schatz: *Hollywood Genres*, pp.128–9.
23 Bhabha: *Location*, p.12.
24 Sobchack: 'Lounge time', p.133.
25 Yau, Esther C.M. and Kyng, Hyun Kim, 'Guest editor's introduction', in

'Asia/Pacific cinemas: a spectral surface', *Positions: East Asia Cultures Critique* 9/2 (Fall 2001), p.285.

26   Bhabha: *Location*, p.9.

27   In fact, in the second instalment, *Stairway to the Distant Past* (1996), Hama's implied father, a killer who 'received his orders directly from G.H.Q. during the occupation', and who is referred to only as either 'the man in white', or, notably, 'the white man', is played by the actor who was made famous as the Japanese lover in Alain Resnais's *Hiroshima, Mon Amour* (1959). Hama, to this extent, is the direct descendent of the violent atrocities of the war.

28   Jackson, Martin A., 'The uncertain peace: *The Best Years of Our Lives*' in John E. O'Connor and Martin A. Jackson (eds), *American History/ American Film: Interpreting the Hollywood Image* (New York: The Ungar Publishing Company, 1988), p.156.

29   Jackson: 'Uncertain peace', p.160.

30   Jackson: 'Uncertain peace', p.160.

31   Schrader, Paul, 'Notes on Film Noir' in Barry Keith Grant (ed), *Film Genre Reader II* (Austin: University of Texas Press, 1995), p.223.

32   Bhabha: *Location*, p.168.

33   Sobchack: 'Lounge time', p.163.

34   Cited in Bhabha: *Location*, p.11.

35   Wilson, Ron, 'The left-handed form of human endeavor: crime films during the 1990s' in Wheeler Winston Dixon (ed), *Film Genre 2000: New Critical Essays* (Albany: State University of New York Press, 2000), p.147.

36   Bhabha: *Location*, p.5.

37   Bhabha: *Location*, p.12.

38   Schatz: *Hollywood Genres*, p.149. Notably, Kano becomes an elected official, through illegal and violent means, in *Stairway to the Distant Past*.

39   Cawelti, John G., '*Chinatown* and generic transformation in recent American films', from Gerald Mast and Marshall Cohen (eds), *Film Theory and Criticism*, 2e (New York: Oxford University Press, 1979). Reprinted in Barry Keith Grant (ed), *Film Genre Reader II* (Austin: University of Texas Press, 1995), p.244.

40   Bhabha: *Location*, p.38.

41   Conley: 'Noir', p.201.

42   Sobchack: 'Lounge time', p.167.

43   Sobchack: 'Lounge time', p.151.

44   Bhabha: *Location*, p.11.

45   Bhabha: *Location*, p.160.

46   Bhabha: *Location*, p.11.

47   Sobchack: 'Lounge time', p.160.

48   Bhabha: *Location*, p.170.

PART FOUR

HOW THE WEST WAS WON?
ASIANISATION AND BEYOND

12

Gary G. Xu

Remaking East Asia, Outsourcing Hollywood

Remaking films from Hong Kong, Japan and South Korea has become a major trend in Hollywood since 2002, which saw *The Ring* (Gore Verbinsky, US, 2002), remade from the Japanese film *Ringu* (Nakata Hideo, Japan, 1998), become a box office success. A short list of recently remade East Asian films includes *Dark Water* (Nakata Hideo, Japan, 2002; Walter Salles, US, 2005); *Chaos* (Nakata Hideo, Japan, 1999; in production, US); *The Grudge* (Shimizu Takashi, Japan, 2000; Shimizu Takashi, US, 2004); *Shall We Dance* (Suo Masayuki, Japan, 1996; Peter Chelsom, US, 2004); *Il Mare* (Lee Hyun-seung, South Korea, 2000; *The Lake House,* Alejandro Agresti, US, 2006); *My Sassy Girl* (Kwak Jae-yong, South Korea, 2001; in production, US); *My Wife is a Gangster* (Cho Jin-gyu, South Korea, 2001; in production, US); *Infernal Affairs* (Andrew Lau Wai-keung and Mak Siu-fai, HK, 2001; *The Departed*, Martin Scorsese, US, 2006); *Kairo* (Kurosawa Kiyoshi, Japan, 2001; *Pulse*, Jim Sonzero, US, 2006); and *The Eye* (Oxide Pang and Danny Pang, HK, 2003; in production, US). Both *The Ring* and *The Grudge* were so profitable that their sequels have already come out: *The Ring 2* in 2005 and *The Grudge 2* in 2006.

Hollywood has had a long history of remaking commercially successful foreign films. Previous remakes were mostly based on European films, but there were East Asian precedents as well. Kurosawa's *The Seven Samurai* (1954), for example, was remade as a western, *The Magnificent Seven* (John Sturges, US, 1960). None of the previous remaking trends, however, could match the current fashion of remaking East Asian films in scale, intensity, publicity or profit. There are various explanations to this phenomenon. One explanation is that all the remakes are simply isolated and random events, and that the trend will not last long once the film industry finds other new profitable venues. The remaking trend could very well be a fully contingent event, since behind almost all the remade films are the passion and effort of one individual: Roy Lee. A Korean American, Roy Lee started his Hollywood career as a lawyer before he discovered *Ringu*. He successfully introduced *Ringu* to DreamWorks, who agreed to buy the remake right from Nakata Hideo for $1.2 million. The remake cost DreamWorks another $40 million, a hefty amount for any East Asian film, but a meagre figure compared to the typical cost of $100 million to $250 million for a Hollywood summer blockbuster. The film proved to be a phenomenal success, raking in $130 million domestically and $230 million worldwide. Ironically, *Ringu*, which was one of the highest grossing Japanese films ever made, made $6.6 million in Japan, whereas its remake *The Ring* made $8.3 million in only the first two weeks on the Japanese market.[1] The success of *The Ring* gave Roy Lee instant credibility, which resulted in a series of remakes based on East Asian films, including the highly acclaimed Scorsese film *The Departed*. Nakata Hideo continued to march into Hollywood, having two more of his films remade, one of which, *Ring 2*, he directed himself. Most of these films were or are being produced by Roy Lee, who is now fittingly dubbed the 'king of remakes'.

For some critics and industry insiders, however, Roy Lee succeeded only because he was in the right place at the right time. The remaking trend happened not simply because of one individual, but because of the systematic exploitation of exotic cultures and fast action by Hollywood. The remaking trend is attributed to East Asia's rich supernatural tradition, as represented in the eighteenth-century Japanese short story collection *Tales of Moonlight and Rain* (*Ugetsu Monogatari*), which was adapted into two acclaimed films: the eponymous film version by Mizoguchi Kenji in 1953 and *Kwaidan* by Kobayashi Masaki in 1964. Indeed, there is a certain aura in Japanese ghost fiction and films, often filled with women's grudges against men who deserted or injured them.[2] Unlike most ghost stories in the West that seek moments of shock and harmless thrills, the Japanese ghost stories tend to allow the aura to linger, to permeate, or to literally haunt the audience rather than shock and thrill them. But there is another side to the contemporary Japanese ghost films. As John Chua aptly points out in his doctoral dissertation on the horror film genre, what makes Nakata Hideo's *Ringu* adaptable is its already Americanised features: American suburban life style, the strong-minded yet vulnerable female as the 'final girl', unambiguous sexuality, and thrilling yet non-threatening horror. These features met DreamWorks' demand to make *The Ring* a profitable PG-13 instead of an R-rated film that is almost synonymous with box office disaster. Chua further notes that Nakata Hideo's *Ringu* was already a remake of a 1995 version that was much darker, horrifying and sexually ambiguous. The biggest difference was in the gender identity of the ghost:

> Sadako, the victim-turned-ghost who kills those people who have seen her apparition, is revealed in the original story to be a hermaphrodite. She becomes a ghost because a doctor rapes her, then kills her upon discovering her dual sexuality. The original story also suggests that Sadako telepathically motivates her rapist to kill her, a difficult if not politically incorrect idea to incorporate within American narratives. This frank sexual ambiguity and erotic violence, described relatively graphically as flashbacks in the novel and shown onscreen in the first movie adaptation, would be much too vivid for mainstream American audiences.[3]

Without ambiguity, be it psychological or sexual, there would not have been aura. After all, aura is something that cannot be safely contained or explained away by modern rationality – something that one can vaguely feel but can hardly locate or identify. If there is ever 'aura' in Japanese ghost films, it is self-consciously filtered out in Nakata Hideo's and Shimizu Takashi's remakes. In this sense, *Ringu* was already Hollywoodised before it was remade as *The Ring*.

Since the current remaking trend includes not only the horror genre but also romance, comedy and action films, the linkage between the East Asian supernatural aura and the remaking success is further disputable. Some have attempted other explanations: Mark Cousins, for example, contends that the art of commercial cinema has been perfected in the hands of the East Asian disciples of Hollywood:

> *Dark Water*, *The Eye* and *The Ring* films unnerved Hollywood because they beat it at its own game. They found new, subtle, inventive ways of doing what producers in southern California have spent a century perfecting: jangling audiences' nervous systems.[4]

The 'new, subtle' ways Cousins refers to include slow building of tension, hinting at unseen horrors, and using sound more evocatively. Cousins is right in suggesting that the current remaking trend should not be regarded as an isolated phenomenon; East Asian cinema's creative imitation of Hollywood is based on East Asia's long history of film industries, whose accumulation of talents and artistic expressions is finally being recognised and materialised.

We must note, however, that there is an Orientalist overtone in Cousins' enthusiasm for the recent success of East Asian cinema. 'Each of the latest new wave of Asian films', he comments, 'is highly decorated, tapestry-like, with an emphasis on detail, visual surface, colour and patterning, and centred on a woman, or feminized men'.[5] What Cousins refers to are such films as Zhang Yimou's *Hero* (China/HK/US, 2002) and *The House of Flying Daggers* (China/HK, 2004), Wong Kar-wai's *2046* (HK, 2004), and Kore-eda Hirokazu's *Nobody Knows* (Japan, 2004). That these films were not remade had to do with their arthouse appeal, which is associated with non-linear narratives and loosely woven plots that would not translate into commercial success. For Cousins, these films display a collective 'Asian aesthetic', exotic, erotic, feminine, seductive, decorative, that makes Asian films attractive to American audiences through either direct theatrical releases in North America or remakes. We can probably put a positive spin on Cousins' assertion, emphasising that the attractiveness of the 'Asian aesthetic' paradoxically exposes the inherent racial/sexual discrimination and the tendency to exoticise the *other* in Hollywood cinema. But the critique of Hollywood's 'othering' strategy only reinforces and endorses Cousins' generalisation, which needs to be challenged. Asian cinema is not exclusively populated by feminised men. Suffice it to mention Kitano Takeshi's stoicism, John Woo's 'aesthetics of violence', Chow Yun-fat's coolness in his trademark gun-wielding image, Hou Hsiao-hsien's masculine heroism, and Jiang Wen's worship of revolutionary sublime. These directors and actors have either entered Hollywood or become darlings of film festivals. If we follow Cousins' generalising logic, shall we say that Hollywood or the entire Western cinema has been masculinised by East Asian films?

There is another major problem in Cousins' argument; he speaks non-discriminately of popular East Asian films and Hollywood remakes of East Asian films, while the differences between these two forms of film could not be bigger. East Asian films cast ethnically East Asian stars who speak in their native tongues. The requirement of subtitling limits the circulation of these films to North American art theatres, with the rare exception of *Crouching Tiger, Hidden Dragon* (Ang Lee, China/Taiwan/US/HK, 2000), *Hero*, and Kitano Takeshi's *Zatoichi* (Japan, 2004). The remakes, on the other hand, rely on Hollywood's star powers and mostly white actresses and actors such as Naomi Watts (*The Ring*), Sarah Michelle Gellar (*The Grudge*), Richard Gere and Jennifer Lopez (*Shall We Dance*), Matt Damon, Leonardo

DiCaprio and Jack Nicholson (*The Departed*), who speak English and stay comfortably in American or Americanised East Asian settings. The most ironic arrangement is in *The Grudge*, which, despite the setting in Japan, stars *Buffy the Vampire Slayer*'s Sarah Michelle Gellar as an expatriate American social worker. There could have and should have been an exploration of cultural tensions for Westerners in Tokyo, similar to that revealed in *Lost in Translation* (Sofia Coppola, US, 2003), but the director simply switches the main role from a Japanese to an American in a clear awareness that Gellar's white face and screen persona are more than enough for the film's acceptance in North America. As Roy Lee told me, Andy Lau, a megastar in Hong Kong, who gave a stellar performance in *Infernal Affairs*, wanted a role, however minor, in the remake *The Departed*, but it simply was not possible to insert an Asian face in the scenes of Boston mafia.[6] From the original to the remake, the switch of ethnicity should not be overlooked. Inherent in the switch are ethnic stereotyping and a reduction of the real multi-ethnic America in favour of a mono-ethnic filmic fantasy. *What has been remade is not only the story but also ethnicity.* While the originals are ethnically specific, albeit Hollywoodised, representations, the remakes are completely severed from the original ethnic soil and become solely the product of Hollywood homogenisation. The remakes, therefore, have nothing to do with the supernatural aura, the long development of East Asian cinemas, or the peculiarly 'Asian' aesthetic based on cultural and ethnic specifics.

The question remains unanswered: why has remaking East Asian films become such a popular trend at the turn of the millennium? Conversations with Roy Lee yielded several interesting clues from which I finally was able to draw a conclusion. First of all, Lee mentioned several times that he did not have a particular interest in Asian horrors. All he saw was market potential. If East Asian remakes became no longer profitable, he would easily switch to other venues for his film productions. Secondly, Lee emphasised repeatedly how cheap it was to make films in East Asia. East Asian film-makers were more than happy to sell the remaking rights to Hollywood, for the fee paid by Hollywood studios, albeit a small portion of the remaking cost, would most likely recuperate what they originally spent on making the films. Thirdly, Lee did not need to search hard for profitable East Asian films. The films came to him; film-makers sent him videos, and they even asked him to read their scripts before their films went into production. It is thus not exaggerating to say that many East Asian films aimed at commercial success now have a built-in 'remaking mentality', which self-consciously measures the films against Hollywood standard and actively exercises self-censorship. Fourthly, all of the originals of Lee's films had been tested well in East Asian cinema markets – *Ringu*, *Ju-on*, *My Sassy Girl* and *Infernal Affairs* were mega hits in East Asia. Lee's trust in the testing effect of East Asian markets reveals an assumption that North America and East Asia share similar patterns of consumption. Cinema consumption used to follow a unidirectional trail of popularity: whatever proved successful in North America would most likely be welcomed in East Asia as long as those countries open their markets to Hollywood. There are exceptions, for sure. Hollywood's occasional stumbling in East Asia has various causes, most of which are related to different local policies or historical specificities. *Mission: Impossible III* (J.J. Abrams, US, 2006), for example, did not gain Chinese audience's favour because its representation of Shanghai with a fading colonial flavour does not fit well with the ultra modern image Shanghai is now proudly known for. In general, however, the box office hits of Hollywood are darlings in Japan, China and Korea. Now, thanks to transnationalism, the unidirectional trail has traffic in both directions; whatever proved successful in East Asia would most likely succeed in North America as long as the original ethnicity is changed to mainly white and Western.

Having considered all the important factors, I would assert that the current remaking trend corresponds to East Asia's new status as the world's production centre. As much as computer chips, flat panel screens, automobile parts, DVD players, and almost the entire Wal-Mart inventory, are increasingly being produced out of China, Taiwan, South Korea and Japan, the film industry is slowly but steadily shifting some of its production to East Asia. This observation might sound outrageous for some, because Hollywood products are still mainly the result of collaborations among American corporations, directors, performers and other supporting personnel. But film production is a long and complicated process. The big studio must begin with an idea, which is then developed into a prospectus before the studio is committed to hiring an expensive screenwriter who will then go through numerous rewrites before the script will ever get in the production pipeline. Once the production is given the green light, everything will have to be in perfect sync in order for a film to come into existence: budgeting, casting, shooting, digital imaging, editing and so on. A small glitch at any of the junctures could doom the entire film. Market testing of the film will then follow. Numerous test screenings will send the film back for endless changes in order to suit the audience's tastes. The premiere date will then be set, advertising campaigns orchestrated, and marketing machines are operating in full gear. This long and arduous process of mass industrial production is why sequels, no matter how diluted they are in comparison with the originals, are continuously being churned out by Hollywood factories. Through a simplified process, a sequel that grosses $100 million at the box office is most likely more profitable and less risky than its original, which grossed $150 million. The same is true for remakes. A plot full of dramatic twists is ready to be built into a successful screenplay; the mise-en-scène has been carefully laid out so that the remake's director only needs to make slight changes; and most importantly, the market has been tested. As Tad Friend puts it: 'Roy Lee's Asian initiative enables Hollywood, in effect to test fully realized cinematic ideas in front of millions of people, and then go forward with remakes of movies that are already proven hits.'[7] Remakes are potentially more profitable than sequels because the sequels can hardly improve on the originals while the remakes, with the added value of 'Hollywood' as the biggest name brand for cinema, would almost certainly surpass the originals in box office.

Remaking is therefore Hollywood's way of outsourcing. Outsourced are the jobs of assistant producers who are the initial script screeners, of the personnel involved in the scripting process, of supporting crew for various details during production, of marketing team, and, increasingly, of directors. Sooner or later, the unions within the Hollywood system will come to realise the outsourcing nature of remaking. But at least for now, the remaking is making Hollywood leaner, stronger, more efficient, more profitable, and more dominant than ever. This is an irreversible but well-disguised trend. The changed ethnicity serves well to disguise this trend; as much as the glamour of the Hollywood star system is designed to make people forget that cinema is a big industry, the white faces in the remakes cover up the significant contribution of East Asia as the provider of intensive labour required by the film industry.

The title of *Ringu* is indicative of the gains and losses of remaking as outsourcing. Originally named *The Ring*, this original must yield the 'original' title to the remake and is forced to use the Japanese transliteration of 'ring' as its 'authentic' title. The Japanese film industry might have gained recognition and a small share of the remake's profit, but the gain for the 'native', symbolised by the letter 'u' added to 'ring', is precisely what has been lost: the original ethnicity, the aura, the intellectual property, and the identity and history of the entire national film industry. How is this 'loss by gaining' any different from outsourcing in the computer industry? Through outsourcing labour intensive jobs such as software engineering, the American hi-tech industry is able to sustain its remarkable growth, while at the same time generating a new white-collar middle class in Shanghai and Calcutta. China and India have benefited greatly from this kind of outsourcing in terms of urbanisation, Westernisation, improvement in living standards; but the gain can never compensate for the losses: failure to develop their own software industries and intellectual properties; reliance on American trade and labour policy; and vulnerability to the high cost of the repackaged end product such as Microsoft Windows.

To further elucidate my point, I provide here a brief reading of *The Departed*, which is based on all three instalments of the famous *Infernal Affairs* trilogy. Initially sought after by Brad Pitt and his production company, the remake was taken over and directed by Martin Scorsese. It has every element that Scorsese is known for: catholic morals, allusion to previous films, action, dark aura, violence, foul language, tough masculinity and lyricism, found amidst the most improbable circumstances. Compared to the original Hong Kong trilogy, many changes have been made in the remake. The original has a strong Buddhist theme: the Chinese title, *Wu jian dao*, refers to the Avici Hell, the most feared underworld in all the hells described in Buddhist canons. The suffering in the Avici Hell is non-stop and uninterrupted; time becomes eternal and the suffering lasts forever. For the protagonists in *Infernal Affairs*, their endless careers as undercover cop/gangster are no different from the Avici Hell. To resume their original identities does not help either; the only way out is death and thus eternal salvation. The deaths of the 'good' cops, therefore, are not nearly as excruciating and honourable as in *The Departed*, which depicts the passing of the police troopers in terms of sacred sacrifice and heroism. Furthermore, the background shifts from Hong Kong to Boston; the love triangle between Matt Damon, Leonardo DiCaprio and the psychiatrist, played by Vera Famiga, is made much more explicit and more significant to the plot; and more importantly, in terms of cinematography, the remake has far more close-ups than the original.

Why the close-up? Because it demands more of the actor and it highlights the stars in the only way befitting the Hollywood star system. The three major stars – Damon, DiCaprio, Nicholson – all give superb performances in expressing their intense emotions through having their faces scrutinised by the close-up. Damon must always appear to be disguising his nervousness and his guilty conscience; DiCaprio plays to the full his straddling of the fine line between moral righteousness and ruthless gang violence; and Nicholson, despite his supreme evil, shows a fatherly side from time to time. Even the minor characters, such as those played by Martin Sheen and Mark Walberg, shine with star power.

In comparison, the original trilogy features almost exclusively medium and long shots, thus placing much less emphasis on the stars than on the *place*. Andy Lau and Tony Leung, superstars in their own right, are virtually expressionless, showing no emotion through their facial changes. One may cite this as the perfect example of the 'inscrutable Chinese', the stereotypical portrayal of the 'Oriental's cunningness' hidden behind frozen facial expressions. While the inscrutable Chinese has been proven to be symptomatic not of the Chinese as a people but of Western colonialism and capitalism that made deep, 'penetrating' cultural contacts impossible,[8] Lau and Leung have long shown how capable they are of rich facial expressions in such films as *The Fulltime Killer* (Johnny To, HK, 2001) and *Happy Together* (Wong Kar-wai, HK, 1997). One of the possible explanations for their expressionless performance lies in what the films demand: the interchangeability of characters against Hong Kong's cityscape. The interchangeability is first of all related to the films' main themes: good and bad are almost infinitely reversible underneath any disguise or appearance. It also has to do with a critical and allegorical reflection on Hong Kong itself as a mere facade. The film calls attention to this possibility: what matters is the shining surface of urban prosperity. Hong Kong as a British colony or as a Chinese territory window-dresses China's rise; the actual people living behind the facade are meaningless and exchangeable. Recall the most impressive and memorable sequence in the first instalment of *Infernal Affairs*: Andy Lau and Tony Leung walk toward each other on the top of a high-rise. The background is magnificent, high mountains on one side and the Victorian Bay on the other. More impressive is the reflection of the two characters on the glass wall of the neighbouring high-rise: shimmering, fleeting, the two reflections quickly glide toward each other for the ultimate face-off. The shadowy reflection is precisely what this Hong Kong original is about. The characters, not the locale, are interchangeable; the locale owes its very existence to the glass walls or the urban facade.

Scorsese has preserved the rooftop scene, but mainly for the theatrical intrigues. Gone are the impressive skyline and the glass-wall reflective of Hong Kong's coloniality; what is left is the nitty-gritty of the violent Irish gangster life or the emotionally intense Hollywood stars showing their star power. None of Scorsese's stars are interchangeable; they each have their own traits that are maximised by their performances. While the characters are not interchangeable, the locale, however, can be easily switched to any other American city. It is Boston, but it could also be New York, Chicago or Los Angeles. The locale only serves as a backdrop against which the actors perform and the actions take place.

To summarise, *The Departed* departs from *Infernal Affairs* in down-playing the importance of the particular locale and in relying on Hollywood star power. While the audience and the critics alike praise the film's complex plot that is unusual for a Hollywood product, the film's East Asian origin is unrecognisable due to the changes made by Scorsese. Except for the Chinese gang and the mysterious 'computer chips', the film does not seem to have anything to do with China. But it is precisely the computer chip episode that ironically points to the film's reliance on the original's intensive labour. This episode, entirely added on for the remake, is the most unconvincing and incongruous part of Scorsese's film. Nicholas's Irish gang, adept in drug trafficking and blackmailing, suddenly has a knack for hi-tech and steals the computer chip for a Chinese gang. The two sides conduct their transaction as if they are trading cocaine. This, of course, is Scorsese's way of taking a jab at the Chinese government. He implies that the Cold War continues and that the Chinese government salivates over the computer chip because it can be made into a precision guide for China's missiles. At stake in the new Cold War is who owns intellectual properties and develops national hi-tech defence industries. This forcible insertion of the shadow of the Cold War destroys the film's narrative integrity, inherited from the original: the story of individual redemption and dark violent psychological drama turns into a tale of Western technological and moral superiority over the dark Chinese force. Ironic, indeed, and not without Scorsese's trademark dark humour built up in the film's denial of its own origin.

What does the remaking/outsourcing mean for East Asian national cinemas? While it is still too early to predict the implications, immediate impacts already begin to show. The success of East Asian films in North America enables Zhang Yimou to continue with his big budget film-making. His latest productions, *The House of Flying Daggers* and *The Curse of the Golden Flower* (China, 2007), have once again entered the mainstream American cinema market. The lone 'superstar' among Chinese film directors, Zhang Yimou is inching closer to the status of 'national treasure', evidenced by the assignment of directing an eight-minute segment for the closing ceremony of the 2004 Athens Summer Olympics and the entire opening ceremony of the 2008 Beijing Summer Olympics. He certainly desires as much attention from Hollywood as possible, but he does not need to settle for low budget and sensationalised films ready to be remade. Holding the flag of 'authentic national culture', Zhang Yimou will facilitate Hollywood outsourcing by attracting and training talents in commercial cinema. Zhang Ziyi's recent success is but one small example. In the meantime, Zhang Yimou's young colleagues, Jiang Wen (*In the Heat of the Sun*; *Devils on the Doorsteps*), Wang Xiaoshuai (*Beijing Bicycle*) and Lou Ye (*Suzhou River*), are finding that the road of art film-making is getting narrower. With talents, experience, name recognition, and readiness to collaborate with commercial cinema, they will most likely become China's Nakata Hideo and Shimizu Takashi. As for China's Jia Zhangke (*The World*, *Still Life*), Taiwan's Tsai Ming-liang (*Goodbye Dragon Inn*) and Hong Kong's Fruit Chan (*Hollywood Hong Kong*), who are least likely to succumb to Hollywood homogenisation, they will continue to fight their lonely and uphill battle. Their colleagues, such as Chen Kuo-fu (*Double Vision*) and Johnny To (*Fulltime Killer*), will probably become avid promoters of Hollywood outsourcing. Although Hollywoodisation is irreversible, unexpected outcomes could still be possible. Facing the pressure of outsourcing, Chinese film-makers are increasingly collaborating with the Japanese and the South Koreans to assert an East Asian identity. Trans-East Asian cinema just might become an interesting by-product of the unexpected success of remaking East Asian films.[9]

References

1 These numbers were gathered from Friend, Tad, 'Remake Man: Roy Lee brings Asia to Hollywood, and finds some enemies along the way', *The New Yorker*, 2 June 2003.

2 For Walter Benjamin, aura has to do with involuntary memory, which comes from the abysmal ocean of one's deeply hidden memories and is only triggered by sheer chance; aura is also based on the associations that 'tend to cluster around the object of a perception', associations that were quickly disappearing due to the perceptive certainty in mechanical arts invented at the dawn of the modern era. Those mechanical arts include photography and cinema. See Benjamin, Walter, *Illuminations*, in Hannah Arendt (ed and intro), Edmund Jephcot (trans) (New York: Schoken Books, 1978, p.186). Of course, it is possible that Benjamin did not fully realise the representational potential of the mechanical arts. But his understanding of aura provides a key to dissecting Hollywood horror films: the audience scream and peep through their fingers, not because fear is reverberating in their repressed anxieties and insecurities, but because they are secretly and joyfully embarrassed by the transference of their fear onto the mechanical shallowness in the film's predictability, conventionality, and non-ambiguity devoid of aura.

3 Chua, John, *The Horror, the Horror: The Repetition and Compulsion of a Genre*, PhD dissertation (University of Illinois, 2004).

4   Cousins, Mark, 'The Asian Aesthetic', *Prospect* 104, November 2004, p.2.

5   Cousins: 'The Asian Aesthetic', p.4.

6   The Chinese tabloids claimed the opposite: that Andy Lau turned down the offer to perform a minor role in the remake of *Infernal Affairs*.

7   Friend: 'Remake Man', p.43.

8   See Rey Chow, *The Protestant Ethnic and the Spirit of Capitalism* (New York: Columbia University Press, 2002).

9   There have been ample examples of collaboration among East Asian national films. The Shaw Brothers' success in the 1950s and 1960s, for instance, was their wide acceptance in areas outside China, Taiwan or Hong Kong. The Japanese pushed for 'pan-Asian cinema' during the Second World War. No matter how large the scales of these previous collaborations, however, the contemporary East Asian collaborations are potentially more cohesive, better organised, and more defensive in facing the Hollywood threat. This 'trans-East Asian cinema' is unique due to today's market condition and 'glocalisation' – the effort to change the local by the global and, in response, the influence on the global of the local.

13

Nikki J.Y. Lee

Salute to Mr. Vengeance!:
The Making of a Transnational
Auteur Park Chan-wook

> T-shirt manufacturers and poster printers take note: Park Chan-wook is
> officially a star director. That doesn't mean that his films are all going
> to be hits, but it does mean that he's joined Quentin Tarantino, Wes
> Anderson, Spike Jonze and the Coen brothers in the ranks of those cult
> auteurs whose every new offering is greeted by the rejoicing and
> fevered chatroom posting of their fans. . . . From now on, expect Park's
> work to keep grabbing headlines at festivals, and to keep cropping up in
> magazines' Best Films Ever polls.[1]

In 2004, the Cannes International Film Festival handed its Palme d'Or
over to Michael Moore's *Fahrenheit 9/11* (US, 2004) – a result that
many interpreted as a critical comment upon the US invasion of Iraq,
made at the very moment of the US presidential elections. In the same
year, Park Chan-wook's *Oldboy* (South Korea, 2003) won the festival's
Grand Jury Prize (often described as 'the Second Best Prize' by the
South Korean media). The Cannes jury that year was chaired by *Kill
Bill* director Quentin Tarantino, whose particular cinematic predilections go some way to explaining why *Oldboy* enjoyed such acclaim at
the festival. Certainly, Park's *Oldboy* is exactly the kind of movie that
Tarantino might be expected to like. The film took its plotline from a
Japanese manga of the same title, but was then developed and transformed into something else entirely. A middle-aged man is kidnapped
and incarcerated for 15 years without knowing why or by whom. When
he is finally released, he has only one thought in mind – to track down
his captors and then take his revenge. Stylish, violent and full of energy,
Oldboy features numerous notorious scenes that have been much talked

about, including the eating of a live octopus, the pulling out of teeth with a hammer, and the extended corridor scene where the main character fights against a small army of gang members in the style of *seul contre tous*.

Armed with the support of Cannes' glorious logo and with Tarantino's endorsement, *Oldboy* has enabled Park to join the small rank of celebrity auteur directors who project a brand image in the world of what Timothy Corrigan calls 'the commerce of the auteurist'. Corrigan underlines that '[d]espite their large differences, theories and practices of auteurism . . . share basic assumptions about the auteur as the voice or presence that accounts for how a film is organized'.[2] In order to understand the contemporary practices of auteurism, Corrigan argues that merely de-humanising or de-romanticising auteurism will not suffice, suggesting instead that the practices of auteurism need to be re-contextualised 'within contemporary industrial and commercial trajectories', and in light of 'any national film history and industry'.[3] For example:

> In the United States . . . the industrial utility of auteurism from the late 1960s to the early 1970s had much to do with the waning of the American studio system and the subsequent need to find new ways to mark a movie other than with a studio's signature.[4]

While Corrigan's observations centre upon Hollywood film history and industry, how should the concept of the 'commerce of the auteurist' be understood in terms of transnational film culture? As the commerce of the auteurist does not merely operate within national boundaries, the need to consider what may be termed the *transnational commerce and practices of auteurism* becomes vital. If contemporary practices of auteurism in the US are related to the 'industrial desires, technological opportunities, and marketing strategies' of the Hollywood film industry,[5] the practices of transnational auteurism are embedded in the material conditions and commercial strategies of international institutions and networks of circulation. While considering the role of auteur as that of 'a cultural agent', Corrigan states that 'the auteur must now be described according to the conditions of a cultural and commercial intersubjectivity, a social interaction distinct from an intentional causality or textual transcendence'.[6] To what extent, therefore, can Corrigan's statements explain the contingencies of the commercial and cultural currencies that circulate around one director as an outcome of 'a social interaction' in 'the transnational commerce of the auteurist'?

In order to answer such questions, this chapter considers the transnational and multi-faceted trajectory of Park Chan-wook's 'becoming' as an (international) star director. Park's case provides an interesting example of how one director from 'the Far East' is engaged in the contemporary practices of transnational auteurism.

The bestowing of the Cannes award ensured that the international fame of both Park and *Oldboy* was sweeping enough to attract the attention of Hollywood executive producers. As a result, the remake rights for two of Park's films – *Oldboy* and *Joint Security Area JSA* (South Korea, 2000) (hereinafter *JSA*) – were snapped up by Hollywood studios, and Park has been approached by several Hollywood companies offering him projects such as a proposed remake of Sam Raimi's *The Evil Dead* (US, 1981). Meanwhile, back in South Korea, the Cannes award appears to have played a significant role in authorising Park's status as a 'national auteur director' representative of Korean national cinema. In this sense, Park achieved the same high rank as Im Kwon-Taek, whose 99th film, *Chihwaseon* (South Korea, 2002), garnered Best Prize for Director at Cannes in 2002 and cemented his reputation as a 'national director'. Responding in a similar manner to how they had earlier favoured Im, the South Korean government awarded a national medal for cultural contribution to Park Chan-wook, Choi Min-sik (who plays the role of the main character in *Oldboy*, Oh Dae-su) and producer Kim Dong-ju. Such recognition echoes the Korean public's perception of Park's success at Cannes; Park is not perceived as a cult director, but rather as an 'internationally celebrated' national talent.

In light of these differing commercial currencies and auteurist discourses that circulate transnationally around Park Chan-wook, I will first examine how Park's celebrity-auteur director status is established inside South Korea. In so doing, I will pay particular attention to domestic narratives concerning the development of his career and critical appreciations of his films. Second, drawing upon examples from the US and UK, I will then analyse the processes through which Park has gained an international reputation as cult auteur director. However, in considering these two seemingly separate domains, I do not mean to suggest that the domestic sphere is any less transnational or more provincial than the international sphere. Both local and international film cultures participate, in vitally important ways, in the formations of transnational auteurism. The construction of cultural values around ('foreign') directors is habitually reconstituted in transnational processes and thus contingent upon local configurations. In short, the commerce of the auteur is never a transcendent nor an absolute phenomenon.

Tamed as a National Celebrity: Park Chan-wook at Home in South Korea

In the world of contemporary Korean cinema, Park Chan-wook is considered an ideal model of success. He is looked up to among younger directors as someone who earned both critical and box office success with films that manifest a cinephile taste within the mainstream system.[7]

In early 2006, Park appeared in a television commercial for a Korean oil company, cast as one among 100 celebrities loyal to a particular oil brand. The commercial begins with a young man in a car shouting: 'I'm an assistant director of Park Chan-wook, the director who won the award at Cannes! Because these days he never stops singing the commercial song of this oil brand, I cannot but become addicted to this brand, too.' Director Park is then depicted singing this commercial song while sitting in his director's chair, in a seemingly self-indulgent and happy mood. Park's fame as 'the director who won the award at Cannes' does not appear to require any further comment – for example, the actual titles of the movies he has made are never mentioned. Instead, the way a television commercial identifies Park through the public media in South Korea is as 'the director who won the award at Cannes'.

The cultural currencies that circulate around Park as star director domestically diverge from those that characterise and support his international fame. For example, while Park is known internationally as a cult director of extreme violence who made his name with the so-called 'revenge trilogy' (*Sympathy for Mr. Vengeance* (South Korea, 2002), *Oldboy* and *Lady Vengeance/Sympathy for Lady Vengeance* (South Korea, 2005)), he is by contrast recognised in the domestic arena as a national celebrity and commercial auteur – a successful mainstream director with a cultish bent. However, in considering the Korean media narratives that articulate the development of Park's career, it is important to be aware of the extent to which Park's domestic fame is not only locally driven, but also the inevitable outcome of complex transnational phenomena.

South Korean public memory concerning Park Chan-wook's reputation as director differs from the briefer history of the recent establishment of his fame in the US and UK. Whilst in the international arena it is *Oldboy* that set him on his path to overseas success, back home in South Korea it was *JSA* that had earlier made his name in the domestic market. Park's third feature film, *JSA* was released in South Korea in early September 2000, where it rapidly became the nation's all-time biggest box office hit, outpacing the record that had been set just one year previously by *Shiri* (Kang Je-gyu, South Korea,

1999). *JSA*'s production cost and high revenue intake secured its privileged place among a group of films marketed as 'Korean blockbusters'. Its narrative concerns the inhumane impact of the persistent Cold War ideology underpinning relations between North and South Korea. The film engages with such weighty subject matter by crossing thriller genre conventions with numerous comic elements.

Before *JSA*, Park had made two feature films, *The Moon is What the Sun Dreams of* (1992) and *Threesome* (1997), as well as the short film *Trial* (1999). The two early features demonstrate the same preoccupation with questions of style, violence and serious social and political themes that can be found in his recent 'revenge trilogy'. However, these earlier films remained a lacuna in the consciousness of the Korean public until Park's recent international emergence.

Because as a first-time director Park had little control over casting for his debut film, he invested instead in stylistic experiments and the more technical aspects of film-making[8] – indeed, one South Korean reviewer summed up his impression of the film by noting its 'desire of style and style of desire'.[9] After the subsequent commercial failure of this debut effort, Park did not make another film for five years. His second feature, *Threesome*, was destined for the same unspectacular box office performance as its predecessor. In South Korea, one review of *Threesome* was called 'Impossible Dream of a Cinephile',[10] with the title referring to Park's reputation at that time for being a knowledgeable film critic who loved and often wrote about B-movies. Park contributed film reviews to several magazines, such as the monthly *Screen*, and in 1994 published a collection of his reviews in book form under the title *The Discrete Charm of Watching Films – Videodrome*.[11] The two feature films and numerous reviews formed the basis of a small cult following that grew up around Park's activities as both film critic and cinephile film director. As a result, *JSA*'s national success as a popular and financially successful Korean blockbuster was not uniformly welcomed by all of Park's followers, one of whom posted the following message on the discussion board of the movie's official homepage: 'Bye, director. Now we return director Park to the mainstream public.'[12]

JSA therefore marks a crucial transition in Park's career. In interviews held around the time of the film's release, Park repeatedly announced that he was able to make 'well-made' films which communicated well with the mainstream audiences.[13] The box office success of the film certainly appeared to attest to his ability to make successful popular films after putting to one side his hyper-enthusiasm for cult movies. He therefore started to become recognised as a director with the talent and ability to make popular Korean blockbusters and hence able to contribute towards the bolstering of the national film industry.

JSA also became the first film of Park's to be screened at prestigious European film festivals, after it was invited into competition for the Golden Bear Awards at the 2001 Berlin International Film Festival. The Berlin festival had long taken an interest in Korean films, especially those dealing with the issue of the division of the peninsula. Many South Korean newspapers consequently reported this news in high expectation of the film winning a major award, even though such exaggerated expectations eventually proved groundless. Despite its great significance in Park's career, *JSA* was only ever released as a DVD title in the US and UK in 2005 – in other words, after the Cannes success of *Oldboy*.

Park's turn to the mainstream, however, was hardly in vain. When interviewed about his next project, he could assert with confidence: 'now, I'll make a film as I like'.[14] *Sympathy for Mr. Vengeance* is the fruit of Park's return to his own film culture, albeit one that failed at the Korean box office, where the extremity of the film's style, themes and violence appears to have alienated audiences. South Korean critics, however, celebrated Park's new-found versatility as a talented director able to make both popular mainstream films and also more cutting-edge 'artistic' creations.[15] Simply put, it is at this point that Park begins to be accepted in South Korea as an auteur director able to cross over between commercially successful film-making and the expression of an artistic individual vision.

Even though this specific articulation of the commerce of Park as celebrity director may be firmly located within a domestic arena, it is in fact not merely locally based, but also solidified through the mediating presence of international institutions such as the Cannes International Film Festival. As has already been noted, Cannes is perceived in South Korea as a highly influential cultural institution, carrying the authority to decide upon, and hence endorse, the artistic value of specific films in the international domain. *Sympathy for Mr. Vengeance* was invited for the Director's Fortnight at Cannes in 2003, just one year after it was initially released in South Korea. The result of this arrangement was that the film had to be held back from any international screenings for a further year because the Cannes screening was required to be a 'world premier'. Moreover, the fact that the film's international release was delayed for so long suggests that its Korean distributor must have been desperate (and determined) to see it screened at Cannes. Indeed, *Sympathy for Mr. Vengeance*'s 2003 debut at Cannes established Park's name on the international film festival circuit and led to the initial invitation for *Oldboy* to be screened in the Director's Fortnight section the following year. As the news broke in Korea that *Oldboy* would play in the Official Competition instead, public expectation that it might walk away with a prize at Cannes rose accordingly. The news that Tarantino would chair the jury merely intensified the sense of anticipation.

It is important to remember in this context that international film festivals strive to 'discover' and present interesting 'new' cinemas and new auteur directors, so as to feed distributors', journalists' and audiences' desires for something fresh and exciting. Paralleling the increased international profile of contemporary South Korean cinema, prestigious European festivals such as Cannes, Venice and Berlin have recently 'discovered' and celebrated a string of the country's directors, including Im Kwon-Taek, Lee Chang-dong, Kim Ki-duk and Hong Sang-soo, as well as Park Chan-wook. Im's *Chunhyang* (2000) and *Chihwaseon* (2002) were picked for Cannes' Official Competition, with the latter awarded the Best Prize for Director. Venice highlighted the work of Lee Chang Dong (*Oasis* (2002)) and also bestowed an award upon Kim Ki-duk's *3 Iron* (2004), while Berlin gave its Best Director's Award to Kim's *Samaria* (2004). Park's *Oldboy* was itself not the only Korean film originally to be invited to Cannes' Official Competition in 2004. Before it was announced that *Oldboy* would be moved into this section, it was expected that Hong's *Woman is the Future of Man* (2004) and Im's *Low Life* (2004) would also be included. However, after the announcement, Im pulled his film from consideration at Cannes, claiming that it would not be completed in time for exhibition at the festival. It was later invited to Venice in September 2004.[16]

At the same time, however, it is the local film industry and government which offers a range of auteur directors for presentation and discovery in international markets. Cannes' choice of Park over Im or Hong appears to have motivated Korean film policy makers to promote popular directors over art-cinema directors as representative of the national cinema. For example, in 2006 the KOFIC (Korean Film Council) began publishing an English-language book series on contemporary South Korean directors such as Park Chan-wook, Bong Joon-ho and Ryu Seung-wan. These three directors were selected as the focus of initial publications in the series, precisely because they are the ones who have to date made films that are both internationally acclaimed and also commercially popular domestically.[17]

Attitudes prevalent elsewhere in Korean media coverage also signal the terms of such a cultural transition. Reporting on *Oldboy*'s award, domestic public media raised the thorny issue of orientalism and Im's films in a forceful manner. The issue at stake here was the question of whether it was 'Western Orientalism' that had made possible the awarding of Im's Best Prize for Director at Cannes in 2002.[18] Such matters had been discussed before, but never so publicly or with such severity. In making a contrast with Im's award, some South Korean commentators advanced the opinion that *Oldboy* impressed at Cannes because of its supposedly universal or familiar styles, themes and generic thriller elements.[19] Such critics even expressed scepticism about Im's films by suggesting that their adherence to traditional Korean aesthetics was no longer valid given the expanding and potentially very prosperous international markets for South Korean cinema.[20] Conversely, promoting popular auteur directors into the global spotlight was regarded as a crucial means for branding the freshness and newness of Korean national cinema.

In deferring to and relying so heavily upon the assumed authority of international cultural institutions, Korean nationalist film culture embraces the extreme and cult movie connotations of Park's films. While *Oldboy* proved to be successful at the domestic box office – drawing more than 3 million admissions nationwide and ranked as the sixth biggest hit of 2003 – neither its incest plot nor graphic violence provided cause for concern in the minds of the Korean public and film critics. Instead, what really excited the Korean public and media appears to have been the later news that *Oldboy* had won the Grand Jury Prize at Cannes. Indeed, Korean media reports broadcast this news in such celebratory tones that it seemed to have been viewed as the best result that a Korean film had ever achieved abroad. *Oldboy* was thus characterised as a 'well-made commercial film'[21] and – riding a wave of national buoyancy – was even re-released into Korean movie theatres.

Commercially successful and critically acclaimed, Park Chan-wook is therefore positioned by a version of the 'commerce of the auteurist' in South Korea, deeply embedded in nationalist film culture and industrial practices. Within this commercial economy, Park as a representative South Korean director comes to embody symbolic currencies which sustain this nationalist identification with South Korean cinema as a unitary whole. Park's auteurist aura – a commercial strategy, to be sure – is identified as that which not only sells his films, but also guarantees the quality of South Korean cinema. It is in this sense that the domestic value of Park as star director is not detached from but rather interrelated with the international domain. While this aura is shaped within the culture and economy of the local film industry, it is also structured in relation to international forces.

Salute to Mr. Vengeance: Via Cannes, Accompanied by Tarantino

What kind of particular currencies and brand effects are layered on to Park Chan-wook as a result of the international circulation of his films? The simple fact that Park's overseas reputation differs from domestic responses does not necessarily mean that international perceptions are tainted by misconception, whereas domestic reception is somehow more 'authentic'. Corrigan suggests that 'the auteur as a commercial presence ... becomes part of an agency that culturally and socially monitors identification and critical reception'.[22] Extending Corrigan's argument into the transnational sphere, it becomes possible to see how Park's status as auteur director forges new instances of 'identification and critical reception' in diverse specific contexts.

The recent establishment of Park's international star status is inextricably linked to complex processes of transnational reception. Consider in this respect the fact that the transnational circulation of films inevitably results in the asynchronous release of specific titles in different markets. The arrival of a particular film in a certain territory is not only often delayed or subject to a cultural time-lag, but the creation of these differing temporal orders also impacts upon a film's release in different technological formats or 'versions' (e.g. theatrical release, DVD, 'special edition', amongst others). In turn, this temporal displacement can contribute towards the construction of varied local critical responses, which build up specific interpretative paradigms designed to elucidate a director's body of work and cinematic predilections. For example, in the US and UK it is *Oldboy* which established the formative vantage points from which knowledge and opinion concerning Park Chan-wook and his films has been generated. As a result of this, viewers who first encounter Park through *Oldboy* – or indeed through *Sympathy for Mr. Vengeance* – will inevitably receive encouragement to perceive Park as *the* director of revenge and violence. As Park's international fame spreads as a result of the Cannes award, attention becomes focused on certain sensational traits: the extreme violence of his films, their stylistic excess, and the theme of revenge.

Oldboy was the first of Park's films to be released in the US, playing theatres in select major cities such as New York and Los Angeles in March 2005 – slightly less than one year after its glory day at Cannes in May 2004. *Sympathy for Mr. Vengeance* – a film now firmly established as the first segment of Park's 'revenge trilogy' – was released in the US in August 2005, at the very time that *Lady Vengeance* was being greeted with enthusiasm by Park's now dedicated fans at several international film festivals. The US release of *Lady Vengeance* followed soon after in April 2006.

The order of arrival was somewhat different in the UK, where the first of Park's films to be released theatrically was *Sympathy for Mr. Vengeance* in May 2003. Indeed, the film was only given a very limited release in a couple of theatres in central London at that time, in a promotional strategy designed to tie-in with the film's virtually simultaneous UK release on DVD. *Oldboy* was released on a far wider nationwide scale in October 2004, and, subsequent to its success, *Lady Vengeance* then landed in the UK in February 2006. While Park's much earlier films are scarcely even mentioned in the UK, the Korean box-office hit *JSA* was released direct-to-DVD in this territory in 2005, where it was clearly expected to ride on the wave of *Oldboy*'s emerging fame.

The specific release patterns discussed above confirm that the value of a film – like the value of any commodity – cannot be pre-determined, but emerges instead in its movement through 'larger networks of circulation'.[23] When it passes through transnational sites of reception, such as international film festivals, the locality of a film often becomes displaced as it is endowed with new layers of meaning and significance. However, it is not only films, but also film directors to whom such new currencies become attached. Analysing the transnational currencies that circulate around Park Chan-wook requires an examination of the specific role that the Cannes International Film Festival plays as an influential international institution, as well as the particular career path taken by Quentin Tarantino as another celebrity/cult director.

After winning his prestigious award and being exposed to the world's press at Cannes in 2004, Park's *Oldboy* attained new levels of value. For example, it is very difficult to find any US or UK reviews that fail to mention the Cannes award and its linkage with Tarantino. *Oldboy* and Park are thus measured in relation to the aesthetics and excessive style of extreme and violent B-movies, or 'Tarantino brand' movies. Indeed, upon the film's release in Los Angeles, one US critic discontent with *Oldboy*'s fame even wrote a review in the form of a letter addressing Tarantino directly:

> Of course – as you know perhaps better than anyone else – we happen to be living at a time when all things Asian and extreme, from *manga* to anime to the way outré offerings of Takashi Miike, are enjoying a halcyon moment in the fickle universe of fanboy enthusiasms. . . . What puzzles me even more, dear Quentin, is your own strong affection for this particular picture.[24]

Given that Tarantino's *Pulp Fiction* (US, 1994) had won the *Palme d'Or* at Cannes in 1994, however, it is no coincidence that Tarantino was invited to play such a prominent role at the festival in 2004. The decision to appoint him as chair of the jury one decade on was a symbolic gesture that honoured both director and the host event itself – it allowed Tarantino to pay Cannes back for its support and recognition, and the festival to parade its ability to make new cinematic discoveries that it can then take pride in. Tarantino's Cannes connection thus reveals an instructive instance of Cannes' engagement in 'the commerce of the auteurist' around Hollywood directors. The awarding of the *Palm d'Or* to Tarantino for *Pulp Fiction* in 1994 marks a turning point, as it both endorses his innovative and unique 'trash-art' vision while also appearing to embrace the aesthetic tastes of the mainstream Hollywood film industry.[25]

The rise of Tarantino's auteur-celebrity status appeared to signal Hollywood's move towards the adoption of new tastes and filmic styles – in short, the acceptance of 'postmodern aesthetics'. His films are often interpreted in exactly these kinds of terms, through discussion of such elements as 'fragmented structuring', 'an intertextual acknowledgement of fictionality'[26] and 'the "copy" that blurs the boundaries between past and present, between the real and the re-enacted and the linear and the circular narrative'.[27] Implicit even in his very first film, *Reservoir Dogs* (US, 1992), the core of Tarantino's filmic style may be thought of as 'pastiche'. His later films, such as *Kill Bill Volume 1* (US, 2003) and *Kill Bill Volume 2* (US, 2004), may certainly be considered pastiche because of the homage they pay to the various film genres, such as those coming from Hong Kong and Japan, which have inspired him. In this regard, Tarantino's popular auteur status is emblematic of the social acceptance of postmodern auteurs, not merely as creators but also as collectors and mediators of other filmic genres and traditions.

David Desser remarks that Tarantino's cinematic style epitomises a new form of cinephilia that 'leads to the flattening of difference in the erasure of national origins and boundaries, offering up in their place an intertextual chain of homages, references, borrowings and reworkings'.[28] Desser considers that *Reservoir Dogs* and *Pulp Fiction* are closely associated with 'the cinephiliac appreciation of Hong Kong cinema' and 'the emergence of something like a global action genre'.[29] According to Desser, the combination of film availability in video format (VHS, DVD, VCD), as well as the internet, contributes to the emergence of this new film style and global cinematic genre. Yet while Desser's emphasis upon this new media environment is valid, it is important that the role that Cannes and other film festivals play in these processes are not ignored. Tarantino has enjoyed both cult fame and mainstream popularity, and the cultural currencies that circulate around him as an auteur director have been gained in part through the awarding of his prestigious prize at Cannes.

Park entered the international film scene backed by Cannes and by Tarantino. His international cult fame has thus been constructed at the juncture where conventional labelling practices concerning auteur/ national cinemas supported by Cannes overlap with the domain of cult films and mainstream Hollywood, as exemplified by the 'Tarantino brand'. As a result of all this, Park appears to have been assigned a similar position to that of Tarantino as international 'cult auteur' director, who crosses over between the cult world and the mainstream entertainment industry. However, yet another dimension needs to be added to further complicate the characteristics of Park's transnational reputation – namely, the way in which his nationality also underlines the varied evaluation of his films. Yet unlike other representative 'Korean' directors like Im Kwon-Taek and Hong Sang-soo, the cultural currencies that contribute to the building of Park's auteur status do not originate merely from the ghetto of foreign language 'art cinema' circuits. Instead, they are situated within precisely the same kinds of new transnational film cultures that Desser considers in his discussion of the cult popularity of Hong Kong cinema in the 1990s.

Just as the fact that 'Tarantino's films emerged in the age of video is no coincidence',[30] it is also no wonder that Park is similarly a well-known cinephile who watched an abundance of films on VHS before establishing his fame in part through the medium of DVD. Certainly, Park's transnational authorship is caught up in the increased international circulation of Asian DVD titles from Japan, Hong Kong, South Korea, and elsewhere. Given the delayed and limited theatrical release of many foreign language films, the new video formats, and in particular DVD, can often function as more effective means for delivering films to fans scattered around the world but also connected up via the internet. As one reviewer comments:

> Thanks to the proliferation of region-coded DVD's that can be viewed on multisystem players, the forty-two-year-old Park enjoyed a cult following well before his movies debuted theatrically in the U.S.[31]

The international fan-base of Park, which has therefore formed around the medium of DVD, exhibits an affinity between fan and medium that once again privileges particular generic features of so-called 'extreme cinema'. Barbara Klinger indicates that '[t]his predilection for the shiniest new machines on the part of the high-end-phile precipitated, in the early years of DVD, a skewing of playback technologies in terms of gender'.[32] According to Klinger, the core purchasers of DVD players have been a group of 'younger, well-to-do white men', and the ancillary DVD market has therefore reflected the tastes of this particular group who prefer 'high-octane' genre films.[33] This demographic description chimes with somewhat degrading comments concerning Park's fan-base, made on occasion by some reviewers: 'Here was a film that could have been created explicitly to secure the allegiance of youngish, nerdish male DVD addicts.'[34] *Oldboy*'s Cannes award appears to mark the culmination to date of the cult following that has grown up around Park's DVD fan-base, and it has helped Park to move into the broader and influential domain of the mainstream.

The success of the Asia Extreme DVD brand provides a further example of how Park's transnational authorship, closely linked to the medium of DVD, is established through international networks. The cultish genre preferences, exotic fantasies, and corresponding forms of fan spectatorship nourished by this new medium, appear to converge in the transnational routes that Park's films travel along. For example, 'Asia Extreme' is the brand that the UK film and video distributor Tartan established in 2001 for the DVD release of titles from Japan, South Korea, Thailand, Hong Kong, and elsewhere. Beginning with *Sympathy for Mr. Vengeance* in 2003, Tartan has been responsible for distributing Park's films in the UK and US, and – along with Kim Ji-woon's *A Tale of Two Sisters* (2003) – *Oldboy* was placed at the forefront of Tartan's marketing strategies when the company launched its branch in the US in 2004.[35] In the UK, meanwhile, the unexpected levels of success achieved by this particular label in the DVD market immediately led to the creation as well of numerous other labels such as Optimum Asia. It may be suggested therefore that Park's Cannes award established crucial opportunities for the 'Asia Extreme' brand to draw attention from not just the mainstream public in the UK and US, but also from highbrow audiences as well as a broader fan-base.[36] In this way, the Cannes award helped consolidate Park's position as one of the leading directors of films which enrich the cinematic terrain, while also popularising the cultish repertoire of 'Asia Extreme'.

Transnational Authorship in Flux

With the release of *Lady Vengeance*, the transnational commerce of Park Chan-wook appears to enter a new phase in both the domestic and international spheres. The film was released in South Korea in August 2005, whereupon it achieved a similar scale of box office success to *Oldboy*, becoming the fourth most commercially successful film of 2005 and drawing 3.2 million admissions nationwide. This box office success was due to a number of factors, including: the high anticipation surrounding the latest work of a director who had earlier made the film *Oldboy*, which had won such a prestigious award at Cannes; Park's resulting brand image as an externally-validated star director; the public's curiosity regarding the dramatic transformation of TV drama star Lee Young-ae into a violent female avenger; and the widespread expectation that *Lady Vengeance* would win another big film festival prize, this time at Venice.[37] Indeed, if the South Korean public was in any way disappointed with *Lady Vengeance*, it was because the film failed to win any prestigious awards at Venice. To be sure, the film did win some awards there, such as the Little Lion Prize and the CinemAvvenire Award. However, these are nowhere near as impressive as a Golden Lion or a Silver Lion, whose symbolic high cultural pedigree the Korean public media understands and respects.

On the other hand, if there was any disappointment at the international level with this last segment of Park's so-called 'revenge trilogy', it was because the film lacked the compelling energy and speed of *Oldboy*, and because it proved to be altogether less violent and more restrained.[38] As violent energy was diluted, however, reviews approaching Park's films from different angles than those merely of revenge and violence began to gain ground. Some reviewers underlined the sublime character of the themes of revenge, salvation and atonement by comparing his films to Greek myths whose stories develop around the theme of incest, as well as individual choice in the face of moral dilemma.[39] Such approaches led towards a re-evaluation of Park's films and the claim that their profound themes transcend the stylish superficiality of a Tarantino. Consideration of this example demonstrates that the transnational commerce of a popular auteur director is never fixed or static. Instead, it is a fluid process dependent upon various factors, including the diverse ways in which subsequent films are placed in relation to existing configurations of the film industry, public culture and audience response – whose expectations and needs may or may not then be satisfied or else defied.

In conclusion, the case of Park Chan-wook suggests that another analytic prism needs to be added to the consideration of the commerce of contemporary popular auteur directors. The commercial and discursive currencies surrounding Park as international star comprise diverse transnational spheres, which in turn also impact upon the director's position in the domestic film industry as well as the critical evaluation of him at home in South Korea. In new commercial markets for Korean cinema in the US and UK, Park's brand value is constructed in light of distinct critical and commercial currencies. The commerce of an auteurist such as Park is therefore a transnational phenomenon that transcends the given boundaries of any national film culture. The commerce of Park as a transnational auteur-director organises 'identification and critical reception' around a series of encounters between varying domestic and international industrial needs, networks of circulation and specific reception environments.

References

1   Barbar, Nicholas, 'Manners Maketh the Man, Buddy', *Independent on Sunday*, 12 February 2006.
2   Corrigan, Timothy, 'Auteurs and the New Hollywood': in John Lewis (ed), *The New American Cinema* (Durham & London: Duke University Press, 1998), p.41.
3   Corrigan: 'Auteurs and New Hollywood', p.42.
4   Corrigan: 'Auteurs and New Hollywood', p.40.
5   Corrigan: 'Auteurs and New Hollywood', p.40.
6   Corrigan: 'Auteurs and New Hollywood', p.42.
7   KOFIC (Korean Film Council) and *Cine 21, Park Chan-wook: Savior of Violence* (South Korea: Korean Film Directors Series, 2005).
8   Park Chan-wook: *Savior of Violence*, p.27.
9   Bae, Byungho, 'Style of Desire, Desire of Style', *Cinema News*, 4 March 1992, p.8.
10 Gu, Jeong-a, '*Threesome* – Impossible Dream of a Cinephile', *Cinema Forever* 2 (1997), p.134.
11 The book is currently out of print. Responding to the recently increased demand, it was re-edited and re-published under the title *Homage of Park Chan-wook* (Seoul: Maumsanchaek, 2005).
12 Lee, Dongjin, 'Park Chan-wook, I Hate Gun-Fight Scenes. That's Why I Can't Make Films Like *Shiri*', *Chosun-Ilbo*, 18 September 2000.
13 Kim, Youngjin, 'Park Chan-wook Interview: I Can Make Well-made Films Too', *Film 2.0*, 7 September 2000; Oh, Dongjin, 'Park Chan-wook Interview: B-rate Movie? No, It's a Well-made movie', *Film 2.0*, 17 April 2000; 'Park Chan-wook Interview: I Will Make Films as I Like From Now On', *Cine21*, 26 September 2000.
14 'Park Chan-wook Interview: I Will Make Films as I Like From Now On'.

15   Lee, Jihun, 'The Chilling Blade Slices Off the World', *Film 2.0*, p.67, 29
      March 2002; Yu, Unseong, 'I Support *Sympathy for Mr. Vengeance*',
      Cine21, 347 (2002).

16   '57th Cannes Announces This Year's List of Films Invited', *United News*,
      23 April 2004; 'What the *Oldboy*'s Award Means?', *United News*, 23 May
      2004; 'The Big Victory of *Oldboy*', *Donga-Ilbo*, 24 May 2004; '*Low Life*
      Invited to the Competition Section at Venice', *Kukmin-Ilbo*, 30 May 2004.

17   The title of each book is *Park Chan-wook: Savior of Violence, Bong Joon-
      ho: Mapping Reality within the Maze of Genre,* and *Ryu Seung-wan: The
      Action Kid.* Each is downloadable from the KOFCIC website
      <www.koreanfilm.or.kr>

18   Lee, Jongsu, 'The Victory of Korean Cinema That Takes Off
      Orientalism', *Seoul Sinmun*, 24 May 2005.

19   For example, Lee, Dongjin, '*Oldboy* Wins at Cannes: The Meaning',
      Chosun-Ilbo, 24 May 2004.

20   Yang, Seunghui, 'Park Chan-wook of *Oldboy* that Shines with The Grand
      Jury Prize of The Cannes', *Munhwa-Ilbo*, 29 May 2004.

21   *United News*: '57th Cannes Announces This Year's List of Films Invited'.

22   Corrigan: 'Auteurs and the New Hollywood', p.43.

23   Harbord, Janet, *Film Cultures* (London; Sage, 2002), p.40.

24   Foundas, Scott, 'To: Quentin Tarantino, From: Scott Foundas, Re:
      Beware of Imitations', *LA Weekly*, 23 March 2005, <http://www.laweekly.
      com/film+tv/film/oldboy-network/818/> accessed 15 January 2007.

25   See Boggs, Carl and Pollard, Tom 'Postmodern Cinema and Hollywood
      Culture in an Age of Corporate Colonization', *Democracy & Nature* 7/1
      (2001), pp.159–81.

26   White, Glyn, 'Quentin Tarantino' in Yvonne Tasker (ed), *Fifty
      Contemporary Filmmakers* (London: Routledge, 2002), p.344.

27   Ritter, Kelly, 'Postmodern Dialogics in *Pulp Fiction*: Jules, Ezekiel, and
      Double-Voiced Discourse' in David Blakesley (ed), *The Terministic
      Screen: Rhetorical Perspectives on Film* (Carbondale and Edwardsville:
      Southern Illinois University Press, 2003), p.293.

28   Desser, David, 'Hong Kong Film and the New Cinephilia' in Meagan
      Morris, Siu Leung Li and Stephen Chan Ching-kiu (ed), *Hong Kong
      Connections: Transnational Imagination in Action Cinema* (Durham and
      London: Duke University Press, 2005), p.214.

29   Desser: 'Hong Kong Film and the New Cinephilia', p.217.

30   Desser: 'Hong Kong Film and the New Cinephilia', p.217.

31   Cashill, Robert, 'Lady Vengeance', *Cineaste*, Summer 2006, p.57.

32   Klinger, Barbara, *Beyond the Multiplex: Cinema, New Technologies, and
      the Home* (Berkeley: University of California Press, 2006), p.63.

33   Klinger: *Beyond the Multiplex*, p.64.

34   Barbar: 'Manners Maketh the Man, Buddy'.

35   Pearce, Judge Joel, 'On the Emerging Korean Cinema: An Interview with Tony Borg', <http://www.dvdverdict.com/interviews/tonyborg> 2005, accessed 15 January 2007.

36   Amongst Korean movies theatrically released in the UK in 2004, *Oldboy* achieved the highest box office record (total revenue £315,698); Lee, Minjeong, 'The Success of "Asia Brand" Video/DVD and UK Independent Distributor Optimum Releasing', *KOFIC Regular Overseas Report*, June 2005, pp.20–3, <http://www.kofic.or.kr/contents/board/index.aspx?Op=bv&MenuId=527&id=143&noticenum=55&currentpage=3> accessed 15 January 2007. *Oldboy* also became the best-selling DVD title of the Asia Extreme brand. In an interview, the head of Tartan, Hamish McAlpine, remarks that Park Chan-wook is an ideal case since they can promote him as a part of 'Asia Extreme', but also as an artistic 'auteur' director; Lee Minjeong, 'Asia Extreme – UK distributor Tartan Interview', *KOFIC Regular Overseas Report*, January 2006, pp.21–5, <http://www.kofic.or.kr/contents/board/index.aspx?Op=bv&MenuId=527&id=166&noticenum=78&currentpage=2> accessed 15 January 2007.

37   For example, Choi, Munhui, '*Lady Vengeance* Goes to Venice', *Cine21*, 28 July 2005.

38   For example, Lee, Nathan, 'With "Lady Vengeance", Park Chanwook Completes a Trilogy, a Bit More Restrained', *The New York Times*, 28 April 2006.

39   Elley, Derek, 'Sympathy for Lady Vengeance', *Variety*, 1–7 August 2005, p.19.

14

Leon Hunt

Asiaphilia, Asianisation and the Gatekeeper Auteur: Quentin Tarantino and Luc Besson

'Silly Caucasian girl likes to play with samurai swords' runs the taunt of O-Ren Ishii (Lucy Liu) to The Bride (Uma Thurman) in *Kill Bill Volume 1* (Quentin Tarantino, US, 2003), but what happens when critically feted (mainly) 'Caucasian' boys play with Asian genres, stars and aesthetics? The 'Asianisation' of Euro-American cinema has been dependent on 'gatekeeper' figures – producers attuned to cults surrounding Hong Kong, Japanese and South Korean cinema, auteurs displaying their connoisseurship of Asian cinema or acting as patrons to cult Asian films and directors. This essay compares Quentin Tarantino and Luc Besson as two such gatekeepers.

There are arguably two types of transnational gatekeeper. The first is a *connoisseur*, who both incorporates aesthetic influences from East Asian action cinema and is referential towards 'cult classics' from (mainly) Japan and Hong Kong. Tarantino's public persona embraces his Asiaphile fanboy credentials, which have been evident throughout his career, culminating in *Kill Bill*'s full-scale pillaging of Hong Kong and Japanese genre cinema. He has acted as 'patron' to Asian cinema, whether distributing Asian films, lending his name to the Western promotion of *Hero* (HK/China, 2002), or through his more recent association with Park Chan-wook.

The second type of gatekeeper *incorporates* East Asian cinema in a non-referential and non-cinephile way. He is attuned to demographics and crossover cults, absorbing Asian talent into Hollywood or Hollywood-style vehicles, or remaking them. Joel Silver is one such figure, as producer of *The Matrix* trilogy (US, 1999, 2003) and of several English-language vehicles for Jet Li. It is into this second group that

Luc Besson seemingly fits. Besson's incorporation of Asian cinema is superficially similar to Hollywood's; less interested in intertextual 'quotes' than injecting Asian stars and choreographers into otherwise Westernised generic formats in such films as *Kiss of the Dragon* (US/France, 2001), *The Transporter* (US/France, 2002), *Danny the Dog/Unleashed* (US/France, 2005) and *The Transporter 2* (US/France, 2005). On the other hand, Besson's company EuropaCorp has distributed, and more recently funded, genre films from East and South East Asia. Besson is a more contradictory figure than Silver because of the liminal position he occupies; not quite 'Hollywood' and yet not fitting neatly into a French 'national cinema' model either.

A comparison of Tarantino and Besson illuminates some of the characteristics of 'core' transnational cinema and tests out the limits of the Western Asiaphile's creative 'ownership' of East Asian (and South-East Asian) cinema. Tarantino appears to embody Ding-tzann Lii's notion of *yielding*, a synthesis of 'dominant' and 'peripheral' cultural forms that 'transcends both self and the Other'.[1] His public statements indicate a desire to *be* an 'Asian film-maker':

> I wanted to immerse myself so much in that style of filmmaking so that the things that they did would be second nature to me ... I was like someone who lived in Hong Kong in the Seventies.[2]

This immersion in the other has its limits – *Kill Bill*'s narrative suggests an inability to introject into Chinese and Japanese subjectivities. *Incorporation* transforms the other unilaterally,[3] rather than blending into it, most blatantly in Hollywood remakes of East Asian 'cult' successes. But this distinction is perhaps best seen as a matter of degree rather than polarised opposites. When EuropaCorp distributed *Ong-Bak* (Thailand, 2003) it was along familiar 'Westernised' lines – the film was dubbed, rescored and edited to downplay the more 'local' aspects of the story.[4] But Besson's co-opting of Hong Kong and Thai Martial Arts cinema is ambivalent. His use of Jet Li compares very favourably with the Hollywood vehicles that wasted both the star's fighting and acting skills. On the other hand, the apparent search for a white Martial Arts star (Jason Statham, Cyril Raffaelli, David Belle) has led Besson to adopt *le parkour* as an indigenous equivalent to Jackie Chan and Tony Jaa, a cinema about movement, energy, the body in urban space.

From 'Asian Grindhouse' to 'Asia Extreme': Tarantino and *Kill Bill*

Tarantino and the Wachowski brothers are the most conspicuous Asiaphile film-makers working in Hollywood, but there is a significant difference in the level of cult capital displayed in their films. The *Matrix* franchise draws mainly on a comparatively 'known' and contemporary set of East Asian influences – Sci-Fi anime, Tsui Hark, Yuen Wo-ping and Jet Li. One can almost hear Tarantino snorting in fanboy derision as he lays out his own intertextual mosaic – Shaw Brothers (with particular nods to Zhang Che, Liu Jialiang and Wang Yu), Bruce Lee's *Game of Death*, Kaji Meiko (star of the *Lady Snowblood* and *Female Convict Scorpion* films),[5] the 'true account' Yakuza films of Fukasaku Kinji, the stylistic delirium of Suzuki Seijun, the 'extreme' cinema of Miike Takashi, violent anime, the 'Lone Wolf and Cub' films (re-packaged in the US as *Shogun Assassin*), not to mention the resonances brought to the film by the actors Sonny Chiba, Gordon Liu and Kuriyama Chiaki, the choreographer Yuen Wo-ping and the Japanese animation house Production IG. That this only scratches the surface of *Kill Bill*'s East Asian referents is indicative of why the annotation of the film has been enthusiastically taken up on the internet, in books and articles and interviews with the director.[6]

Tarantino operates within what Aaron Anderson calls 'an economy of connoisseurship'.[7] For Anderson, asserting Tarantino's authorship of his Asian homages involves downplaying the input of collaborators like Yuen Wo-ping, stating that Tarantino acted as fight choreographer after preliminary consultations with Yuen. True or not, this certainly accords with the promotion of the film. Yuen is credited as 'Martial Arts Advisor' and never mentioned on *The Making Of Kill Bill Volume 1*, included on the DVD. On *The Making Of Kill Bill Volume 2*, David Carradine claims that Tarantino 'basically was the choreographer ... he doesn't need anybody else'. Tarantino talked extensively of his admiration for action directors and his desire to join the pantheon – 'the whole idea on *Kill Bill* was to test the limits of my talent'.[8] Insofar as this dovetails into fantasies about 'being Asian' (albeit in *la mode retro*), it also suggests a desire to slay the Asian cinematic 'father', just as characters in the film either slay their Asian mentors (Elle Driver's poisoning of Pai Mei) or relegate them to positions of subservience (The Bride's commandeering of Hattori Hanzo).

Sheng-mei Ma characterises the Asiaphile movie fan as someone who 'yearns for the non-self, an essentialized entity never part of Westernness'.[9] This desire to blend into an 'Orientalised' other contrasts with

Julian Stringer's account of Western fan cults surrounding Hong Kong cinema. Unlike the subcultural desires of white youth to 'be black', Stringer discerns 'little concomitant desire ... to assimilate, introject, and express their worldview through Chinese style and culture'.[10] He concludes of this racial economy that 'you can *have* the Chinese, but you can *be* black'.[11] Both of these seemingly opposed views have some purchase on Tarantino's immersion in Asian genre cinema. The fantasy of 'being Asian' is bound up with authoring 'Asian cinema', and even being able to speak directly to an Asian audience – 'they are going to have a context for where some of this stuff is coming from'.[12] The fantasy of 'having' Asian is reflected in the iconic presence of Asian stars 'collected' by the fan curator. Gordon Liu, Sonny Chiba and Kuriyama Chiaki may carry more subcultural capital than the more widely known Asian stars adopted by mainstream Hollywood, but it is hard to escape the impression that they function as action figures to be collected rather than creative collaborators or characters to be explored in the same depth as their American counterparts.[13] An example of this is Tarantino's 'triple crown', his 'three favourite stars of kung fu from three different countries': Chiba from Japan, Liu from Hong Kong and David Carradine from the US.[14] Chiba and Liu function primarily as facilitators of The Bride's 'Asianisation' (just as Yuen Wo-ping is positioned in relation to Tarantino's authorship). Carradine (as the eponymous Bill) functions rather differently, both because his character is more complex and because his presence invokes his 'yellowface' performance in the *Kung Fu* TV series. He is a racially mobile figure; skilled in Japanese and Chinese Martial Arts, playing Kwai Chang Caine's flute from the series that gave him cult immortality, and blending into O-Ren's animated origin story as the silent killer who 'passes' for Japanese.

Tarantino's connoisseurship is perhaps best captured by David Desser's distinction between 'old' and 'new' cinephilia. The cinephile, he suggests, 'loves those moments in the cinema that rise to poetry', and in a pre-VCR, pre-DVD age, those moments are rendered more exquisite by a 'sense of impermanence, or evanescence, of a fleeting moment of experience and epiphany'.[15] 'New' cinephilia, closer to cult consumption than traditional canon-building, belongs to the age of DVD and VCD. Not only is it possible to possess a film, but these new formats give rise to a new relationship with global cinema. When this new cinephilia is manifested by young film-makers, it takes the form of 'a distinctly non-canonical referencing', drawing on 'an instant canon rather than relying on the classics'.[16] No film epitomises this more than *Kill Bill*. Its referentiality frequently takes the form of cinephilia's epiphanic 'moments' – the stare-downs that precede combat, a re-contextualised musical cue that achieves a new poetry, the arterial torrents that follow (after a beat) a deadly sword stroke, a lurid skyline from *Goke – Bodysnatcher From Hell* (Japan, 1968), the mid-battle shifts to black-and-white in Zhang Che's mid-1970s films. And yet, while Tarantino is the quintessence of the new cinephile, *Kill Bill* also suggests an attempted resurrection of an 'old', but non-canonical, cinephilia that draws on memories of Asian cinema's former theatrical ghetto in North America – the 'grindhouse'.

Tarantino's Asiaphilia conflates two historical periods – periods separated by viewing technologies, exhibition patterns, promotional discourses and conceptual understandings of Hong Kong and Japanese genre cinema. On the one hand, Tarantino was forever telling inter-viewers that this was his grindhouse movie – 'I think *Kill Bill* has the same relationship with 70s grindhouse cinema that *Raiders of the Lost Ark* has with 1940s and late 1930s movie serials'.[17] This is a nostalgic relationship to East Asian cinema, identifying Tarantino as part of a Euro-American generation that was having formative encounters with kung fu and *chanbara* films, Japanese monster movies and gangster films in downmarket cinemas.[18] The grindhouse is open to exotic thrills, but not sensitive to cultural difference – it literally 'grinds ups' diverse cultural forms into the amorphous category of 'exploitation cin-ema'. In the grindhouse, Asian genre cinema bears the marks of its translation and repackaging – bad dubbing (parodied in a deleted scene from *Kill Bill Volume 2*), versions prepared specifically for Western consumption, like *Shogun Assassin* – its similarities to other 'exploita-tion' cinemas (particularly from Italy) more pronounced through proximity. Tarantino's postmodern grindhouse suggests a longing for the pre-DVD consumption of East Asian thrills; exotic, dangerous, mysterious. *Kill Bill Volume 1* opens with three title cards – the Shaw Brothers logo gives way to a cheesy 'And Now Our Feature Presentation' (we are watching a 'Shaws film' *in* the virtual grindhouse), but both are preceded by the Miramax logo to suggest that 'Asian trash' has been re-positioned as part of Hollywood's 'smart cinema'. On the other hand, Tarantino references an East Asian cult cinema that has thrived as part of the new cinephilia, such as what he calls 'this violent pop cinema coming out of Japan'.[19] The new Asiaphilia is epitomised by the British distributor Tartan Metro's 'Asia Extreme' banner, which promises 'exotic and dangerous cinematic thrills'.[20] Japan in particular functions as a pleasurably violent other within this formation. Tarantino made considerable capital out of preparing a bloodier ver-sion of *Kill Bill Volume 1* for the Japanese market, claiming that Japan 'can handle this stuff better. They just think it's funny'.[21] While this appears to authenticate the 'harder' version for the Asiaphile cultist, it also, as Gary Needham observes, constructs 'a kind of innate desire for cruelty and extreme violence as a typical trait of Japanese film audiences'.[22]

Kill Bill's most substantial Asian influence is *Lady Snowblood* (Japan, 1974), in which Kaji Meiko plays a swordswoman literally born for vengeance. The film exerts a formal, as well as narrative, influence, with its chapter headings, self-conscious use of panels from the original Manga during a flashback sequence, and a snowbound climax that is invoked in the confrontation between The Bride and O-Ren. Kaji's 'demon of the netherworld' can be seen as the inspiration for both The Bride and O-Ren, but it's hard to see the equivalence between the fantasies of empowerment that Tarantino discerns in his two 'Lady Snowbloods':

> I'm kind of secretly hoping that *Kill Bill* inspires some thirteen-year-old girl to put up a poster of Uma Thurman in her Day-Glo track suit, or maybe causes some Asian teenager who doesn't have any role models to look up at Lucy Liu on the screen and feel empowered.[23]

Leaving aside the question of whether Asian (does he mean Asian *American?*) teenage girls are short of role models, there's a glaring asymmetry in what *Kill Bill* offers to its imagined audience(s). O-Ren is the most developed of the film's Asian characters, perhaps because of her hybridised identity (Japanese-Chinese-American), but she is pathologised by her appetite for revenge and power. Her animated incarnation as avenging nymphet aligns her with the homicidal Go-Go and frames her within a fantasy of 'extreme' Asia. The Bride is 'Asianised' in the course of her vendetta, both through her mastery of Chinese and Japanese Martial Arts and the zen-like epigrams that punctuate her journey in *Volume 1* – this 'silly Caucasian girl' can play *very* nicely with samurai swords, thank you. She may cast her 'womanhood' aside (as *Lady Snowblood*'s theme song puts it), slaughtering Vernita Green in front of her daughter, but she ultimately reclaims it via Hollywood's favourite trope for recuperating violent women – motherhood. Ultimately, while Tarantino finds Asia 'cool', his sympathies remain with Asianised white protagonists, while the film reproduces Orientalist tropes of impenetrable psyches and exotic otherness.

The Art of Displacement: Luc Besson, *Film d'action* and Asian Cinema

During one of *Ong-Bak*'s celebrated action scenes, as Tony Jaa vaults over and slides under cars, side-somersaults between sheets of glass and leaps through a ring of barbed wire, it would be easy to miss graffiti invitations to two Western film-makers, Steven Spielberg and Luc Besson, to work with the film's makers. Spielberg is an obvious referent for global ambition, but what was it about Besson that made him seem an appropriate recipient for this message? Was it EuropaCorp's distribution of Asian, and particularly Thai, films, or was there some other sense in which Besson was a kindred figure? Either way, the French producer-director (unlike Spielberg) responded to the invitation, both by distributing *Ong-Bak* in France and subsequently building other links with the Thai film industry, including producing *Nam Prix* (Thailand, 2006) for EuropaCorp Japan.[24]

Susan Hayward characterises Besson as a 'self-made film-maker' who has 'beaten the Americans at their own game'.[25] Like Tsui Hark in Hong Kong, another producer-director who could in his heyday be said to have 'beaten the Americans at their own game', he has a knack for initiating popular cycles and series (the *Transporter* and *Taxi* films), both absorbing and 'localising' influences from Hollywood, and injecting political subtexts into hyperactive, youth-oriented genre films.[26] As a director, Besson was associated with the glossy, stylised *cinema du look*. As a producer, he is central to the emergence of *film d'action* in France, influenced by both Hollywood and Asia and described by Hayward as a high octane cinema of attractions, like EuropaCorp's *Taxi* series (France, 1998, 2000, 2003), constructed around 'high speed car chases, cheap gags and martial art-inspired fight scenes, all set to a hip-hop musical score'.[27] *Film d'action* is frequently seen as antithetical to 'authentic' French national cinema. According to *Variety*, 'Besson eschews the idea of intimate, personal films in his own language, instead using his European base to make English-lingo films that have a Hollywood style but with Euro DNA'.[28] In this equation, Besson both betrays and is betrayed by his 'Frenchness'; his cinematic 'DNA' gives him away as he attempts to pass himself off as a Hollywood film-maker. French Martial Arts films, as Peter Hutchings suggests, are particularly vulnerable to being perceived as 'second-hand appropriations' – French copies of American copies of Hong Kong films.[29]

The *film d'action* can be seen as one of three types of French Asiaphile cinema. Besson is joined by Christophe Gans, who has adapted a Japanese manga (*Crying Freeman*, France, 1995), added kung fu to a historical film about the Beast of Gevaudan (*Brotherhood of the Wolf*, France/Canada, 2001) and adapted a Japanese console game set in a Gothic American town (*Silent Hill*, US/France/Canada/Japan, 2006). The second type can be found within commercial Art cinema, such as Olivier Assayas' *Irma Vep* (France, 1996). Finally, Nicole Brenez identifies a strand of East Asian cinephilia in more experimental avant-garde films. Film-makers such as Agatha Dreyfus and Xavier Beart find in Hong Kong action films a 'liberating lever to reconstruct the problem of movement'.[30] Brenez contrasts a cinema engaged with the 'non-figurative phenomenon of psychic energy',[31] with the debased 'mimetic repetition' of Besson and Gans,[32] but I'm less certain that some of the recent Besson productions aren't in their own populist way concerned with the 'secrets of movement'.

EuropaCorp's main excursions into Martial Arts cinema are the *Transporter* films and two Jet Li vehicles, all four filmed in English and deploying Hong Kong fight choreographers (Yuen Wo-ping on *Danny the Dog* – Cory Yuen on the others). *The Transporter* is nominally credited to action director Cory Yuen, but Louis Leterrier's credit as 'artistic director' suggests that Yuen was brought in mainly to add some Hong Kong flair to the fight scenes and stunts. The sequel confirms this impression when Yuen's onscreen credit is downgraded to action choreography and Leterrier's upgraded to director proper. Both films can be seen as part of Western cinema's search for the Great White Hope of Martial Arts movies; where once karate champions like Chuck Norris attempted to fill Bruce Lee's shoes, now Hong Kong fight teams transform action men like Keanu Reeves and (in this case) Jason Statham into overnight kung fu stars.

According to Kwai-cheung Lo, 'Hollywood's westernization of Hong Kong action stars is always criticized for being like a love relationship in which one partner tries to change the very things in her lover that attracted her in the first place'.[33] While *Kiss of the Dragon* is certainly no *Once Upon a Time in China*, it does give the impression of having examined how Jet Li's persona works in his modern-day Hong Kong films. The film maps the kung fu star's chaste chivalry onto the emotionally withdrawn heroes of Besson's earlier films, particularly *Leon* (France/US, 1994). Hayward describes Jean Reno's eponymous hitman as an 'automaton ... apparently without feeling ... regressively turned back within himself', even 'seemingly autistic',[34] a characterisation that largely applies to Li's single-minded Mainland cop. *Danny the Dog* offers Li a weightier dramatic part, but does so by regressing the hero even further. If Leon is a '12-year-old within a 40-year-old body',[35] then Danny (Li) seems to have had his development arrested at an earlier age. Raised as a human pitbull, he alternates between unremitting violence (dog collar off) and childlike fragility (collar on).[36] Both of the Li films possess an abstract sense of geo-cultural specificity. *Kiss of the Dragon* is set in Paris, but one in which everyone speaks English and tourist landmarks are rarely out of shot. *Danny the Dog* opts for a Glasgow seemingly devoid of anyone Scottish, but populated by Chinese orphans, Afro-American men, white American girls and a crew of largely Cockney hoodlums that seem to have strayed from a Guy Ritchie film.

Banlieue 13/District 13 (Pierre Morel, France, 2004) re-inscribes 'Frenchness' onto *film d'action*, but also shifts its Asian cinematic referent from Hong Kong to Thailand; or rather, a Thai film made under the spell of Hong Kong cinema. The film can also be seen as an action-movie variant on *cinema de banlieue*, films set in outer-city, mainly multi-ethnic housing estates such as *La Haine* (France, 1995).[37] In 2010, the eponymous volatile *banlieue* is walled off by a nervous government. When a stolen fragmentation bomb finds its way into the 'danger zone', undercover cop Damien (Cyril Raffaelli) and Leito (David Belle), an inhabitant of *B-13*, are sent in to retrieve it. Damien is upright but naive, and Leito, a subaltern knight-errant who steals heroin in order to destroy it, is right to be cynical about the mission – the film's ultimate villain isn't the local ganglord, but the Secretary of State for Defence, who staged the theft in order to cleanse the troublesome district. At a lean 80 something minutes, *B-13* offers a populist subtext within a series of body-centred action spectacles.

B-13's English-language tagline was 'No Wires, No Special Effects, No Limits', a nod to Jackie Chan's *Rumble in the Bronx* ('No Fear, No Stuntman, No Equal') by way of *Ong-Bak* ('No Stuntmen, No Wire Action, No Computer Graphics'). We are invited to see David Belle and Cyril Raffaelli as French equivalents to both Chan and Jaa. As pretender to the martial arts throne previously occupied by Chinese men, Tony Jaa was promoted as a 'spectacle of the real', but *Ong-Bak* was also seen as remarkable for coming from a national cinema with no international reputation for making Martial Arts films. More than this, it was widely seen as *beating Hong Kong at its own game*. If *Ong-Bak* superseded the Hong Kong action film for some fans, it did so by both knowingly drawing on it – its country-boy-in-big-city plot is familiar to every Bruce Lee fan – and 'localising' it by combining *muay thai* with the kind of dangerous stuntwork associated with classic Jackie Chan. *B-13* is Western action cinema's first attempt at a 'spectacle of the real', but there's more going on than an attempt to co-opt Asian 'authenticity'. What Morel and Besson learn from *Ong-Bak* is the importance of localising Hong Kong Martial Arts cinema, of finding an indigenous equivalent – after all, as one viewer observes, this film, too, 'is from a nation that is not known for kung fu movies'.[38] While *Ong-Bak* has its own national fighting art to draw on, France clearly doesn't, but what it does have is *le parkour*, the 'Art of Displacement'.

In the words of the film's press notes, *parkour* is 'a philosophy of action-based movement in an urban environment in which objects such as buildings are absolutely to be scaled rather than circumvented'.[39] It has a more aestheticised offshoot in 'Freerunning', which favours a more spectacular approach to the economy of *parkour*. *Parkour*'s claims to national specificity lie not only in its subcultural *banlieue* origins, but its earlier roots in the theories of George Hebert that influenced the training of French soldiers during the Vietnam War. With cultural links to the French 'encounter with Asia', modern *parkour* clearly also invites comparison with the bodily spectacle of East Asian and South East Asian action cinema. In his 1980s action films, Jackie Chan interacts with the mutating physical, cultural and technological space of modern Hong Kong, developing a new style of action based on 'dynamic movement and reconfiguring of space'.[40] In *Ong-Bak*, Tony Jaa is the country boy transplanted to the cosmopolitan, global city of Bangkok, but quickly adapts his skills to traversing a series of human and material obstacles. *Parkour* as subcultural practice can be seen as a reclaiming of urban space, thus *B-13*'s dystopian narrative provides the perfect generic framework for the oppositional athletic body to resonate as it does in the best kung fu movies, to *mean something* as well as thrill the spectator. The tower blocks of *B-13* are sparser than the obstacle courses faced by Chan and Jaa – apart from a rope hanging conveniently outside a window, the film doesn't throw parallel sheets of glass or ropes of barbed wire at its heroes with quite the same gleeful abandon. But the real Parisian *B-13* is also where real-life *traceurs* (practitioners of *parkour*) train, again locating the film and the athletic body within a culturally specific context.

While it has some way to go to catch up with kung fu, *parkour* is scarcely new to the screen. It made quite an impact in a BBC promo *Rush Hour* (2002), featuring *parkour* founder and *B-13* star David Belle, and the documentaries *Jump London* (Channel 4, UK, 2003) and *Jump Britain* (Channel 4, UK, 2005). Currently, global action cinema is making more use of *parkour* and Freerunning, most famously in *Casino Royale* (US/UK, 2006). One of James Bond's biggest setpieces finds our hero in pursuit of Sebastien Foucan, another *parkour* pioneer and the founder of Freerunning. Unlike Belle in *B-13*, Foucan is used as stuntman (and choreographer) rather than a star, and subordinated to the role of villainous ethnic other in the kind of imperialist adventure one expects of the Bond series. Just like Hong Kong action before them, *parkour* and Freerunning seem to be in the process of being disembedded by global action cinema.

In French cinema, *parkour* has appeared in sequences in *Taxi 2* and *Crimson Rivers II: Angels of the Apocalypse* (France, 2004), but is rather more central to EuropaCorp's *Yamakasi – Les Samourai des Temps Modernes* (France, 2001). The latter features members of the original *yamakasi*, the group of *traceurs* founded by Belle, but seems unable to find a satisfactory narrative to showcase the art. *B-13* re-positions *parkour* in the light of *Ong-Bak,* as a wire-free, CGI-free, gravity-defying spectacle. The casting of David Belle lends it an additional layer of authenticity. One online viewer draws analogies with another innovative icon: 'Watching B13, I feel like one of the first guys to see Bruce Lee. The styles are amazing.'[41]

As remarkable and graceful as Belle is, however, he alone cannot provide a spectacle comparable to Tony Jaa's amazing feats, and the film must distribute its authentic star-body across two different performers. Cyril Raffaelli, a martial artist, former circus performer and stuntman, who worked with Jet Li on *Kiss of the Dragon*, brings a more noticeably Hong Kong-inspired style of action to the film. While Belle and Raffaelli are clearly intended to complement each other's skills, Raffaelli (who also choreographs) brings *parkour* into the orbit of Martial Arts. Each of the two stars is given a signature action sequence by way of introduction. The opening chase sequence featuring Belle sees him bouncing off walls, jumping through a tiny window (Figures 1 and 2), evading his pursuers 'like a bar of soap'. He moves in and out of apartment blocks, up and across walls, leaping from balcony to balcony, roof to roof. One online viewer complains that the action suffers from '"Hollywood style" over-editing … David Belle & Cyril Raffaelli have *real* skills … so why chop most of the best moves into 3 separate shots, so we can't really appreciate them?'.[42] *B-13* doesn't luxuriate in the moving body to the same degree that *Ong-Bak* does, and its editing style is less committed to the legibility that Bordwell discerns in Hong Kong action.[43] Nevertheless, several of Belle's gravity-defying leaps do take place in a single take (Figures 3 and 4). Raffaelli's introductory sequence, an extended combat in a casino, offers a mixture of gunplay and kung fu that is more familiar from Hong Kong action cinema – somersaults and flips, stuntmen performing 'bad' landings, a beautiful mid-air spinning kick used to disarm a gunman, and a running two-footed drop kick borrowed from *Danny the Dog*.

Figures 1 & 2. Shots from the opening chase sequence of *Banlieue 13*

Western discourses surrounding Hong Kong action aesthetics broadly take two forms. On the one hand, there is a celebration of the *representation* of dynamic movement and inner power – the aesthetics of speed, the ecstatic pulse of kinetic spectacle, the 'secret of movement'.[44] The 'secret' of this aesthetic, while it has connections to local cultural forms, lies in the plasticity of the medium, and thus it is a secret that can escape the boundaries of 'national cinema' and blend into other cinemas, whether they be Hollywood blockbusters (like *Kill Bill*) or French avant-garde films. On the other hand, Hong Kong (and more recently, Thai) cinema as a 'spectacle of the real' both continues to obsess fans more than scholars, and is less easy for Western cinema to incorporate. For Jackie Chan, the 'real' was an important way of resisting Hollywood, by offering something it couldn't reproduce – I imagine that Tony Jaa and his collaborators see his skills similarly. What is especially notable about *B-13* is that it not only incorporates notions of

Figures 3 & 4. One of David Belle's single take gravity-defying leaps in *Banlieue 13*

the real into its promotion, but that it also seems to have been consumed by some viewers within this frame of reference.

Both *Ong-Bak* and *B-13* were bought for North American release by Magnolia Pictures, whose boss Eamonn Bowles seems to have seen them as similar kinds of exotic action. 'I just sat there slack-jawed', he claimed after seeing *Ong-Bak* at the Toronto Film Festival, 'I could not believe what (Jaa) was doing'.[45] The following year, he promised that *B-13* would be 'a complete revelation for action fans', and that Belle and Raffaelli performed some of the 'most amazing stunts I've ever seen'.[46] Such hyperbole should perhaps not be taken too literally. What is more striking is the way that the French movie was able to duplicate some of the internet buzz surrounding *Ong-Bak*. Some viewers even compared the two films:

Anyone who enjoyed this film should check out *Ong Bak* which features similar, if not better, real-time stunts and amazing action.[47]

If you've seen the street chase scene in *Ong-Bak: The Thai Warrior* and thought that it was a refreshing change from all the wire work present in most action films today, that pales in comparison to the chase scenes in *Banlieue 13*. Watching David Belle escape from an apartment building while chased by thugs is like watching poetry in motion ... Every action scene in the movie is real; there is absolutely no wire work of any kind.[48]

Banlieue 13 manages to neither incorporate nor yield to Hong Kong and Thai action. Instead, it seems to emerge from a dialogue about how to make a 'body cinema' that combines global appeal with local resonance. In this dialogue, it is by no means clear which is the 'dominant' cinema and which the 'peripheral' one.

Kill Bill is most poignant (and thrilling) when it captures the imprint East Asian action cinema has left on the Western cinephile imaginary over the last 30 years. On the other hand, in the post-*Crouching Tiger* era, it feels decidedly regressive to see a global Martial Arts film return to fantasies of white warriors triumphing over the 'Orient'. The fantasy of 'Orientalist' immersion blurs the desire to 'be' and 'have' Asian, reminding us that the Asiaphile-connoisseur still operates with a 'politics of cultural appropriation'.[49] Tarantino's outlook can be seen as simultaneously reverent and aggressively territorial, his desire to 'walk with the giants' of Martial Arts cinema replaying the colonial trope of conquest. Besson's EuropaCorp films circumvent the desire to 'go Orientalist', and at their worst, seemingly adopt an opportunistic relationship to Asian popular cinema. But they display an ongoing fascination with the physical stardom embodied by Asian action cinema, whether through mimicry (the *Transporter* films), cultural adaptation (Jet Li's persona) or finding parallels between different kinetic regimes (kung fu/*muay thai/parkour*). *Banlieue 13*'s legacy may prove to be a mixed blessing – it has finally given the Western Martial Arts film a transcendent white body. But it also suggests that *film d'action* sees Asian action cinema not only as a peripheral resource to be plundered, but a pioneer of 'glocal' popular cinema.

References

1   Lii, Ding-tzann, 'A colonised empire: reflections on the expansion of Hong Kong film in Asian countries' in Kuan-hsing Chen (ed), *Trajectories: Inter-Asian Cultural Studies* (London and New York: Routledge, 1998), p.134.

2   Topel, Fred, 'Tarantino talks *Kill Bill Volume 2*' in Paul A. Woods (ed), *Quentin Tarantino: The Film Geek Files* (London: Plexus, 2005), p.183.

3   Lii: 'A colonised empire', p.134.

4   Although it was possible to see the original version in France, too.

5   The theme songs from both series (sung by Kaji) appear in Volume 1 and 2 respectively.

6   See, for example: Machiyama, Tomohiro, 'Quentin Tarantino reveals almost everything that inspired *Kill Bill*' in Paul A. Woods (ed), *Quentin Tarantino: The Film Geek Files*, pp.172–8; Holm, D.K., *Kill Bill: An Unofficial Casebook* (London: Glitter Books, 2004); '*Kill Bill* references guides', *The Tarantino Wiki*, <http://www.tarantino.info/wiki/index.php/ Kill_Bill_References_Guide> accessed 28 November 2006.

7   Anderson, Aaron, 'Mindful violence: The visibility of power and inner life in *Kill Bill*', *Jump Cut: A Review of Contemporary Media* 47 (2004), <http://www.ejumpcut.org/archive/jc47.2005/KillBill/index.html> pp.6, 7, accessed 28 November 2006.

8   *The Making of Kill Bill Volume 1* (DVD extra).

9   Ma, Sheng-mei, *East-West Montage: Reflections on Asian Bodies in Diaspora* (Hawaii: University of Hawaii Press, forthcoming).

10 Stringer, Julian, 'Problems with the treatment of Hong Kong cinema as camp', *Asian Cinema* 8.2 (1996/7), p.58.

11 Stringer: 'Problems', p.60.

12 Machiyama: 'Quentin Tarantino reveals almost everything', p.177.

13 In the case of Chiba, he barely takes the action figure out of his box.

14 Machiyama: 'Quentin Tarantino reveals almost everything', p.174.

15 Desser, David, 'Hong Kong and the new cinephilia' in Meaghan Morris, Siu Leung Li and Stephen Chan Ching-ku (eds), *Hong Kong Connections: Transnational Imagination in Action Cinema* (Durham and HK: Duke University Press/Hong Kong University Press 2005), p.208.

16 Desser: 'Hong Kong', p.216.

17 *The Making of Kill Bill Volume 1*.

18 For more on this, see Desser, David 'Consuming Asia: Chinese and Japanese popular culture and the American imaginary' in Jenny Kwok Wah Lau (ed), *Multiple Modernities: Cinemas and Popular Media in Transnational East Asia* (Philadelphia: Temple University Press, 2003), pp.167–78 and Desser, 'The Kung Fu craze: Hong Kong Cinema's first

American reception' in Desser and Poshek Fu (eds), *The Cinema of Hong Kong: History, Arts, Identity* (Cambridge and New York: Cambridge University Press, 2000), pp.19–43.

19   Machiyama: 'Quentin Tarantino reveals almost everything', p.175.

20   Needham, Gary, 'Japanese cinema and Orientalism' in Dimitrios Eleftheriotis and Gary Needham (eds), *Asian Cinemas: A Reader and Guide* (Edinburgh: Edinburgh University Press, 2006), p.11.

21   Dinning, Mark, 'The Big Boss', *Empire* 173 (2003), p.92.

22   Needham: 'Japanese Cinema and Orientalism', p.11.

23   Cabot Black, Henry, 'Quentin bloody Quentin' in Paul A. Woods (ed), *Quentin Tarantino: The Film Geek Files*, p.167.

24   Frater, Patrick, 'EuropaCorp hot for Thai sauce: Besson's shingle continues into Asia', *Variety*, 24 June 2005, <http://www.variety.com/article/VR1117925032?categoryid=1043&cs=1> accessed 9 November 2006.

25   Hayward, Susan, 'Luc Besson' in Yvonne Tasker (ed.) *Fifty Contemporary Filmmakers* (London and New York: Routledge, 2002), p.51.

26   Susan Hayward, for example, reads Besson's earlier films as director against the disenchantment that marked the Mitterand regime, an era of corruption, recession and unemployment, while it is common to map Tsui's films onto the period between the Sino-British Joint Declaration (1984) and Hong Kong's return to Chinese sovereignty (1997).

27   Hayward: *French National Cinema*, p.298.

28   Nicole LaPorte, 'Despite the lures, international helmers resist Hollywood', *Variety*, 5 June 2005, <http://www.variety.com/article/VR1117923919?categoryid=19&cs=1&query=luc+and+besson&display=luc+besson>

29   Hutchings, Peter, 'Le Kung Fu: Martial Arts and national (in)Authenticities in contemporary French cinema', Unpublished Paper, European Cinema Research Forum, University of Northumbria, 1995.

30   Brenez, Nicole, 'The secrets of movement: The influence of Hong Kong action cinema upon the contemporary avant-garde' in Meaghan Morris *et al.*, *Hong Kong Connections: Transnational Imagination in Action Cinema*, p.164.

31   Brenez: 'The secrets of movement', p.169.

32   Brenez: 'The secrets of movement', p.173.

33   Kwai-cheung Lo, *Chinese Face/Off: The Transnational Popular Culture of Hong Kong* (Urbana and Chicago: University of Illinois Press, 2005), p.155.

34   Susan Hayward, *Luc Besson* (Manchester and New York, Manchester University Press, 1998), p.61.

35   Hayward: *Luc Besson*, p.61.

36   The dog collar imagery caused the film some problems in China.

37   For more on *banlieue* cinema, see Tarr, Carrie, *Reframing Difference: Beur and Banlieue Filmmaking in France* (Manchester and New York: Manchester University Press, 2005).

38   Huerta, A. Joseph, Amazon Customer Reviews.

39   Leyland, Matthew, 'District 13', *Sight and Sound* 16, 6 (2006), p.44.

40   Tateishi, Ramie, 'Jackie Chan and the re-invention of tradition', *Asian Cinema* 10, 1 (1998), p.78.

41   Huerta, A. Joseph, Amazon Customer Reviews.

42   Simon Booth (UK), Internet Movie Database User Comments, <http://www.imdb.com/title/tt0414852/usercomments>

43   Bordwell, David, *Planet Hong Kong: Popular Cinema and the Art of Entertainment* (Cambridge, Massachusetts and London: Harvard University Press, 2000), pp.163–8.

44   See, for example, Bordwell, *Planet Hong Kong*, Brenez, 'The secrets of movement'; and Martin, Adrian, 'At the edge of the cut: An encounter with the Hong Style in contemporary action cinema' in Morris *et al.* (eds), *Hong Kong Connections: Transnational Imaginations in Action Cinema.*

45   Mohr, I., 'Magnolia's "Warrior" a welcome dinner guest', *The Hollywood Reporter*, 2004, <http://www.hollywoodreporter.com/thr/columns/apple_corps.jsp> accessed 21 June 2004.

46   McClintock, Pamela, 'Magnolia fits in District', *Variety*, 21 November 2005, <http://www.variety.com/article/VR1117933384?categoryid=13&cs=13&cs=1&query=luc+and+besson&display=luc+besson>

47   'Fat Bob', Amazon Customer Reviews.

48   Richard from Toronto, Internet Movie Database User Comments, <http://www.imdb.com/title/tt0414852/usercomments?start=10>

49   Hamamoto, Darrell Y., 'Introduction: On Asian American film and criticism' in Hamamoto and Sandra Liu (eds), *Countervisions: Asian American Film Criticism* (Philadelphia: Temple University Press, 2000), p.13.

15

Sheng-mei Ma

Brush and Blade in East-West Cultures

Unsheathe

The apparently contradictory pairs in the title turn out to have blood
ties that go back to the nineteenth century. These cultural opposites,
after the initial shock and revulsion of colonialism, begin to attract each
other, driven by the urge to be one: East and West, brush and blade, the
literary and the martial. In the West, nineteenth- and early twentieth-
century colonial loathing of the Orient gradually gives way to high
modernist and postmodernist idolisation; the demonic, dehumanising
non-West metamorphoses over time into a dream-self. Whereas
Conrad, Forster, Maugham and Orwell – all implicated in colonialist
ideology to various extent – project irrationality and acephalic violence
onto non-Western cultures, their initial shock evolves into a phallic sign
of empowerment in contemporary Hollywood and independent cinema. Nearly a century ago, novelists dreaded the blade of wrath in the
hands of the colonised. Today's film-makers circulate the ideal oneness
of the poetic and the manic, borrowed from the East, for a receptive
global market. Yet the diametrically opposed sensibilities spring from
the same root of 'Orientalism'. A colonialist attempt to inflate and to
lose itself, Orientalism has formulaically polarised the West's 'shadow'
into the aesthetic and the abominable: geisha and samurai, chrysanthemum and the sword,[1] Madame Butterfly and Dragon Lady, Charlie
Chan and Fu Manchu, castrated celestial and the Yellow Peril. The
binarism renders each of its attributes indispensable to the other.
    When high modernists inherit an 'Orientalist' legacy, dialectical
clashes often come in the metaphor of thunder, whose abruptness and

raw force embody a conceptual cataclysm that destroys and enlightens. Thus, in the flash of the Montashigi blade as it is unsheathed,[2] in the shock of Kali's bloody tongue,[3] modernist and avant-gardist such as Yeats and Bataille intuit an apocalyptic vision. Modern, secular and 'scientific', the West transfers its need for myth and magic to the phantasmagoric Orient. Accordingly in literature, Pound borrows from what he believes to be Chinese ideograms a medium to inaugurate modernist poetry, alleging that Chinese sentence structure gives the desired *'transference of power'* like 'a flash of lightning . . . between two terms, a cloud and the earth'.[4] Imagistically, Pound weds two disparate, intangible realms: language and nature, half-understood Chinese and modernism-in-the-making. Pound further closes with three Chinese ideograms, 'sun', 'rise' and 'East', all of which, in his split-word analysis, come to pictorialise their meaning. 'East' is taken to visualise the sun amidst trees, hence sunrise in the East. Not only the language of the East, but the East itself, becomes the rock on which modernist poetry is founded. Likewise, the drought of Eliot's *The Waste Land* ends in an Oriental epilogue as 'What the Thunder Said' pronounces *'Datta'*, *'Dayadhvam'*, *'Damyata'* (Give, Sympathize, Control). In both cases, high modernists are speaking in tongue, and unintelligible Oriental tongues to be exact, to usher in a new era. The brush is the blade of annihilation and of creation.

These cultural opposites attract because East and West share the same 'blood', only forced apart schizophrenically. Science and logic favour the analytical over the synthetic, a preference conducive to the maintenance of boundary and power. One particular duo is implied by 'brush and blade': the name and the named. While blade betokens violence, the naming of violence through the sword's classical, elegant nomenclature – King Arthur's Excalibur, *Crouching Tiger, Hidden Dragon*'s Qingming Sword, or *Kill Bill*'s Hattori Hanzo Sword – effects a sublimation. Bloodshed and death, which are, ultimately, what is being named, retreat in the chain of signification, abstracted first as the named sword, then as the name of the sword, a proper name in foreign words without dictionary definition, whose linguistic elusiveness intimates wonder and mystique.

Blood is the missing link between brush and blade as well as the true signified; it alludes to both the physical and the spiritual, both the body's essential fluid and the essence of 'race', 'nation' and 'spirit'. Rather than a 50–50 split between human biology and human mind, 'blood', in its role as the Holy Spirit to the Trinity with brush and blade, privileges the unseen, the veiled and the spiritual, over the materialistic, the human senses and the empiricist. In both films and literature herein, the master narrative entails that only by sacrificing the physical blood can one attain the spiritual counterpart. Although these texts on brush and blade are written in invisible blood, as it were, the fact that brush enjoys top billing, preceding blade, demonstrates the belief that the spirit is superior and gives meaning to the matter. Philosophically, Nietzsche's Oriental Superman Zarathustra admonishes thus: 'Write in blood', a ritual of self-sacrifice that elevates human drama of blood-letting by the sword.[5] The proverb 'the Pen is mightier than the Sword' serves a similar function to rein in and euphemise human aggression. In the Old Testament, the Word, the Voice from the Burning Bush and the Unnameable 'I am' take precedence over idols and images. Derrida labels this Greco-Judaic-Christian tradition 'logocentrism' that valorises the Word.[6] This age-long belief in brush over blade runs counter to the human history of unrelenting war and struggle. Althusser's idea of ideological interpellation of individuals as subjects helps explain why traces of blood are missing in these tales jointly written by brush and blade.[7] Ironically, whereas these tales laud spiritual triumphalism, their very existence must be understood in a materialistic framework. The trend of swordplay films elegising sacrifice, in our present day, aims to cash in on the box office. Market driven colonialism, a century ago, breathes life into nationhood and masculinity in Conrad *et al.*

In Freudian psychoanalysis, the sword is a phallic fetish, whose power is acknowledged and disavowed at once, whose potential stems from the originary trauma of a boy's inference that the maternal penis has been castrated. The copulation of brush and blade constitutes a fetish of power as well in the Lacanian nexus of signs. Lacan argues that rather than a one-to-one correspondence between the signifier and the signified, the signifier acquires meaning through its connection with other signifiers. The structure of language creates the effect of signification. A word no longer points to the thing, but to other words. Instead of the Freudian Patriarch suggested by the word 'father', Lacan coins the term 'Name-of-the-Father' to underline his idea of linguistic self-reflexiveness. Lacan proceeds in 'The Signification of the Phallus' to analyse the phallus as a sign: The phallus 'can play its role [of signifier] only when veiled, that is to say, as itself a sign of the latency with which any signifiable is struck'.[8] The more obscure the phallus, the more transformative possibilities with which it is vested. In fact, since its debut in Freud's psychoanalysis, the penis has been an absent presence, or a present absence.[9] The sword is a perfect phallic symbol not only for its aggressiveness but for its occluded-ness – encased in the scabbard, untainted by the blood it has shed, the erection of the penis implied. Layers of veiling come to be crystallised not in 'Name-of-the-Father', but 'Name-of-the-Sword'. The 'Name-of-the-Sword', in turn, sets off a signifying effect, the centre of which is the absence of the object, a void behind the name. The phallic sword can also be taken to figure, in Bataille's *Erotism: Death and Sensuality*,[10] as both an instrument of love or eroticism and an instrument of death. Yoking together seemingly unrelated spheres, all these thinkers, Pound and Eliot included, manifest a shared desire to, in a single stroke of wedding antitheses, grasp the totality, or oneness, of things. In essence, theorists are in search of a systemic explanation that is constructed by human speech, but goes beyond it in a way evoking the so-called 'oceanic feeling' in mysticism.[11] They are after the unnameable, like the vowel-less, well-nigh unpronounceable YHWH in Judaism or the 'You-Know-Who' in *Harry Potter*.

Global Phallus

At one of the entrances to the Bronze Exhibit Hall in Beijing's Forbidden City stands a *Shaoyu* sword, dating from the late Spring-Autumn period (652–476 BC). As if made of steel, the blade shines after 2,500 years. Like a silent spell, 20 ancient characters are inscribed in gold down the middle on either side. The blade and the words cut through time, constituting an aura of power, where violence and culture – even grace – are immanent in the symbols of sword and script. Arising out of the Asian dialectical philosophy of yin and yang, of *Wen* and *Wu* (the literary and the martial), the calligraphic brush and the sword have long defined masculine empowerment in Asian culture and, in recent decades, Asian films. The adage '*litouzhibei*' ('strength penetrating to the back of the paper') complements calligraphy in the metaphor of swordsmanship, namely, the force of the brush goes through rice paper in the same manner that a sword severs its target. '*Li*' ('strength') alludes not so much to muscle strength as *qi* (breath or inner strength), elevating the calligrapher from the physical world. The precursor to Chinese swordplay films, *wuxia xiao shuo* (novels of chivalry), frequently juxtaposes the book and the sword, as in the leading contemporary practitioner of this genre Jin Yung's *Shujian enchou ji* (*The Chronicle of Book and Sword, Favour and Hate*). In the West, heroic feats must also be performed through art. Achilles and Odysseus are indebted to Homer, the hero with the pen; *Beowulf* and *Sir Gawain and the Green Knight* owe their existence to anonymous Old English and Middle English bards; the symbolic loss of swords of Antony, Othello and others depends on Shakespeare's poetry; Don Quixote with his makeshift lance requires a Cervantes.

The contemporary medium crystallising the union of sword and art is global cinema. As the world shrinks in the vein of David Harvey's time-space compression,[12] film-makers omnivorise various warrior traditions, Western and Eastern, for the late capitalist market. Dominated by post-Fordist circulation of capital, information and images, television and cinema are key players in this globalisation. Reality is increasingly interwoven with what Jean Baudrillard terms hyperreal simulacra.[13] Drawing from the *aura* of various heroic traditions for profit-making, global cinema routinely flattens these traditions to the point of a 'funhouse of hyper-real media images and . . . of floating signifiers in the postmodern carnival'.[14] But let us return for a brief moment to Old Asia, the source of this global film style, before the coming of the barbarians.

Asian swordplay films at their best resemble the brush that traces the way of the sword, ideographic stroke copying the stroke of the blade. The samurai leader in Kurosawa Akira's classic *Seven Samurai* (Japan, 1954) wields a sword during battle; subsequently, he picks up the brush to cross out enemy kills and strategise against remaining bandits. In the Hong Kong swordplay classic *Five Tigers Killing a Dragon/Brothers Five* (Lo Wei, HK, 1970), one of the heroes fights with a pointed metal brush. Not surprisingly, he happens to be the tactician of the group. A recent barbarised example of this style is Zhang Yimou's *Hero* (China/HK, 2002), which repeatedly aestheticises violence through calligraphy: one of the protagonists, *Canjian* (Broken Sword, named after the half-sword he uses), persists in his writing of *jian* (sword) while arrows fly around him; with his sword, he even composes two gigantic characters *tianxia* ('under the sun' or 'in the world') in the desert sand. The episodes of composition are captured in slow-motion, body and brush/blade synchronised in a dance. The finale arrives when the First Emperor of Qin turns his back on the assassin to contemplate the hanging scroll with the single character, *jian*. Invariably, these action sequences in *Hero* consist of the counterpoint of stasis and dynamism, prolonged shots of stillness magnifying the explosion of movement.[15] *Jing* and *dong* (quietism and motion), or *wen* and *wu*, works like day and night, each issuing from and pregnant with the other.

Complementarity lodges itself in the 'dramaturgy' as well: these scenes of violence unfold through *naming* of violence. The shower of arrows of death is literalised by the written word, *jian*, and the writing of it. Fundamentally opposite activities, writing and fighting accentuate each other, the former's stillness, persistently the focal point of the camera, anchoring the latter's movement. Even during fight scenes, characters keep a stoic, expressionless, dispassionate facade with down-cast eyes, as if the core of self is removed from and coolly observes the fighting self. Moreover, at least two fights, at the chess house and on the lake, are conducted in the contestants' minds, with their eyes closed, bodies frozen, the imagined battles proceeding in black-and-white and in slow-motion stunts. That brush receives higher regard than blade in this swordplay film manifests itself in the narrative structure as well. The *Rashomon*-esque versions of the assassination attempt are not arrayed as varying angles and possibilities, but vertically from human greed and deception to sacrifice and undying love. Unequivocally superior, the brush also prevails in that the 'words' or calligraphy of Zhao survives beyond Qin's military might and the obliteration of the State of Zhao.

The second key scene of *naming* of violence is shot on location amidst the barren beauty of Xinjiang. To dissuade the swordsman Nameless from assassinating the Emperor of Qin, *Canjian* renders *Tianxia* (the world) in the desert sand, which pictorialises, in effect, a map of what would become China. Sparing the Emperor's life means that he would eventually seize vast territories prophesied in *Tianxia* and would found the Chinese Empire, which continues to the present day. Qin's control, however, exacts an extreme form of violence historically called *fenshu kengru* ('burning books and burying scholars alive') and '*shu-tongwen chetongkuei*' ('one written script, one width for carts'). Differences in terms of written scripts, ideas and lifestyles are suppressed in the rhetorical magnanimity of *Tianxia*, simultaneously an imperial self-inflation and an odious ethnocentrism. In the film's closing moments, the Emperor confides in the assassin that he would conquer a '*Da – da – de jiangtu*' ('vast – vast – territory'), sweeping his right arm in an arc, his mouth opened wide to utter '*da*', his face tense with ambition and disdain, as if swallowing the entire space. In the name of 'the world', carnage is perpetrated and then absorbed into the oblivion of history.

The film concludes as the Emperor, 'enlightened' by his meditation on the scroll of 'Sword', grasps the true meaning of '*sa*' ('to kill'), which is '*bu sa*' ('to not kill'). Utilising four-word proverbs in pseudo-classical Chinese, the language chosen to underscore the faraway time period, the Emperor explicates the three levels to swordsmanship: *renjianheyi* ('The swordsman and the sword are one'); *shouzhongwujian, xinzhongyujian* ('No sword in the hand, the sword in the mind'), which kills with the mythical *qi* of sword; and *shouzhongwujian, xinzhongwu-jian* ('No sword in the hand, no sword in the mind'), which refrains from killing altogether. Zhang Yimou appears to sanction peace, yet ends his film with the assassin's death in a swarm of arrows. The Emperor's Zen-like awakening fails to apply to politics, the order of execution given under the pressure of the court. The true awakening is the assassin's in sparing the Emperor and sacrificing himself. Brush and its attendant values – peace and spirit – are eulogised through film-making, but somehow defused by it; even the elegant, pithy four-word proverbs are soon buried under the excessive, kitschy special effect of violence. Throughout *Hero*, Zhang manifests Althusserian interpella-tion of Chinese nationalism and global cinema's commercialisation, reflecting China's emergence as a superpower and his personal quest for financial success, name recognition and perhaps an Oscar.[16] The string of China's top tourist attractions shot on location gives the impression that this film is a collection of picture postcards or a scrap-book, relishing in Zhang's aestheticism rather than venturing beyond the material world. Repeatedly, Zhang dwells obsessively on *his* blade, or trademark cinematography, in the heavy-handed artistry and exu-berant colour schemes, now coupled with mind-boggling special effects. Zhang's recent swordplay films, including *The House of Flying Daggers* (China/HK, 2004), are so derivative of Ang Lee's *Crouching Tiger, Hidden Dragon* (HK/US/Taiwan/China, 2000) in soundtrack and visu-als that they are symptomatic of an auteur-to-be lapsing into recycling rather than innovating. Take, for instance, the subject of brush and blade. Zhang Ziyi in *Crouching Tiger* gives away her swordswoman identity when her brushstrokes reveal hidden strength. Originally meant to give the blade's heroism a spiritual dimension, Zhang Yimou blows up the twins in such an extravaganza of special effect and cine-matography that it unwittingly parodies the swordplay genre. While Zhang resorts to traditional Chinese thinking of 'dialectic concepts',[17] in the Emperor's inference of 'to not kill' from 'to kill', the film-maker evinces a similar dialectical reversal: from his early career of well-wrought art-house products to recent global-cinema commodities.[18]

Zhang Yimou's assassin, Nameless (yet another typical Chinese inversion), confesses to the Emperor that his special move is *shibu yisha* ('Ten Step One Kill'), named after his accurate coup de grace within a ten-step circumference. Here, Zhang continues the swordplay and kung fu film convention of 'naming the move', a particular form of the coun-terpoint of brush and blade. In action sequences, a specific martial skill is routinely named and even described before or during its execution. Such meta-narrative moments contain not only action but self-referentiality to action, not only violence but its legend, which defuses violence. Predating Judith Butler's performativity and devoid of the stringent level of self-reflexivity, this tradition of performance has been dubbed by Brecht as the 'alienation effect' utilising de-familiarisation.[19] For example, Stephen Chow's comical *Kung Fu Hustle* (HK/China, 2004) narrates and displays a number of famous kung fu techniques, all of which have been constructed discursively within the long history of Hong Kong cinema: Double-Ringed Arms, Yang Family Spear, Lioness' Roar, Toad Kung Fu, climaxing with the most potent of all, Buddha's Palm, a *deus ex machina* to claim final victory. Even the supposedly unique Buddha's Palm reprises other films, such as Tsui Hark's *Once Upon a Time in China* series (HK, 1991–3).

Given the Western tradition of heroes and bards,[20] Hollywood and independent films of the last decade or so, Jim Jarmusch's *Ghost Dog: The Way of the Samurai* (US, 1999), Tom Cruise's *The Last Samurai* (US, 2003) and Quentin Tarantino's *Kill Bill Volume 1* and *2* (US, 2003, 2004), have somehow looked eastward to appropriate the kinship of brush and blade. A benign form of Orientalism that projects more longing than loathing onto Asia, these film-makers, nevertheless, rehearse much of the Oriental discourse. Admittedly, Asians perpetuate their own myth, such as in Stephen Chow's naming of the kung fu moves and in Zhang Yimou's increasingly unabashed self-'Orientalisation', yet it appears that the further film-makers are situated vis-à-vis the subject of brush and blade, the more prone they are to stylisation and stereotypes, i.e. the repetition of an Orientalist repertoire. Figuratively, Western film-makers who have never acquired the skill of calligraphy are destined to paint the Orient in broad strokes. Jarmusch *et al.*, as a consequence, name elements of an Orient far more denuded than Chow's or Zhang's, while performing it – samurai's seppuku, geisha's tea ceremony, Shaolin long staff, Drunken Boxing (via Jackie Chan and *The Matrix*'s Neo), and so forth. When it comes to brush and blade, the difference between Asian and non-Asian practitioners is one in degree, not in kind. Hence, the action of the black samurai *Ghost Dog* in the urban ghetto is interrupted, commented on and foreshadowed by inter-titles, all citations from the eighteenth-century *Hagakure: The Book of the Samurai*.[21] *The Last Samurai* opens with Japan's genesis of God's blade steeped in the ocean, followed by the single character of 'Samurai', and the voiceover of 'honour', a banal Oriental move to deify the tragic heroes of samurai in modernity. The opening credits to *Kill Bill* show kanji (Chinese ideograms borrowed as one of the Japanese scripts) cut horizontally by a sword, with blood dripping down from the wound. This appears to be a spinoff from *The Matrix*'s film still of Neo and others against a backdrop of green vertical Japanese words and numbers.

This nostalgia for heroes with swords at a time of politicians with nuclear footballs is intriguing.[22] Now that the 'blade' is 'dead', the 'brush' of film-making and cultural representations tries frantically to keep its partner alive. The tragic beauty of individual heroism befits swords more than guns, guns more than machine guns, machine guns more than bombs, for the simple reason that one-to-one combat, with the valour and honour it entails, becomes progressively impossible in a remote controlled warfare of indiscriminate killing and massive casualties. Many swordplay classics mourn the outdated swords: every samurai killed in *Seven Samurai* dies from gun shot; the battle in *Kagemusha* (*The Shadow Warrior*, Japan, 1980) is decided by musket volleys that ruthlessly cut down charging cavalries; *Once Upon a Time in China I* (Tsui Hark, HK, 1991) also concludes with a kung fu master's death by bullets. The movie-going public exhibits such an anachronistic taste for swords that it bespeaks a suppressed anxiety over (post)modernity, one that seeks relief in equally far-fetched scenarios of a samurai 'retainer' Ghost Dog; of a Civil War veteran Algren, played by Tom Cruise, training Japanese soldiers in firearms use; and of an over-the-top revenge saga that culminates in the killing of Bill. While Jarmusch and Tarantino, with their independent and art-house sensibility, tweak the Eastern swordplay genre through irony, parody, pastiche and montage, Cruise of the twenty-first century revitalises vintage Orientalism of the kind Tom Clavell perpetrates in his 1975 two-volume *Shogun*.

Cruise's title gives away the white man's imaginary. Like *The Last of the Mohicans* (US, 1992) and *Dances with Wolves* (US, 1990), *The Last Samurai* is so named to acquire a romantic tragic glow associated with extinction and self-alienation. In the name of the demise of the samurai lineage, Cruise recycles mainstream masculinist fancy over the endgame of a racial other: Mohican braves, the Wild West or Japanese samurais. Tinged with white liberal guilt, all these texts adopt the point-of-view of a lone white male, deeply dissatisfied with his own culture, venturing into an alien land and gradually identifying with it. These films alleviate the neurosis over past violence against Native Americans and over American imperialist thrust into Asia in the wake of Commodore Perry; what the blade has done to the racial other, the brush tries to undo. Yet the cathartic cleansing requires sacrificial blood, the re-inscription of Orientalist discursive violence. The linguistic and cultural labyrinth of the Orient turns out to be a well-rehearsed style; the Orient is predictably fetishised, while remaining, forever, beyond grasp.

Granted, Zhang Yimou generates swordsmen's quasi-spiritualism on the basis of Chinese calligraphy and wordplay, yet for Western

film-makers, this more or less literal 'brush', a system of representations between language and culture shared by Chinese on and off the
screen, becomes radically defamiliarising. Indeed, white protagonists in
The Last Samurai and *Kill Bill* subject themselves as much to a pun-
ishing martial apprenticeship as to a linguistic and cultural disorientation, as much to the mastery of blade as to that of brush, in order to
achieve skills necessary for redemption. The training of Cruise's Algren
in swordsmanship is predicated on his acquisition of the Japanese language, culture and mindset. And that mindset, similar to the Emperor
of Qin's 'to not kill' or Neo's 'no spoon', turns out to be 'no mind'.[23]
Once Algren lets go, entering into a state of ego-lessness, he draws a tie
in sparring and, subsequently, disposes of a fair number of waylayers.
The 1960s Zen cult continues in this magical dissolving of technical,
linguistic, cultural and conceptual barriers, by turning mental faculty,
rationality in particular, on its head. Seemingly a self-effacement in the
immersion into the other's philosophy, Cruise, Kevin Costner's
Western and the Wachowskis' Sci-fi as well, remains quintessentially
Western in the messianic narrative. The no-mind oceanic-feeling
intimates a Christian divinity in yellow face, disguised as an Oriental
trope.

On a more secular level, Algren moves from his captivity by samurai
at an agrarian setting to a disciple of *bushido*, the way of the samurai.
A tale of 'gone native', like his fellow white men Mistah Kurtz and Lord
Jim, it is in fact a tale of 'gone Orientalist'. Surely more conscientious
than Puccini's ugly American Pinkerton, Algren, nevertheless, is next
of kin to Clavell's Blackthorne, the English pilot stranded in Shogunate
Japan in *Shogun*. While Clavell's male fantasy over a heathen paradise
has been cut to a kiss and a shot of bare shoulder against long black hair,
Cruise follows the same Orientalist recipe. Death wish runs amuck in
Clavell's hierarchical Japan, with the samurai mantra of 'take my head'
or 'slit my belly' offered whenever honour is in danger. Algren exhibits
a similar habit as, kneeling and kowtowing, he beseeches the Japanese
Emperor to grant permission to end his life. Awkward phrases such as
'so sorry', 'karma' or 'pillowing (love-making)' punctuate Clavell's
1,000 pages with numbing regularity, a speech defect that Algren picks
up when he apologises: 'so sorry'. Given that linguistic stereotypes
occur in Tarantino and Jarmusch as well, such as Bill's 'Ah so' and
Ghost Dog's 'I'm your retain-a', they are somehow redeemed by the
former's playful, sarcastic delivery and the black accent of the latter.
Both film-makers reinvent visual and auditory clichés. One such
moment is Ghost Dog's hilarious flourish of his gun before reholster-
ing, as if he were sheathing a long samurai sword. By contrast, both

Clavell and Cruise construct romantic stories, which are but glosses of a stylised Japan. The pivotal ritual in the array of stylisation is seppuku, the end of life and the height of aestheticism. A clash of Freudian Eros and Thanatos, Clavell's death poem amidst falling cherry blossoms, in effect, concludes *The Last Samurai*.

Seppuku is self-disembowelment, which should properly end with the beheading of the samurai by a second. The rite of beheading, whether linked to seppuku or not, veers the thesis – of the 'oneness' of brush and blade, self and other, the name and the named – toward colonial stereotype of native violence, but not quite, since all the examples of actual beheading are squarely contemporary, despite being anachronistic in outlook. Clavell's novel teems with severed heads; Cruise obscures the decapitation behind a tree trunk; Tarantino's *Kill Bill* overdoes and parodies the headless gore, on the one hand, and, on the other, minimises and contains it in the scalping of Lucy Liu's O-Ren Ishii. A Japanese culture aficionado, Lian Hearn opens her Otori trilogy with a beheading and repeats it on numerous occasions.[24] Certainly not limited to Orientalist discourse, Kurosawa's *Ran* interweaves beheading into King Lear's losing of his head; the same motif runs through Miyazaki Hayao's *anime*. *Princess Mononoke* (Japan, 1997) culminates in the sacrilegious beheading of God, avenged by the head of a divine dog biting off the offender's arm. *Spirited Away* (Japan, 2001) counts three muttering, jumping heads as part of the evil witch's familiars. Considering the difficulty of severing the neck with bullets, all beheadings are done by swords, with the exception of the supernatural *Princess Mononoke*.

Decapitation means the truncation of head and body, the seats of reason and heart. Symbolically, it severs the two fundamental traits of humanity. More importantly, it literally cuts the body in half. The two-part corpse exposes death in all its rawness, without the semblance of life countenanced by an intact body. As such, decapitation has been banned in most civilised countries as cruel and barbaric. In *Kill Bill*, however, the hyperbolic beheadings with blood gushing out are carnivalesque, celebrating Jamesonian pastiche and flatness as well as postmodern schizophrenia. In the Lacanian-Jamesonian sense of schizophrenia, beheading exteriorises the disrupted 'signifying chain', where 'the interlocking syntagmatic series of signifiers which constitutes an utterance or a meaning'[25] is superseded by a cacophony of images and sounds. The whole 'revenge' genre, to which *Kill Bill* belongs, consists of cause and effect, violence and its reaction. But between what is metaphorically head and body, a schizophrenic wedge intrudes. Instead of the human response of horror and grief, the audience 'sees through' this cartoonish, fake violence. The sensory overload in Tarantino, particularly the excessive, culturally hybridised fight scenes, indexes psychic discontiguousness, but with a sense of post-Kafka ease. An angel of vengeance seeks to marshall violence even greater than the enemy's, consequently becoming the enemy. This is self-evident after the first revenge in *Kill Bill*: Uma Thurman's The Bride turns to find her victimiser/victim's daughter staring at the dead. The Bride comforts: 'When you grow up, if you still feel raw about this, come and find me', thus foreshadowing cycles of violence, for The Bride will have a daughter of her own by the end of the film. Any existential anxiety over the switching of self and other, one of the psychoanalytic definitions of schizophrenia, is shrouded in the rush of nostalgic presentness. Schizophrenia becomes Tarantino, who is so keenly aware of the division that he capitalises on it. Hence, The Bride embarks on the preposterous quest for sword across the Pacific, while poking fun at the martial arts genre's banalities. Tarantino's own quest for Asian filmic style receives its share of self-scrutiny. The somewhat rough-hewn, fraying nature of *Kill Bill* calls attention to the many melanges as incomplete cultural and psychological links. From its opening 'Acknowledgements', montaged citations of East and West characterise *Kill Bill*. The logo of Hong Kong's film studio Shaw Brothers is followed by the blurred inside of a pistol barrel typical of the 1970s Bond movies, each image accompanied by its respective soundtrack. While 'Acknowledgements' keep image and sound intact as a unit, the subsequent film often montages, in Sergei Eisenstein's fashion, the visual and the auditory, so jarringly that it flaunts incongruous collage in each frame. A bloodbath with samurai swords is accompanied by Western spaghetti soundtrack; a black-and-white shot of a doorway against American Southwest's bleak landscape is disturbed not by whistle but a Chinese flute.

The cast exhibits this insouciant schizophrenia as well. Oriental characters are routinely split: the victim O-Ren grows up to be an assassin; the giggling schoolgirl Go-Go thrusts a phallic sword into a paedophile; the comical, bantering sushi bar chef metamorphoses into the solemn Hattori Hanzo sword-maker; the raving chief of Crazy 88, with a Kato Mask and shaved head, becomes the kung fu master Pai Mei, with white beard and long robe. White characters go through similar transformation: Michael Parks plays the Texas Sheriff and the Latin American pimp; The Bride moves from a vegetative state to an avenger, assisted by the Hanzo Sword and the sadomasochistic apprenticeship to Pai Mei. All these narrative movements take the characters inexorably toward the blade, not only owning the Hanzo Sword and Pai Mei's

Five-Point-Palm Exploding-Heart technique, but becoming the named themselves. The name and the named coalesce. Although the passage of time is inherent in these film stars' long silence, until *Kill Bill*, nostalgia is infused with Tarantino's stylistic jouissance, rendering depthless all the intervening years for Sonny Chiba, Gordon Liu and Michael Parks. The violence of time resembles the violence of the fetish sword; both wrinkles and blood are seen and forgotten. Hence, the ludicrously named Five-Point-Palm Exploding-Heart technique endears the memory of Pai Mei, despite all his Zen master cruelty, including hits to the novice's head to induce sudden enlightenment. Even the foulness of racial stereotype and transgressive murder are lightened up; Pai Mei is poisoned by his disciple when he consumes his favourite fish head.

Grisly, Asian-inflected beheading has turned comedic – Bakhtinian – in the postmodern Tarantino. Tarantino's dubious 'trans-cultured pearl' would not have come to pass without centuries of discomfort over the sand of a primitive Orient, one that undergirds colonial expansionism and modernisation's pursuit of happiness in terms of raw materials, labour and market. Coloniality and modernity collaborate in Conrad, Forster, Maugham, Orwell and many others, locating what is opposite to Western progressiveness in native characters and mobs, caught in a state of fury. The blade of imperialism is transferred by the brush of fiction-making onto savage natives' headlessness. Projecting their own violence onto the other, colonialists have resorted to stereotypes of inhumanity as partial justification of imperialism, including cannibalism, head-hunting, and decapitation. As Western modernity defines itself against the 'acephalic rush' of the colonised, modernism is inspired by the alterity of African sculpture, Oriental ideogram, and various non-Western traditions. Nonetheless, the abysmal colonised in colonialist texts is but the shadow to the apocalyptic other in modernist and avant-gardist texts.

References

1   Ruth Benedict's wartime study of the Japanese enemies, *The Chrysanthemum and the Sword: Patterns of Japanese Culture* (New York: Houghton Mifflin, 1946), can be renamed as 'cherry blossom and seppuku', which populates public imagination of the Japanese.

2   Yeats, W.B., *A Dialogue of Self and Soul* (New York: Macmillan, 1959), pp.230–2.

3   Preceded by a graphic illustration, the entry on 'Kali' in *Encyclopaedia Acephalica*, edited by Georges Bataille (London: Atlas, 1995), cites

Katherine Mayo's *l'Inde avec les Anglais*: 'She is black-faced and sticks out an enormous tongue, filthy with blood. Of her four hands, one holds a human head, dripping blood, the second a knife, the third, extended, pours out blood, the fourth, raised in menace, is empty', p.55. The entry also describes in gruesome detail temple sacrifices of goats by beheading.

4   Pound, Ezra and Fenollosa, Ernest, 'The Chinese Written Character as a Medium for Poetry', *Instigations* (1920), p.366.

5   Nietzsche, Friedrich Wilhelm, *Thus Spake Zarathustra*, trans. Walter Kaufmann (New York: Penguin, 1980), p. 152.

6   Derrida, Jacques, *Of Grammatology*, trans. Gayatri Spivak (Baltimore: Johns Hopkins UP, 1976).

7   Althusser, Louis, 'Ideology and the Ideological State Apparatuses (Notes Towards an Investigation)' in Ben Brewster (ed), *Lenin and Philosophy and Other Essays* (New York: Monthly Review Press, 1971), pp.127–86.

8   Lacan, Jacques, 'The Signification of the Phallus' (1966) in *Ecrits: A Selection,* trans. Alan Sheridan (New York: Norton, 1977), p.288.

9   See Freud's 'Fetishism' (1927) in *Sexuality and the Psychology of Love,* trans. Joan Riviere (New York: Collier, 1963), pp.214–19.

10 Bataille, Georges, *Erotism: Death and Sensuality* (New York: Walker & Co., 1962).

11 See Parsons, William B., *The Enigma of the Oceanic Feeling: Revisioning the Psychoanalytic Theory of Mysticism* (New York: Oxford University Press, 1999), especially Chapter 6 'Mysticism East and West'.

12 Harvey, David, *The Condition of Modernity* (New York: Blackwell, 1989).

13 Baudrillard, Jean, *Simulacra and Simulation* (Ann Arbor: University of Michigan Press, 1994).

14 Cvetkovich, Ann and Kellner, Douglas (eds) *Articulating the Global and the Local: Globalization and Cultural Studies* (Boulder, Colorado: Westview Press, 1997), p.11.

15 See Bordwell, David, *Planet Hong Kong: Popular Cinema and the Art of Entertainment* (Cambridge MA: Harvard UP, 2000), 'The alteration of swift attack and abrupt rest is characteristic of the Asian martial arts' – a style Bordwell attributes to both the tradition of martial arts and that of Peking Opera, whereby movements are punctuated with 'moments of pure stasis, the technique of *liang hsiang* ("displaying"). Often underlined by a cymbal crash' or a clapper (*ban*), p.224.

16 Chinese media has often taunted Zhang Yimou for his overzealousness of catering to Western taste in order to be awarded an Oscar.

17 Li Zhilin, 'On the Dual Nature of Traditional Chinese Thought and Its Modernization' in Eliot Deutsch (ed), *Culture and Modernity: East-West Philosophic Perspectives* (Honolulu: University of Hawaii Press, 1991), p.246.

18   Li Zhilin critiques the method of reasoning in traditional Chinese thinking as 'a kind of systematic inference (that is, a system that can be inferred from another system) . . . different from Western prepositional inference. The Chinese inference is also full of dialectic concepts' (p.246). Such systematic inference 'lacked definite rules and procedures and depended simply on analogous inference', leading to 'strained interpretations' (p.247). Li faults traditional Chinese thought for its reliance on 'mystical intuition', 'ambiguous concepts and expressions of infinite capacity' (p.250). It appears Zhang Yimou is doing no less.

19   See Brecht, Bertolt, 'Alienation Effects in Chinese Acting' in John Willett (ed), *Brecht on Theater* (New York: Hill and Wang, 1964), pp.91–9.

20   Thomas Carlyle's anti-democratic, anti-evolutionist *On Hero, Hero-Worship, and the Heroic in History* (1841) includes six types of heroes: God, Prophet, Poet, Priest, Man of Letters and King, which is a mix of the brush and the blade.

21   *Hagakure: The Book of the Samurai* is one of the two Eastern books on martial matters often alluded to in Western popular culture. The other one, even more frequently translated and quoted, is the Warring States period (403–221 BC), Chinese text, *Sun Tzu: The Art of War*.

22   The size of an American football, the device nicknamed 'nuclear football' follows the US President wherever s/he travels. The device contains the mechanism to launch a nuclear strike.

23   The term may have come from Suzuki, D. T., *The Zen Doctrine of No-Mind* (London: Rider, 1949).

24   Hearn, Lian, *Across the Nightingale Floor* (New York: Riverhead, 2002).

25   Jameson, Fredric, *Postmodernism, or, The Cultural Logic of Late Capitalism* (Durham: Duke University Press, 1991), p.26.

Index